INSIGHT GUIDES

MARRAKESH

smart guide

APA PUBLICATIONS

Part of the Langenscheidt Publishing Group

Contents

Areas

A–Z

Atlas

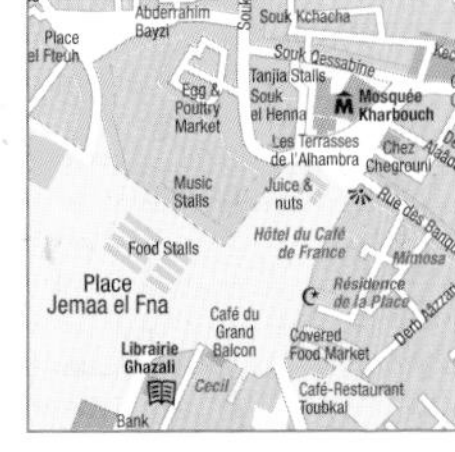

Highlights

▲ **Jemaa el Fna** This lively square buzzes all day, from the early morning orange juice to the food stalls and entertainment at night.

▶ **Koutoubia Mosque** The iconic minaret's design and decoration has been copied ever after.

◀ **Souks** A warren of colourful alleys and streets with a vast choice of shops selling crafts, clothes and spices.

▲ **Ben Youssef Medersa** Get a flavour of the great variety of Moroccan decorative arts at this delightful and tranquil Koranic school.

▲ **Atlas Mountains** The snow-peaked mountains are the best background for the city, and offer a quick escape.

◀ **Majorelle Garden** Exotic garden with bamboo groves, cacti and lily ponds set against an electric-blue Art Deco villa.

Marrakesh

Marrakesh, the Red City, offers an instant dose of the exotic, just a short and often cheap flight from Europe. The old medina, with its winding souks, and the hectic main square of the Jemaa el Fna bedazzle the senses in every way. But Marrakesh is also a buzzing modern city, big, fast and furious, with an increasingly happening culture and nightlife.

Marrakesh Facts and Figures

Population: 1.68 million (city), but over 2 million including suburbs
Area: Marrakesh is the capital of the mid-southwestern region of Marrakesh-Tensift-Al Haouz, close to the foothills of the High Atlas Mountains. The Jemaa el Fna is the heart of the city, which is divided between the old medina, the French-built New Town and the suburbs.
Location: 31°38'N 8°0'W
Language: Arabic is the official language, but many people speak Amazigh (Berber language) and French. English is increasingly spoken in tourist areas.
Climate: Marrakesh has a dry climate with hot summers and cool winters. The best time for visiting is between March and June and from September to December. There is usually snow in the high mountain areas near Marrakesh from December to April, but the higher mountain peaks have snow until June.
Number of overnight visitors in 2008: 5,573,529
Number of food stalls in Jemaa el Fna: over 100

Medina Buzz

Marrakesh may have few museums or conventional sights, and its mosques may be closed to non-Muslims, but that doesn't mean the city has no attractions. One look at the old walled medina and it soon becomes clear where the name of 'Red City' comes from. The walls and many buildings are covered in a deep-red ochre pigment, which makes a perfect background for a whole range of vibrant colours, from mounds of kaleidoscopic spices to pink leatherwear and bright yellow babouches or slippers.

Founded by Almoravid Sultan Youssef ben Tachfine in the 11th century, the old medina retains much of its medieval character, despite the fact that the 21st century has definitely moved in. Recent years have seen Marrakesh change dramatically as many riads, the old courtyard houses, have been sold to foreigners, who have turned them into pleasure palaces for their own use, or more often into luxurious and stylish boutique hotels, the subject of so many magazine features.

The medina may have lost some of its mystery, but it still tends to confound the first-time visitor. One first treads carefully in the well-worn tracks of others, along the main thoroughfares, past the more obvious tourist sights and shops. The crowds can be

Below: traders lay out their wares in the sun in 'La Place', the Jemaa el Fna.

Above: the red-coloured, mudbrick walls of the medina.

overwhelming, the exotic produce and crafts mind-boggling, the persistent salesmen irritating, but the first impression is never anything less than exotic. With a little more confidence and a newly gained sense of orientation, it is easier to wander off in the quieter labyrinthine alleys to admire an amazing palace or a tiny shrine, to sit in a café or stop for a chat with a shopkeeper, and feel the true wonder of the place.

Jet-Set Haven

Marrakesh has always attracted the rich and famous, most of whom used to stay safely tucked away in private mansions or in the fabled hotels such as La Mamounia, outside the walls. Things have changed. The fashion designers, wealthy socialites and interior decorators who started buying the decaying large houses and transforming them into their oriental fantasy set a trend. Now developers are turning their eye to the colonial-era Art Deco buildings of the Ville Nouvelle, the Palmeraie and beyond. Marrakesh has gone to great lengths to entertain these guests and, in the process, earned itself a reputation for wild nightlife and extravagant anything-you-ever-dreamed-of parties with musicians, magicians, snake charmers, fire-eaters and belly dancers. New boutique hotels seem to open every month, each more designed and more luxurious than the last, and with ever more sophisticated spas and pampering possibilities.

Natural Delights

After a few days spent living the exotic dream, life in a medina riad can start to pall and the hectic pace of nightlife in the city begin to wear you down. That is when the snow-capped peaks of the High Atlas mountains exert their pull. Marrakesh is easy to leave: it takes just a short ride to reach the sheer beauty of the mountains and the Berber villages clinging to it, to swim in a lake, to have a picnic by the Ourika river or to go hiking in the foothills of the Atlas. The charming coastal town of Essaouira is only a few hours away by bus or car. Most hotels organise day-trips out into the countryside around Marrakesh. But if that sounds too energetic and all that is desired is a suntan, there are several artificial beaches with huge swimming pools to cool down, just a short drive from the city walls.

Jemaa el Fna

The heart and soul of Marrakesh, the Jemaa el Fna or just 'La Place' (the Square) as locals call it, is lively and life-enhancing. The square pulls the city together, the perfect interlude between the old medina and the modern Ville Nouvelle (New Town). The square is popular with both tourists and locals, who come for a stroll, for a meal or for the street entertainment. Unesco has recognised its importance and declared it a 'Masterpiece of World Heritage'. South of the Jemaa el Fna is the Koutoubia minaret, the other main symbol of the city. The nearby parks and gardens offer a welcome respite from the heat and hectic pace of the nearby souks.

LA PLACE

The square goes back to the city's 11th century beginnings, when it was a parade ground in front of the Almoravid fortress, which was later destroyed and is now under the site of the Koutoubia Mosque. Later, it was used for public executions, hence its name **Jemaa el Fna** ①, meaning 'the Assembly of the Dead'.

Much has changed since then. Now, from the early morning until late at night, the vast space turns into a stage for street performers, snake charmers, magicians, traditional doctors, henna tattooists and noisy chefs. The rooftops of the many restaurants and cafés on the side of the square command great views of the High Atlas mountain peaks, and over the crowds and the activity down below. Behind the buildings north of the square are the narrow entrances to the souks. Southwest of the square is the **place de Foucauld**, a small garden with a tourist information booth and horse carriages for city tours.

SEE ALSO SQUARES, P.120

THE KOUTOUBIA

The 77m (253ft) high **minaret** of the **Koutoubia Mosque** ② dominates the Marrakesh skyline and is the tallest building in town. It will remain so, as local regulations forbid building higher. Standing on the site of earlier mosques, this mosque was built by the Almohad ruler Yaqoub el Mansour. As it is still used for worship, the mosque is closed to non-Muslims, but the elegant minaret, a model for most Moroccan minarets, can be admired, along with the tomb of **Lalla Zohra** ③, from the surrounding **gardens** ④.

SEE ALSO ARCHITECTURE, P.39; GARDENS, P.63; MONUMENTS, P.74; RELIGIONS AND RELIGIOUS SITES, P.94

It used to be hard to slip away by yourself into the souks coming from the Jemaa el Fna. Marrakesh's medina was infamous for its hustlers, and faux guides would accost you and not leave you alone. One of the first things King Mohammed VI did was to train a tourist police, in plain clothes, with the intent of dealing once and for all with these hustlers. Today, there may still be a few dodgy characters around in the more remote parts of the medina, but in general the situation is under control, and visitors feel a lot safer and more relaxed when wandering around.

Left: the evening gathers pace on the Jemaa el Fna.

> The name of the **Koutoubia Mosque** comes from the hundreds of *Koutoubiyyin*, Arabic for booksellers, who used to have their shops in the souk around the mosque. To celebrate the opening of his new mosque, the Almohad Sultan Abdel Moumen, grandfather of el Mansour, displayed one of the four original copies of the Quran compiled by the third Caliph Othman.

AVENUE MOHAMMED V

The **rue de Bab Agnaou**, running down from the southeast side of the Jemaa el Fna, is packed with patisseries, budget restaurants and hotels, and shops selling fake-branded trainers. The city's main artery, between the medina and the Ville Nouvelle, the **avenue Mohammed V**, starts just off the Jemaa el Fna, from the place de Foucauld. To one side of the avenue Mohammed V is the Koutoubia Mosque, and further down you will find the tranquil contemporary gardens of the **Cyber Parc Moulay Abdeslam** ⑤. On the other side are restaurants, and further north, opposite the Cyber Parc, stands the **Ensemble Artisanal**, where a good variety of crafts are made and sold at fixed prices. This is a good place to start your shopping before tackling the souks.

SEE ALSO GARDENS, P.62; SHOPPING, P.111

PLACE BAB EL FTEUH

North of the Jemaa el Fna is the smaller square of **Bab el Fteuh**. It leads to the chic **Mouassine quarter** *(see p.12–13)*, but has at the same time a very down-to-earth feel to it, apart from the über-stylish **Akbar Delights** boutique. Off the square is a wonderful fondouk with warehouses, crafts shops and a great jewellery store, **Boutique Bel Hadj**, set around a courtyard. Further east, alleys lead into an **egg market** and the **olive souk**.

SEE ALSO SHOPPING, P.112, 113

CITY WALLS

The old medina of Marrakesh is surrounded by 16km (10 miles) of well-preserved red pisé (mud-brick) **walls** ⑥, built in the 12th century, and endlessly restored ever after. The walls were once pierced by 20 gates, and defended by more than 200 towers. The best place to start a tour, by horse-drawn carriage, taxi or bicycle, is at the **Bab Jedid** near the Mamounia hotel, and then continue north around the city.

SEE ALSO MONUMENTS, P.74

Below: a snake charmer on the Jemaa el Fna.

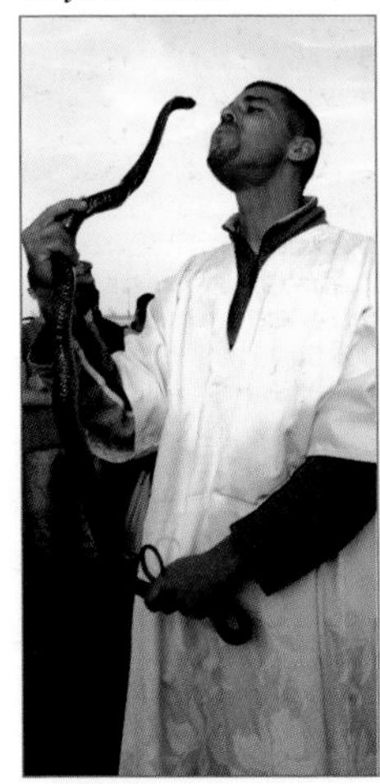

Southern Medina

From the city's very beginnings, the sultans and kings chose to live, rule, play and establish their palaces and pleasure gardens in the kasbah, in the southern part of the medina. Today's royal palace is still in the kasbah, as well as the more modest home King Mohammed VI built for himself and his family, and nearby are the remains of two other sumptuous palaces, Palais de la Bahia and el Badi palace. The Jews played a special role in Morocco, illustrated by the fact that the Mellah or Jewish quarter was adjacent to the king's palace but separated from the rest of the medina. It was once the largest Jewish quarter in all of North Africa.

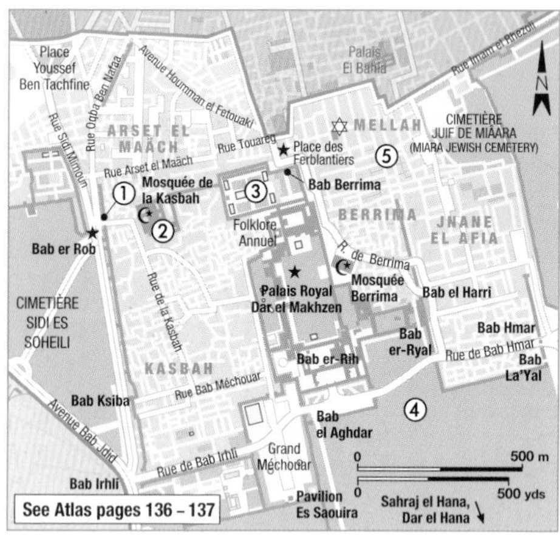

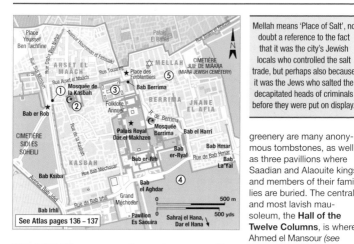

See Atlas pages 136 – 137

Mellah means 'Place of Salt', no doubt a reference to the fact that it was the city's Jewish locals who controlled the salt trade, but perhaps also because it was the Jews who salted the decapitated heads of criminals before they were put on display.

BAB AGNAOU

The official entrance to the kasbah was through the **Bab Agnaou** ①, built in 1185 by Sultan Yaqoub el Mansour. Most of the buildings in Marrakesh are built in pis, but this gate is different, built in the local blue Guéliz stone. Originally Bab Agnaou was guarded by the sultan's black African guards, known as the Gnaoua, people of Guinea. Just next to the Bab Agnaou is the gate of **Bab er Rob**, the entrance for mere mortals into the city itself, now occupied by a pottery shop.

SEE ALSO ARCHITECTURE, P.38; MONUMENTS, P.75

SAADIAN TOMBS

Immediately past the Bab Agnaou is the 12th-century **Kasbah Mosque**, built by the same Yaqoub el Mansour; it is closed to non-Muslims. A separate door in the wall around the mosque leads into the walled gardens. This is where, in the 1920s, a Frenchman discovered by chance the **Tombeaux Saadiens (Saadian Tombs)** ②, the impressive and elaborate tombs of the Saadian Kings. Among the greenery are many anonymous tombstones, as well as three pavillions where Saadian and Alaouite kings and members of their families are buried. The central and most lavish mausoleum, the **Hall of the Twelve Columns**, is where Ahmed el Mansour *(see box, opposite)* is buried.

SEE ALSO MONUMENTS, P.75

EL BADI PALACE

East of the Kasbah Mosque is the busy and picturesque **place des Ferblantiers**, a rectangular

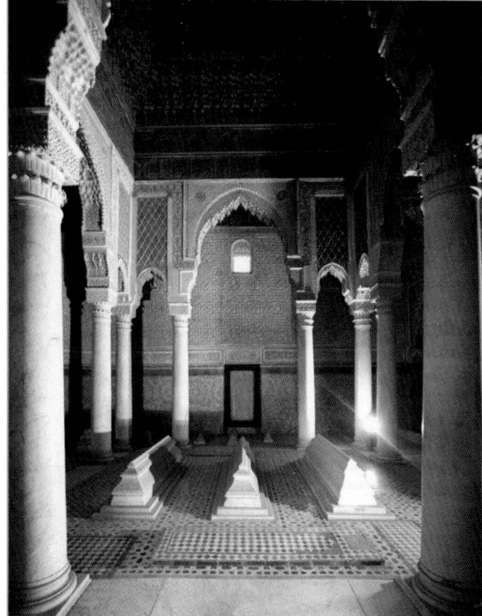

Left: the stately Saadian Tombs.

fondouk courtyard surrounded by workshops of metalworkers. Still a good place to buy brass lanterns, it now has a few café terraces perfect for a cheap alfresco lunch, and the trendy **Kosybar**, serving everything from sushi to Moroccan salads.

The southern gate of Bab Berrima leads to a space between the outer wall that separates imperial Marrakesh from the rest of the city and the massive wall of the **El Badi Palace** ③, topped with storks' nests. The 16th-century palace of Ahmed el Mansour, it was once famously beautiful. Destroyed and stripped of everything by Moulay Ismaïl in 1696, it is now nothing but ruins, albeit atmospheric ones. What is left is a set of sunken gardens and a few pavillions, including the new one housing the stunning **Koutoubia minbar**, or pulpit, from the Koutoubia Mosque.

SEE ALSO KASBAHS AND PALACES, P.68; NIGHTLIFE, P.85; RESTAURANTS, P.100; SQUARES, P.120

Left: the remains of the El Badi Palace.

ROYAL PALACE

Also within the kasbah, behind the **El Badi Palace**, lies the **current Royal Palace** and the home King Mohammed VI built for his family: both are inaccessible to the public. At the back of the royal palace lie the **Agdal Gardens** ④, stretching for a few kilometres south of the medina, and only open when the king is not in residence. The gardens, laid out in the 12th century, have a vast pool, the **Sahraj el Hana**, and the lovely **Dar el Hana** pavilion at the centre.

SEE ALSO GARDENS, P.63

THE MELLAH

In the 16th century the Saadian king moved all Marrakchi Jews into a secure quarter, known as the **Mellah** ⑤, which was separate from the rest of the city, and right next to the palace walls. The main entrance to the Mellah is just off place des Ferblantiers. Very few Jews still live in this area, as most have moved to Israel or to the more cosmopolitan city of Casablanca. The warren of alleys still contains a few **synagogues**, and further east is the **Miara Jewish Cemetery**.

SEE ALSO RELIGIONS AND RELIGIOUS SITES, P.97

The Saadian king Ahmed el Mansour, the Victorious, ruled Morocco from 1578 to 1603. During his reign he seized the goldfields of West Africa, which gave him the nickname *ed Dehbi* or 'the Golden One'. He used his new-found wealth to embellish his capital, Marrakesh, and build the El Badi Palace. The walls and ceilings in the palace were encrusted with gold from Timbuktu, and boats floated on the pools. The palace was only finished a few months before the king died.

Eastern Medina

This mostly residential part of town, home to an increasing number of riads being turned into boutique hotels, is crossed by the rue Riad Zitoun el Jedid and the rue Riad Zitoun el Qedim, running from the Jemaa el Fna to the place des Ferblantiers. These two streets offer off-the-beaten-track shopping and a few hip boutiques. Two private houses, Dar Si Said and Maison Tiskwin, are now interesting museums. The other side of the eastern medina is more commercially inclined, with a warren of souks, a fascinating spice market and an old slave market where today Berbers come from their villages to auction off their handmade carpets and rugs.

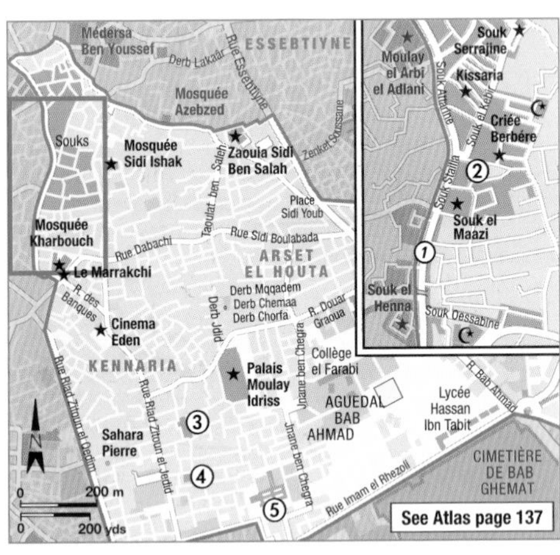

SOUKS

North of the Jemaa el Fna stretches the intricate labyrinth of the **souks** ①, with different trades and crafts grouped together in specific areas. The main drag, the broad **Souk Smarine**, is shaded by a trellis ceiling, and lined with expensive antique shops, shops selling traditional clothing and increasingly, with souvenir shops. Further on, the street splits into the Souk el Kebir and the Souk el Attarine, with the Kissaria in between the two. This was traditionally the heart of the souk, a more intimate market that could be locked at night. From here more specialised souks run off to all sides.

SEE ALSO SOUKS, P.114

RAHBA KEDIMA

To the right off the Souk Smarine is the picturesque square of the **Rahba Kedima** ②. The old corn market is now lined with stalls and shops selling spices, traditional cures and protection against the evil eye. In the middle of the square, mountain women sell their hand-knitted hats and baskets. Vendors will happily explain the ins and outs of love potions, Berber lipstick and amber to protect you from the evil eye. Two entrance ways on the north side of the square lead into the **Criée Berbére**, a narrow space where domestic slaves were sold until 1912. These days it's Berber rugs and carpets that are auctioned off.

SEE ALSO SOUKS, P.114; SQUARES, P.121

The **Café des Epices** on the Rahba Kedima, run by young Moroccans who grew up selling spices in the square, is the most pleasant place to while away the afternoon watching the local goings on. *See also Cafés, p.43.*

RUE RIAD ZITOUN EL JEDID

To the right of the restaurant **Le Marrakchi** on the northern side of the Jemaa el Fna is the rue des Banques, which leads into the rue Riad Zitoun el Jedid, and on to the place des Ferblantiers. At the beginning of this street is **Cinema Eden**, a typical local cinema described in Juan

Right: scarves and spices for sale piled up in the souks.

Left: local life in the souks.

> Shops selling traditional remedies are hung with all kinds of dried animals, like hedgehogs, snakes, porcupines, lizards and desert foxes. These are most likely to be used to make aphrodisiacs or love potions. Women often come to these shops for one that will make their husband stay by their side for ever. Dried herbs are used to make remedies for all sorts of ailments.

Goytisolo's book of the same name. The Spanish writer has lived in this quarter since the 1970s. The street is lined with more quirky and stylish shops than are found in the souks, selling West African jewellery, Tuareg leather work and trendy kaftans in vintage materials. Parallel to this street runs the rue Riad Zitoun el Qedim, with shops selling wares like picture frames made from old car tyres.

SEE ALSO FILM, P.57; RESTAURANTS, P.99

PALATIAL HOUSES

At the end of an alley off the rue Riad Zitoun el Jedid is the signposted **Dar Si Said**, the **Museum of Moroccan Arts and Crafts** ③, worth visiting for the house alone, which was built by Si Said, the brother of the vizier Ba Ahmed. More modest than the vizier's Bahia Palace but nonetheless elegant, it houses an interesting collection of artefacts rescued from kasbahs, as well as crafts and textiles. Nearby is another grand house open to the public, the **Maison Tiskwin** ④. The owner, Dutch anthropologist Bert Flint, an avid collector of textiles and crafts, opened part of his own house as a museum, which illustrates the strong connection between Marrakesh and Timbuktu.

SEE ALSO MUSEUMS AND GALLERIES, P.78, 79

EL BAHIA PALACE

Further south along rue Riad Zitoun el Jedid, closer to the Mellah, is the 19th-century **El Bahia Palace** ⑤, built by the vizier Si Mousa and his son Ba Ahmed. The palace sprawls over 8 hectares (20 acres) with gardens, pavilions and various other buildings. The complex was stripped bare after the vizier died, but still retains much charm.

SEE ALSO KASBAHS AND PALACES, P.68

Mouassine Quarter

Only a stone's throw away from the frenetic pace of the Jemaa el Fna, the fashionable Mouassine quarter, on the western side of the medina, is much, much quieter. The grand riads may have attracted an in-crowd of jet-setter types, but the area retains an authentic neighbourhood feel, with corner shops, little mosques and tiled fountains for ablutions. Some of the shops do reflect the neighbourhood's 'designer' status, however, selling precious antiques, foreign and local designer clothes inspired by the Marrakchi vibe, contemporary candles in vibrant colours, and minimalist Islamic pottery.

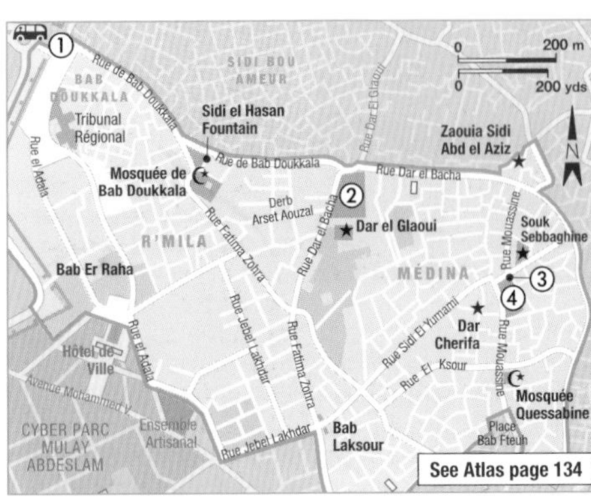

Above: ornate door knocker in the Mouassine quarter.

> *Es Sebti* are the Seven Saints of Marrakesh, and all have a shrine to their name: Sidi Bel Abbès is the most popular and revered saint, a Sufi who died in 1205; the others are Sidi Liyad, Sidi Abd el Aziz, Sidi Youssef ben Ali, Sidi el Ghawzani, Sidi el Suhayi and Sidi ben Slimane el Jazuli. Sultan Moulay Ismail restored the seven older shrines and established a *moussem* or festival which included a pilgrimage to all the shrines. Some people believe that Sidi Bel Abbès is in fact associated with St Augustine, and that he flies around the Koutoubia Mosque every night until all the poor have been fed. *See also Religions and Religious Sites, p.95.*

BAB DOUKKALA

The doors of the Almoravid gate of **Bab Doukkala** ① are now usually closed, as the gate stands a little abandoned and unused to the left of the modern traffic-locked gate. Outside the gate is the city's busy *gare routière* or main bus station, with buses departing constantly for almost every city in Morocco, while just inside the gate are the uninspiring modern law courts. The rue de Bab Doukkala leads to the **Bab Doukkala Mosque**, built in the 16th century by the daughter of a southern chieftain, the mother of the Saadian golden boy, Ahmed el Mansour. The mosque is closed to non-Muslims, who can only admire the graceful minaret, and the lovely **Sidi el Hasan fountain**.

DAR EL BACHA

Further along, on the corner, is the impressive **Dar el Bacha** ②, also known as Dar el Glaoui. This palace was built at the beginning of the 20th century, by the notorious Pasha of Marrakesh, Thami el Glaoui. The biggest jetsetter of all, he entertained statesmen and movie stars in his stately home until the 1950s. Much attention was dedicated to the lav-

Left: freshly dyed wool is hung out to dry.

In the Mouassine area and northern medina you will find many **fondouks** *(see p.38)*, artisans' workshops and lodgings around a courtyard. Some have been turned into hotels, while others are still in use as workshops and shops. Walk in to admire the architecture, and sometimes the garden, or sip a cup of syrupy mint tea while chatting to the traders, who seem more relaxed than those on the main streets.

ish style and the grandeur, less was wasted on tasteful details. Many a wealthy, beautiful or powerful foreign guest was entertained and pampered here, with top French wines, opium, Berber girls or boys and expensive gifts, often paid for with dubious money. The palace now houses government offices, but it is rumoured to be planned as a museum of Islamic art sometime in the future.
SEE ALSO KASBAHS AND PALACES, P.69

SHRINE OF SIDI ABD EL AZIZ

Several fondouks *(see box, left)* line the rue Bab Doukkala, like the one featured in the film *Hideous Kinky*. Most are still in use today, and if the gate is open, you can just wander in to admire the architecture and the woodwork. Further west is the **Zaouia Sidi Abd el Aziz**, the shrine of one of the Seven Saints of Marrakesh *(see box, opposite)*, who died in the city in 1508.
SEE ALSO FILM, P.56; RELIGIONS AND RELIGIOUS SITES, P.96

MOUASSINE MOSQUE

The **rue Mouassine** starts at the colourful **Souk Sebbaghine**, Souk of the Dyers, where freshly dyed wool is draped between the shops to dry. Further south is the ornate **Mouassine Fountain** ③, with carved wooden decoration, and the **Mouassine Mosque Complex** ④. The 16th-century complex, closed to and mostly hidden from non-Muslims, includes mosque, *medersa* (Koranic school) and baths.

The rue Mouassine, the rue Sidi el Yamani and the **Souk Cherifia** offer great shopping opportunities, with anything from vintage and ethnic clothing and jewellery to contemporary designs and organic bath products from the Ourika Valley, at prices lower than in the Ville Nouvelle. Shoppers can relax from bargaining in one of the many courtyard restaurants in the neighbourhood, including the beautiful literary café at **Dar Cherifa** or the trendy **Terrasse des Epices**, with a lounging area on the roof.
SEE ALSO CAFÉS, P.43; MONUMENTS, P.76; RELIGIONS AND RELIGIOUS SITES, P.95; SOUKS, P.115

Below: the entrance to the Bab Doukkala Mosque.

Northern Medina

Walking through Souk Smarine, it may feel like most of the northern medina is nothing but souks, but coming out at the other end one discovers some of the city's main sights – and even better, here they are open to non-Muslims. The Ben Youssef Medersa, the Koubba Ba'adiyin, and the nearby Musée de Marrakech all reveal the typical Moroccan architectural style: no centimetre is left undecorated, but the overall effect is one of balance and tranquillity. Venture even further north to find the most authentic part of the medina, with residential streets, local food markets, smaller mosques, the shrine of Sidi Bel Abbès, and best of all, few other tourists.

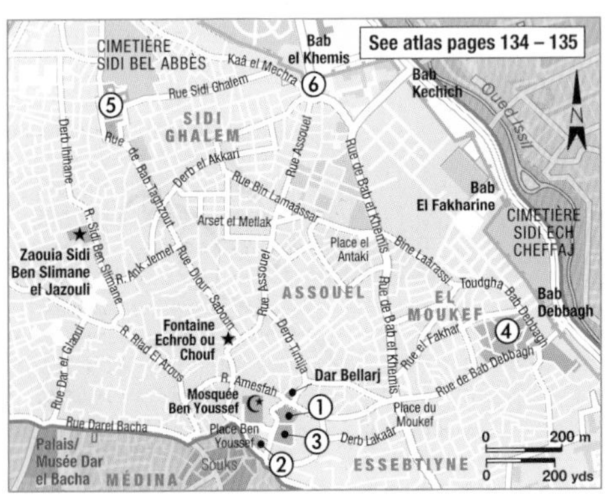

BEN YOUSSEF MEDERSA

On the western side of the place Ben Youssef is the **Ben Youssef Mosque** (closed to non-Muslims), often draped with dyed yarn drying in the sun, hung over the outer walls. Built by the Almoravid sultan Ali ben Youssef in the 12th century, it has been renovated many times. Down the alley to the right of the mosque is the **Ben Youssef Medersa** ①, or Quran school, which can be visited. A long, dark passage leads into an open courtyard flanked with galleries and a prayer room, and student cells on the first floor. The plan is simple enough, but the decoration of *zellij* mosaic, plaster and cedar carving and calligraphy is extraordinary.

SEE ALSO ARCHITECTURE, P.39; RELIGIONS AND RELIGIOUS SITES, P.94

KOUBBA BA'ADIYIN

Facing the Ben Youssef Mosque, the **Koubba Ba'adiyin** ② is behind the wall on the left. When it

Below: in the Musée de Marrakech.

Left: the Koubba Ba'adiyin.

was rediscovered in 1948, a French art historian claimed that 'the art of Islam has never exceeded the splendour of this extraordinary dome'. For the visitor today this may seem perhaps a slight exaggeration, as the small dome is all that is left from a 12th-century structure. However, this is where many shapes, like the horseshoe and scallop window frames so familiar in Moorish architecture now, were introduced for the first time.

SEE ALSO ARCHITECTURE, P.39; MONUMENTS, P.76

ART GALLERIES

Facing the mosque across the square is the Dar M'Nebhi, also known as the **Musée de Marrakech** ③. This sumptuous and beautiful early 20th-century residence houses temporary art exhibitions, but is even worth visiting just for the house. There is a pleasant café in the large, peaceful courtyard, and a small, well-stocked bookshop.

North of the Ben Youssef Medersa is another exhibition space and cultural centre, Dar Bellarj, House of Storks, formerly a hospital for wounded storks.

SEE ALSO CAFÉS, P.42; MUSEUMS AND GALLERIES, P.80

One can spot storks sitting on their nests high up on roofs, towers and walls, everywhere in Marrakesh. Moroccans have a deep-rooted superstition about storks. The storks' strength during their trek from Africa to Europe makes them a symbol of good health and prosperity. They are believed to bring happiness, and a stork's nest on the roof protects the house from evil and bad luck. Because the storks come back to the same nest year after year, and because they nest in couples, they are attributed with a large dose of love magic. It is still by law a punishable offence to destroy a stork's nest or harm the bird.

TANNERIES

An easy walk along the rue Bab Debbagh leads to the gate of the same name in the medina's northeastern corner. Your nose will find the trail to the neighbourhood **tanneries** ④, but they can be tricky to locate exactly. Therefore it may be a good idea to take on the services of one of the young men hanging around the gate, who may also provide a sprig of herbs, handy against the stench of rotting leather.

SEE ALSO SOUKS, P.114

BAB EL KHEMIS

Turn right after the Ben Youssef Medersa, and left down a covered passage which leads towards the rue Assouel, past several 16th- and 17th-century fondouks. On the left is the very ornate **Echrob ou Chouf fountain**, which means, drink and look. Turn left after the fountain towards Bab Tarhzout for the shrine or **Zaouia** of **Sidi Bel Abbès** ⑤. Follow the street eastwards towards **Bab el Khemis**, which has a large **junk market** ⑥ on most days, but is particularly good on Thursdays.

SEE ALSO RELIGIONS AND RELIGIOUS SITES, P.96; SHOPPING, P.110

Guéliz

The Ville Nouvelle divides into the buzzing Guéliz area and the quieter garden suburb of Hivernage. Built by the French, it could not be more different than the medina, with its broad avenues, neat street plan and Art Deco architecture. The avenue Mohammed V runs from the Jemaa el Fna right through Guéliz, and is lined with airline offices, fashionable shops and café terraces from where to watch the Marrakchis on their late afternoon stroll. The Majorelle Gardens and museum are the neighbourhood's only real sight, but definitely not one to miss. The Ville Nouvelle has seen a huge expansion in recent years, not least towards and around the Palmeraie.

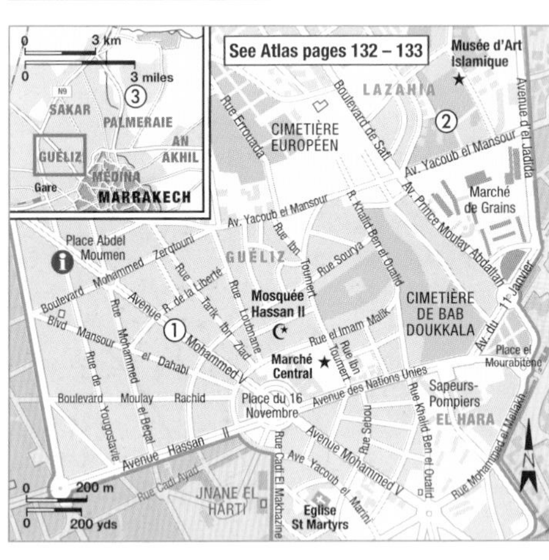

Above: the main drag.

The French city planner Henri Prost started building the Ville Nouvelle in 1913, on the orders of the French Resident General Marshal Lyautey. One main avenue led from the Koutoubia Mosque northwest to the Guéliz hills, the **avenue Mohammed V**, and another avenue ran southwest to the Menara gardens, the **avenue de la Menara**. The name 'Guéliz' is thought to come from a corruption of the French word l'église, church, after the Church of St Martyrs which dominated this part of the city at that time.

ART DECO ARCHITECTURE

The French wanted to keep the medina for the locals, so in the 1930s the colonial power decided to build a new town, the Ville Nouvelle. The neighbourhood still has a wealth of Art Deco and modernist architecture, often obscured by ugly concrete blocks and tourist coaches. The centre of Guéliz used to be the much-loved **Marché Central**, until it was destroyed amidst huge protests in 2006. The soulless new market is on rue Ibn Toumert off the place de la Liberté. One of the oldest buildings, dating from 1918, on the junction of rue de la Liberté and avenue Mohammed V, used to be the tourist office. The **Eglise St Martyrs** on rue Imam Ali is a small town church, painted in the typical Marrakchi red. Walk the **rue de la Liberté**, the **rue de Yougoslavie** and the streets around it for some of the best shopping in town, great restaurants and fabulous architecture.

SEE ALSO ARCHITECTURE, P.38; RELIGIONS AND RELIGIOUS SITES, P.94

AVENUE MOHAMMED V

The broad, tree-lined **avenue Mohammed V** ① connects the New Town with the medina, and cuts right through the middle of Guéliz. The **tourist office** is just off the avenue, on the junction with the rue de

Left: the gloriously colourful Majorelle Garden.

In the 1960s, Beat Generation writers and artists like William Burroughs and Brion Gysin set up home in the **Hôtel Toulousain** on rue Tarek Ibn Ziad *(see also Accommodation, p.35)*, where they held smoke-infused sessions with local musicians.

Yougoslavie. The bustling downtown area is situated between the **place du 16 Novembre** and the **place Abdel Moumen**, and covers most of the streets leading off this stretch. Expats and wealthy Moroccans love the car-friendly streets, as opposed to the mostly pedestrian medina, the Western-style shopping and restaurants, and the generally relaxed pace of it all. In the 1970s, most tourists stayed in this part of town, avoiding the run-down medina. Then with the explosion of riad renovations in the 1990s, the focus was on the medina. Now, just recently, as the medina has lost some of its mystery, a return to Guéliz is slowly happening. A sign of the times is the opening of the **Bab Hotel** on boulevard Mansour ed Dahabi, by the hip Moroccan fashion designer Fadila el Gadi.

SEE ALSO ACCOMMODATION, P.35; ESSENTIALS, P.53

MAJORELLE GARDEN

The exotic **Majorelle Garden** ②, designed by the French painter Jacques Majorelle, and restored by the late fashion designer Yves Saint Laurent and his partner Pierre Bergé, who owns the villa next door too, are worth the short taxi ride. Majorelle's house, now a museum with a small but lovely collection of Islamic art, also houses many of his paintings. About 500m/yds west, on rue Errouada, is the **European Cemetery**, with 1930s and 40s French colonists' tombs.

SEE ALSO GARDENS, P.63; MUSEUMS AND GALLERIES, P.81

PALMERAIE

Northeast of Guéliz is the **Palmeraie** ③, the large palm grove from the time of Marrakesh's founder, Youssef ben Tachfine. Nowadays the palm trees are making way for luxurious villas and sumptuous hotels, but it still retains an air of tranquillity and offers good sporting options. The **Circuit de la Palmeraie** is between the roads to Fès and Casablanca.

SEE ALSO GARDENS, P.64; SPORTS, P.118

Below: a *calèche* waits in the Ville Nouvelle.

Hivernage

As well as Guéliz, there is Hivernage, comprising the other part of the French-built Ville Nouvelle. It is a garden suburb with villas and hotels all boasting large mature gardens, including the mother of all hotels – La Mamounia, where one has to dress up to visit the much-loved Moorish garden. A visit here is best combined with a drink on the terrace. Other gardens include the Jnane el Harti, closer to Guéliz, which is perfect for a brief stop and a breath of fresh air, and the Menara Gardens, a favourite with Marrakchi families who come for a picnic or a stroll through the olive orchards.

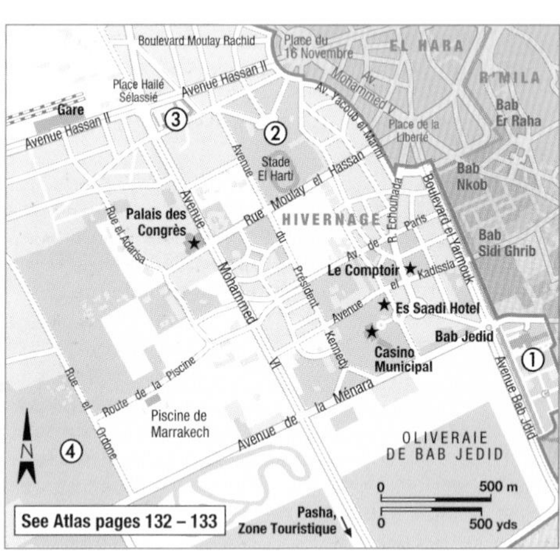

MAMOUNIA HOTEL

A short walk from the Jemaa el Fna, near the Bab Jedid, is the fabled **La Mamounia** Hotel ①, nestled in a corner of the southern medina, but more connected with the Hivernage. Winston Churchill described the gardens, laid out by the Saadians on royal grounds, to President Franklin D. Roosevelt in 1943 when they were both staying here, as the loveliest spot in the world. The hotel, once the queen of all Marrakesh hotels, has suffered from the rise of the smaller, über-luxurious riads. It is rumoured that the glorious Art Deco hotel will reopen, after several years of serious renovations, later in 2009.

SEE ALSO ACCOMMODATION, P.36; GARDENS, P.64

HIVERNAGE

At the heart of Hivernage is another well-established hotel, the **Es Saadi**, with a large, mature garden and a casino. Nearby, on one of the neighbourhood's main streets, the rue Echouhada, is the hottest nightspot in town, **Le Comptoir**, a chic restaurant with belly dancers every night. A stroll through the quiet streets

Below: the tranquil Menara Gardens.

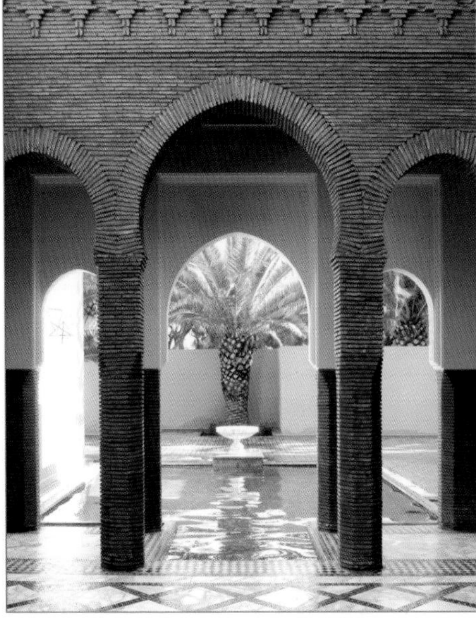

Left: a courtyard in the famed La Mamounia hotel.

with large villas is the best way to enjoy this neigbourhood. Further northwest on avenue du Président Kennedy is the **Jnane el Harti** ②, a pleasant garden with a children's playground.

SEE ALSO ACCOMMODATION, P.36; CHILDREN, P.45; GARDENS, P.64; NIGHTLIFE, P.85; RESTAURANTS, P.105

AVENUE MOHAMMED VI

Still often referred to by its old name, 'avenue de France', but now named after the current king, the **avenue Mohammed VI** claims to be the longest avenue in Africa. This 8km (5-mile) -long thoroughfare cuts from the route de Targa in the north, through the 'new Marrakesh', and will some time in the future see the realisation of the king's aspirations for the city *(see box, right)*. The old railway station is getting a 21st-century overhaul. On the avenue is the totally over-the-top **Théâtre Royal** ③, designed by Charles Boccara, not yet entirely finished, but certainly hoping to attract the big international names, and a grand **Palais des Congrès** built in 1989, also empty and only in use during the annual film festival. **Pacha**, the multicomplex nightclub of Ibiza fame, is a success story that has put Marrakesh on the map for European jet-setters. Cranes and fences hide numerous hotel developments in the soon-to-be **Zone Touristique** (Tourist Zone), a pet project of King Mohammed VI, which will provide tens of thousands of beds for tourists.

SEE ALSO MUSIC, DANCE AND THEATRE P.83; NIGHTLIFE, P.87

In 2001 King Mohammed VI launched his ambitious Vision Morocco 2010, to bring 10 million tourists to Morocco every year. In 2001 2.5 million tourists came to Morocco; this number had reached nearly 8 million by the end of 2008. The strategic tourist development programme should create 600,000 new jobs. In 2010, Morocco will have more than 250,000 hotel beds. A channel tunnel between Morocco and Spain should bring even more tourists; high-speed trains will be introduced and new roads built. It remains to be seen how the plan will fare in the current economic downturn.

MENARA GARDENS

South of Hivernage are the large **Menara Gardens** ④, which gave their name to the airport in Marrakesh. The gardens, laid out in the 12th century, consist mainly of extensive olive groves around a large basin of water with an elegant 19th-century pavilion. The water in the basin has wonderful, much-photographed reflections of the Atlas Mountains and the pavilion.

SEE ALSO GARDENS, P.64

Below: the grand Théâtre Royal.

Ourika Valley

The countryside around Marrakesh is splendid and within easy reach of the city. The quickest escape from the city into nature is to do as Marrakchis do, and head out at weekends for a picnic in the Ourika Valley or a swim in the Lake Lalla Takerkoust. The Ourika Valley is stunning at any time of the year, but particularly in spring, with the blossoms of almond and fruit trees. The terrain is perfect for less arduous trekking than what's on offer in the Toubkal area. Several beautiful gardens growing organic herbs and flowers are now open to visitors. The region is dotted with mudbrick Berber villages, and the vistas are endlessly picturesque.

OURIKA RIVER

The **Ourika River** ①, cutting deep through the High Atlas Mountains, is lined on both sides with a patchwork of neatly kept terraced gardens and orchards with almond and cherry trees, offering a vision of a bucolic paradise. The mudbrick cubic houses of the Berber villages cling precipitously to the mountain. The river almost never dries up, so the gardens produce all year round, and the people here have traditionally always been very powerful, as they controlled the water supply to the city of Marrakesh.

When Marrakesh gets too hot, having a picnic in the shade of trees or a dip in the river is a tempting proposition, but beware of sudden strong flash floods after heavy rainfall, particularly in winter. Many restaurants also have terraces on the river. The entrance to the Ourika Valley is 33km (20 miles) southeast of Marrakesh, and can be reached by bus or taxi.

Above: a Berber woman by the Seven Waterfalls.

GARDENS

The first village in the valley, coming from Marrakesh, is **Tnine Ourika**, which has a souk on Monday mornings, now popular with coach tours from Marrakesh, and a tourist office, the **Centre d'Information Touristique Ourika**, that provides information and a map for trekking in the area. Just across the bridge is the crumbling kasbah **Dar Caid Ourika**, that belonged to the 19th-century Ourika *caid*, or chieftain. Signposts lead the way from the main toad to the botanical garden at **Jardins Bio-aromatiques de l'Ourika (Nectarôme)** ②. The garden grows the organic herbs and plants used in traditional Berber remedies, and offers aromatherapy treatments on the premises using their products. Also signposted is the **Jardin du Safran** ③, which grows the purple flowers of the *crocus sativus* to produce saffron. Several wonderful

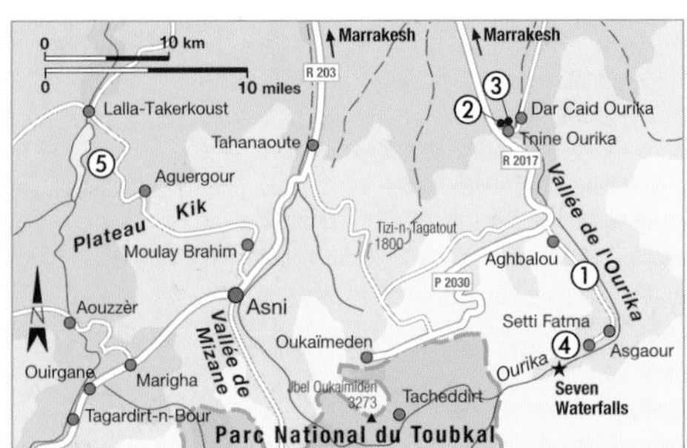

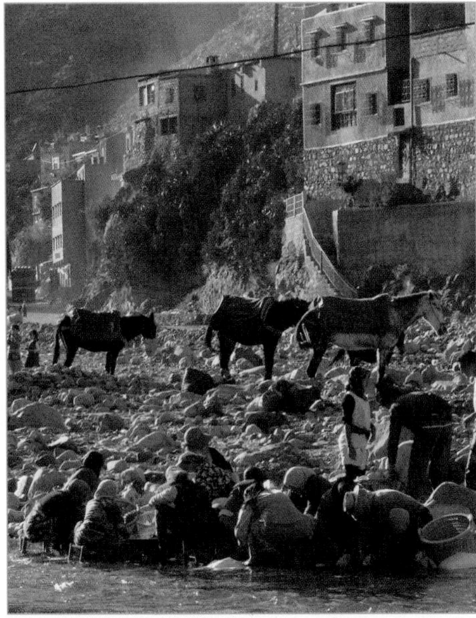

Left: Berber women washing clothes at Setti Fatma.

guesthouses in the valley, with large gardens, can be booked for lunch and organise off-the-beaten-track walks.

Below: mudbrick buildings dot the mountains.

SEE ALSO BERBER CULTURE, P.41; GARDENS, P.65

SETTI FATMA

The pretty hamlet of **Setti Fatma** ④ makes a good base for treks in this area. The most popular one-day walk is to the Seven Waterfalls, about four hours away, for a picnic and a cooling swim. On a bank above the river is the green-tiled koubba or **shrine of Setti Fatma**, not open for non-Muslims, the centre of a four-day *moussem* in August. Information for longer walks is available from the Bureau des Guides in the village.

SEE ALSO FESTIVALS AND EVENTS, P.55

LAKE LALLA TAKERKOUST

Built at the time of the French protectorate, the dam of Lalla Takerkoust not only provides the region of Marrakesh with electricity, but has also created a lovely and large artificial lake, only 40km (25 miles) away from Marrakesh. The lake has several beaches both public and private, for sunbathing and swimming, and rentals for kayaks, pedal boats, jet skis and windsurfs. It's quietest on the northern side of the lake. Around the lake there are opportunities to walk in the surroundings or rent quad bikes. Several restaurants around the lake offer a variety of cuisines, with great views over the lake and surroundings.

SEE ALSO SPORTS, P.116

Every year in August the Berbers of Setti Fatma celebrate the *moussem* of their patron saint, Setti Fatma. This is the most famous of a series of *moussems*, traditional celebrations of the saint's day of local saints, which in fact go back to the pre-Islamic harvest festivals. It's a joyous affair attended by the families of all the surrounding villages, with a huge souk, lots of entertainments and Sufi ceremonies. Recently the authorities have tried to stop the celebration of *moussems*, worried that they were too much of a stage for the ideas of fundamentalists, or on the contrary worried that they could be a target for other fundamentalists who consider these occasions 'un-Islamic'. Some villages cancelled the *moussem* in recent years, to use the money for local development projects instead.

Toubkal Park

Only over an hour and 70km (40 miles) away from Marrakesh is the superb Toubkal National Park in the High Atlas. This area offers unsurpassed views of the snow-capped mountains, total tranquillity and well-established routes for hikers. The town of Asni lies at the foot of the highest peaks, and has a large souk on Saturdays. The pleasant village of Imlil is the most popular departure point for the ascent of the park's highest peak, Jbel Toubkal. Day-trippers from Marrakesh can enjoy the unspoilt scenery of the mountains, with a short easy walk from Imlil and lunch on the terrace of the Kasbah du Toubkal ecolodge.

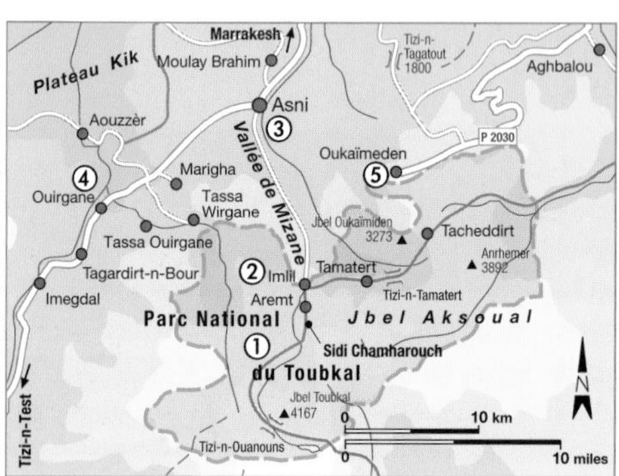

Above: Asni city gates.

PARC NATIONAL DU TOUBKAL

The **National Park of Toubkal** ① in the High Atlas, created in 1942 and covering a surface area of 38,000 hectares (95,000 acres), provides ample opportunities for great hikes. The scenery is incredibly varied, from barren cliffs, steep gorges and snow peaks to lush gardens and orchards, and scenic Berber villages where you can often spend the night in someone's home.

Jbel Toubkal is, at 4,167m (13,671ft), the highest peak and the park's main draw. Experienced hikers in good physical condition can make the climb from Imlil in two days, but three or four days allows for a more leisurely climb. The trail for this climb is clear and can be done without the help of a mountain guide. Between June and September is the best time, but beware that even in summer it can get bitterly cold at the top.

CLIMBING UP

Imlil ② is the main departure point for hikers. The **Bureau des Guides** can provide qualified mountain guides, maps and information; mule owners rent out camping equipment and mules to carry provisions and bags. The small town has a range of accommodation, from the backpackers' hostel to the more palatial **Kasbah du Toubkal**, situated on a rocky outcrop above the village; it is an old kasbah converted into a hotel, run by local Berbers. The girls in the **Dar Taliba School Garden** grow their own vegetables for lunch, and plants to prepare the traditional Berber remedies.

An hour's walk away is the delightful village of **Aremt**, where many villagers offer rooms to stay. From here the trail zigzags up the mountain, past the **shrine of Sidi Chamarouch**, where Berber families come on a pilgrimage to seek a cure for their mentally ill.

SEE ALSO GARDENS, P.65; SPORTS, P.119; WALKS, DRIVES AND VIEWS, P.128

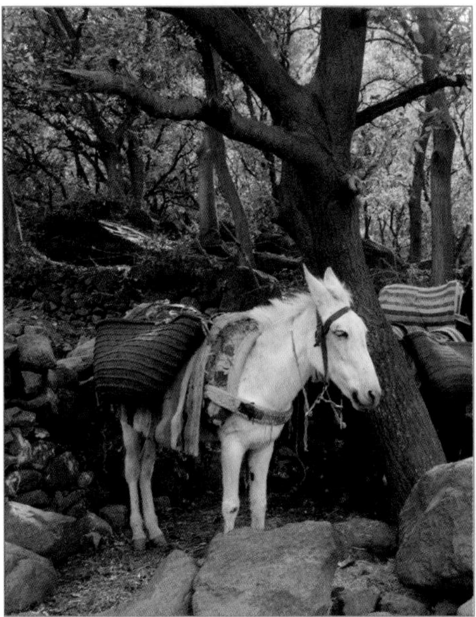

Left: mules can be hired to carry provisions on treks.

ASNI VALLEY

The region's administrative centre is the small town of **Asni** ③. It has a large souk on Saturdays where villagers from all the surrounding area come and trade. In recent years the souk has become a popular stop for coach tours from Marrakesh, so come early for the real thing.

16km (10 miles) south of Asni is **Ouirgane** ④, another base for trekking, less crowded, but also with less facilities. The eco-friendly **Dar Tassa** in the mountain hamlet of Tassa Ouirgane organises treks in the nearby **Takherhort Nature Reserve** to see Barbary sheep, or Aoudad, endemic to North Africa, gazelles and other protected species. Barbary sheep are in fact a species of Caprinae (goat-antelope) found in the rocky mountains of this reserve. Their huge horns curve outwards and backwards and can reach up to 50cm (20in).

SEE ALSO BERBER CULTURE, P.41

OUKAÏMEDEN

About an hour away from Marrakesh is Morocco's main ski resort at **Oukaïmeden** ⑤, 2,650m (8,694ft) high. There is usually snow here from January to early March, and during the peak season there are seven runs, from black to nursery slope, with the highest ski lift in Africa at 3,243m (10,640ft). Snow has been scarce in recent years, but rumours have it that Gulf Arabs are investing to make it the best ski resort in Africa, with artificial snow machines, new cable lifts and more runs. In summer, Oukaïmeden is a good base for trekking.

SEE ALSO SPORTS, P.118

Below: the snowy peaks of Oukaïmeden.

The Tizi-n-Test, the narrow road from Marrakesh to Taroudant through the High Atlas, offers one of the most spectacular, if dangerous, drives in the country. The road passes the splendid Almohad mosque of Tin Mal, on a hilltop beside the road, one of the few mosques in Morocco open to non-Muslim visitors. After that the road climbs to the summit of the Tizi-n-Test pass at 2,100m (6,900ft), past stunning scenery. The descent is very different, but equally exhilarating, as the views open up to the Souss Valley 1,600m (5,250ft) below.

Tizi-n-Tichka

Higher than the Tizi-n-Test, and a beautiful but less strenuous drive, the Tizi-n-Tichka connects Marrakesh with the oases and kasbahs in the south. The road leads through oak and walnut forests first, before ascending to an increasingly barren landscape. Past the Tizi-n-Tichka pass is the lunar landscape of the Middle Atlas and the impressive kasbahs of Telouet and Aït Benhaddou, no doubt familiar from blockbuster movies like *Gladiator* and *Lawrence of Arabia*. The French garrison town of Ouazarzate still feels like something of an outpost today, despite the presence of the film studios and the luxury hotels that house the international movie stars.

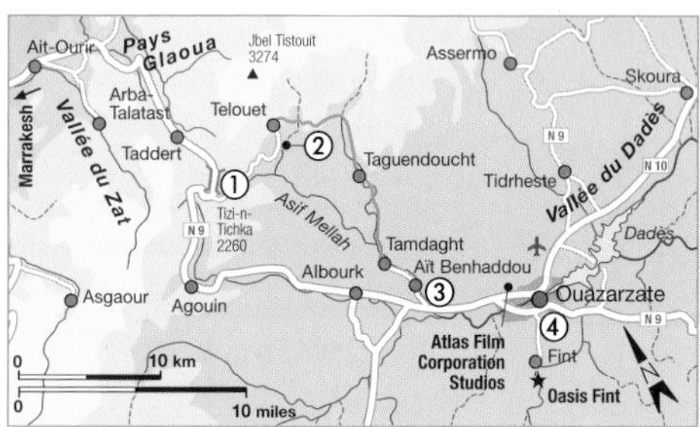

تيزى نتيشكة
COL DU TICHKA
ALT 2260

Above: the road ascends to great heights.

TIZI-N-TICHKA

The **Tizi-n-Tichka** ①, meaning 'gate to the pastures' in Berber language, is a safer, less dramatic road than the Tizi-n-Test to the west of Marrakesh. However, it makes for a great drive through the wonderful mountain scenery, stopping at some Berber kasbahs on the way, before arriving at Ouazarzate, the gateway to the southern oases in the Sahara desert. The road meanders besides the fertile Zat Valley, a favourite with weekend walkers from Marrakesh. After Taddert the road starts climbing up for the last 15km (10 miles) to the summit, 2,260m (7,410ft) high. Children and adults attempt to sell fossils and minerals all along the way. The road can be treacherous in winter and the pass is often closed, so ask before setting out.

The **Atlas Film Cororation Studios** (tel: tel 0524-882 212; www.atlasstudios.com) offer guided tours where you can see the sets used for famous movies filmed in and around Ouazarzate, including *Asterix*, *Kundun*, *Jewel of the Nile* and *Gladiator*. The king has done much to promote Morocco as a country to make films in. Almost every movie set in biblical times or in the Middle East is made here. **North Africa Horse** (tel: 0524-886 689; www.northafricahorse.fr) arrange the stunts and scenes with horses and camels for the films, and sometimes they stage re-enactments of famous movie scenes.

TELOUET

After the pass, the landscape changes dramatically. The **Glaoui Kasbah of Telouet** ② is signposted from the road, and appears across the river from the village of **El Khemis Telouet**, after 21km (13 miles). Once an important stop on the trans-Saharan caravan route, Telouet gathered its wealth from the toll traders were forced to pay. In 1953 the Pasha of Marrakesh, Thami el Glaoui, who was originally from Telouet, was ousted by the Independence movement, so his town lost its importance and the kasbah fell into disrepair. The mudbrick building may be crumbling, but the sheer opulence of the place is still evident from the scale and some of the details.

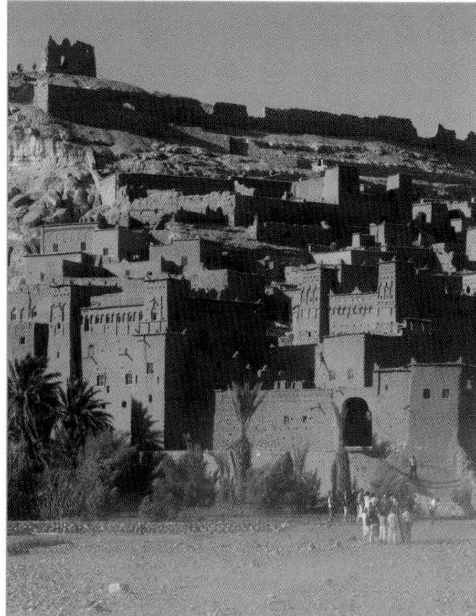

Left: Aït Benhaddou is the quintessential desert kasbah.

The piste from Telouet to Aït Benhaddou, which passes through delightful Berber villages, should only be attempted on foot or by 4WD.

Back on the Tizi-n-Tichka, between the turn off for Telouet and **Aït Benhaddou**, is the charming **I Rocha** hotel, run by a local geologist who is passionate about the mountains and rocks around him and leads walking tours in the area.
SEE ALSO ACCOMMODATION, P.37; KASBAHS AND PALACES, P.69

AÏT BENHADDOU

The **Kasbah of Aït Benhaddou** ③ appears like a mirage across the Ounila river, and seen from the village it almost looks too neat and picture-perfect, particularly after a visit to Telouet. Various film crews have touched up what started life as an 11th-century caravanserai, and later became a series of kasbahs built tightly together. Only a few people still live in the old kasbah, most of whom will open their house for a tip, and there are stunning views from the top.
SEE ALSO FILM, P.56; KASBAHS AND PALACES, P.69

OUAZARZATE

The town of **Ouazarzate** ④ sounds more exotic than it is. Despite the authorities' attempts to spruce up the public squares and the fact that is has over half a million inhabitants, as well as the presence of the internationally renowned film studios, it still retains the feel of an outpost, with little character of its own, and apart from the **Taourirt Kasbah**, not much of interest. The thing it has going for it is the dry warm climate all year round, an airport allowing fast access from other cities and a wide range of hotels. Its an important crossroads, with roads going north to Marrakesh, east to the Dadès Valley and the desert beyond, south to Zagora and west to Agadir. The Taourirt Kasbah stands on the eastern end of town, while the **film studios** are at Ouazarzate's northern entrance.
SEE ALSO FILM, P.57

Below: a traditionally dressed Berber man on the Tichka pass.

Essaouira

A laid-back sea resort 170km (100 miles) west of Marrakesh, Essaouira has long been a hangout for surfers and artists. Once known as Mogador, it was the harbour for Marrakesh and Timbuktu, so it was always home to a mix of Moroccans, other Africans and Europeans. The town took its current shape in the 18th century when the French architect Théodore Cornut, captured by the sultan, redesigned the medina and city walls. The small, whitewashed medina is easily explored on foot, galleries offer work by local artists, the fishing fleet brings in a fresh catch throughout the day, and on a bright day there is always the beach.

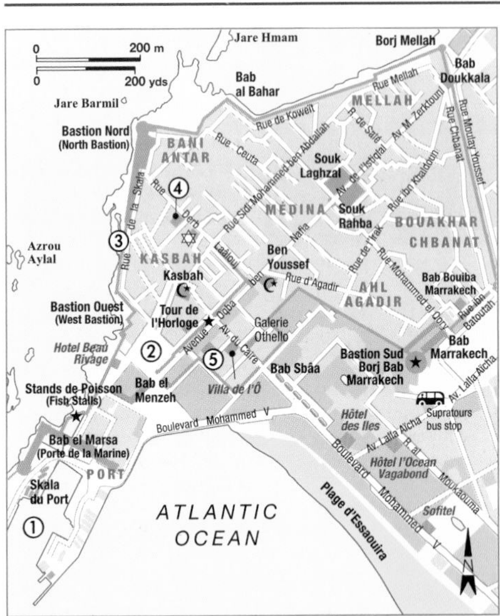

As Essaouira gets more crowded, Marrakchi expats head for the even more laid-back sea resort of Oualidia, about 120km (75 miles) north of Essaouira. Still very under-developed, Oualidia is situated on a lagoon connected to the Atlantic, which offers both safe bathing for families and on the ocean good surfing for surfers. The present king's grandfather, Mohammed V, built a summer villa on the beach, which is now atmospherically crumbling. The town is famous for its oysters and fabulous seafood, offered at many restaurants in town.

THE PORT

The small **Port de Pêche** ① (fishing harbour) is protected by the L-shaped **Skala du Port**, a square-shaped sea bastion, commanding great vistas over the sea, port and uninhabited islands of Mogador. The port is a busy place, with colourful fishing boats coming in and out, nets being repaired, fish being sold and new boats build. Essaouira has the third-largest sardine-fishing fleet in the country. At the far end of the port, the restaurant **Chez Sam**, shaped like a ship, overlooks the boats coming in, but the freshest fish is grilled in front of you at the **fish stalls** just outside the harbour.

SEE ALSO MONUMENTS, P.76; RESTAURANTS, P.107

PLACE MOULAY HASSAN

The most obvious place to start a visit of the medina is **place Moulay Hassan** ②, the large square beyond the port. The square is lined with tall white buildings and many café-terraces. Coming from the port the first alley to the left off the square leads past antique and crafts shops, to the town battlements or **Skala de la Ville** ③ where you can climb up to the tower of the **North Bastion** and walk on the terrace lined with heavy bronze cannon. Below the bastion are the workshops and shops of the **woodcarvers**, who

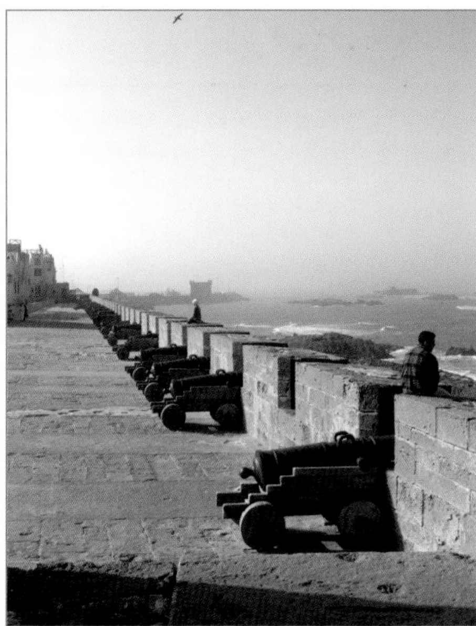

Left: on the ramparts of the Skala du Port.

work the thuja wood Essaouira is famous for, with its rich texture and lovely perfume.
SEE ALSO MONUMENTS, P.77; SQUARES, P.121

MEDINA AND SOUKS

The main thoroughfare inside the medina is the **rue Sidi Mohammed ben Abdallah,** which runs from the place Moulay Hassan to the old Mellah, or Jewish quarter. Off this street to the left is rue Laatouj, which leads to the Skala de la Ville and the ethnographic **Musée Sidi Mohammed ben Abdallah** ④ in the 19th century town house of a pasha. The museum has a delightful collection of jewellery, weapons, crafts, musical instruments and textiles. The streets and alleys on and off the main streets are lined with shops selling **Essaouira crafts**, including woodwork, musical instruments, henna-tattooed goatskin lampshades and beauty products made of argan oil produced in the co-operatives near Essaouira.

Further up the rue Sidi Mohammed ben Abdallah to the right is a wider street leading off to the fish and vegetable market, which has a spice market in the galleries.
SEE ALSO MUSEUMS AND GALLERIES, P.81

Below: at one of Essaouira's woodcarving workshops.

AVENUE OQBA BEN NAFIA

The old Mechouar or parade ground, running alonside the city walls, is now the tree-lined Avenue Oqba ben Nafia. On this street is the long-established **Galerie Frédéric Damgaard** ⑤, which has promoted the Gnaoua artists of Essaouira for years. The Gnaoua were wandering healers and musicians, but with the rise in popularity of modern hospitals, many have taken to painting in their own particular style. There are several other galleries in the kasbah area behind the Galerie Damgaard. The town holds a popular **Gnaoua festival** every year.

On the west side is an archway under the distinctive **Tour de l'Horloge** or clock tower leading into the souks.
SEE ALSO FESTIVALS AND EVENTS, P.55; MUSEUMS AND GALLERIES, P.81

BEACH

South of the town stretches the beach, relatively calm for the Atlantic Ocean. Essaouira is known as the windy city of Africa and the beach is more for water sports, a game of football or long walks rather than sunbathing, as the wind often blows sand right in the face. At the end of the bay stands a ruined fort which is slowly being reclaimed by the ocean.
SEE ALSO SPORTS, P.116

A–Z

In the following section Marrakesh's attractions and services are organised by theme, under alphabetical headings. Items that link to another theme are cross-referenced. All sights that are plotted on the atlas section at the end of the book are given a page number and grid reference.

Accommodation

Visitors are spoilt for choice when it comes to accommodation in Marrakesh, with everything from simple hotels to romantic hideaways, and from the backpacker's haven to the luxury riad, where every minute is an indulgence. Most people head straight for the medina, dreaming of the ultimate riad experience. The area around the Jemaa el Fna is the most centrally located, but has mostly budget hotels. The rest of the medina is more residential. The ideal is to have a mixed stay with a few days in a riad in the medina, and a few days in a hotel in the Palmeraie or in the surroundings of Marrakesh. *See also Riads, p.108–9.*

JEMAA EL FNA

Gallia

30 rue de la Recette; tel: 0524-445 913; www.ilove-marrakesh.com/hotelgallia; $$; map p.139 C1

Attractive and comfortable rooms are arranged around a traditionally tiled courtyard with a palm tree in the middle, a delightful place for breakfast. Well situated off Rue Bab Agnaou near the Jemaa el Fna, and very friendly service. But it's success means it always fills up quickly, so book ahead.

Grand Hôtel Tazi

Corner of avenue el Mouahidine and rue de Bab Agnaou; tel: 0524-442 787; $; map p.138 C1

This is an older-style hotel that is a bit run-down but has bags of character and a bohemian feel. If you dislike expensive, self-consciously chic riads run by expats, this ornate and ramshackle place might be for you. If the room you are shown does not appeal, ask if they have a better one available (ones at the back are quieter). No credit cards.

Below: the Jnane Mogador is a good-value hotel in a classic riad.

Hôtel Ali

Rue Moulay Ismail; tel: 0524-440 522; $; map p.138 C1

Popular choice for backpackers and adventure travellers, and a good place to hook up with hikers and mountain bikers. Cheap and cheerful, with a decent restaurant and buffet on its terrace in summer. Very central location just off the Jemaa el Fna.

Hôtel de Foucauld

Avenue el Mouahidine; tel: 0524-440 806; $; map p.138 B1

This older-style hotel has a gloomy exterior, has lost a star and is no longer licensed (it still allows customers to bring their own alcohol), but it is conveniently located just a stone's throw from the Jemaa el Fna and remains a firm favourite among hikers and adventure travellers. No credit cards.

Hôtel du Trésor

77 derb Sidi Bouloukat, off rue Riad Zitoun el Kedim; tel: 0524-375 113; www.hotel-du-tresor.com; $–$$; map p.139 C2

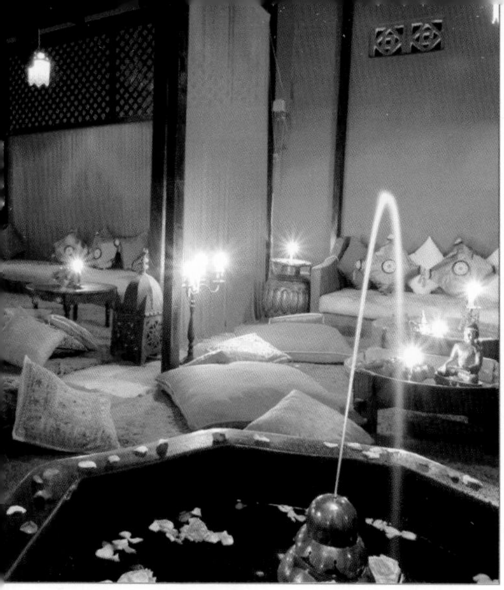

Left: classic Moroccan fantasy style at Dar Fakir.

Prices given are for a standard double room with bathroom, in high season, including breakfast, service and taxes. Note that rates can often be significantly lower if booked online or through a travel agent, or in low season.

$ under 600Dh
$$ 600–1,100Dh
$$$ 1,100–1,600Dh
$$$$ over 1,600Dh

With over 600 riad hotels to choose from, the choice can be overwhelming and the differences between them not always obvious. Several websites specialise in booking riads, including **Marrakech Riads** (tel: 0524-391 609; www.marrakech-riads.net). One way to find the right riad is via the Marrakesh experts **Boutique Souk** (tel: 0661-324 475; UK mobile: 0044-7900-195 261; www.boutiquesouk.com), run by the wonderful Irish Rosena and her French husband Fred. With a portfolio of carefully selected riads for all budgets, they can organise anything from the wildest party weekend to the most romantic wedding party.

This utterly charming little hotel, in a quiet backwater near the Jemaa el Fna, has been lovingly restored by its Italian owner. Most traditional details have been retained, while most new additions were salvaged from old hotels like La Mamounia *(see p.36)* or local junk markets. The 14 rooms are set around a brilliant white courtyard with an orange tree in the middle. The rooms are simple but very tastefully decorated, always with a touch of humour. Very good value.

Jnane Mogador
116 derb Sidi Bouloukat, off rue Riad Zitoun el Kedim; tel: 0524-426 323; www.jnanemogador.com; $; map p.139 C1
Excellent budget hotel in a traditional 19th-century riad with comfortable, spic-and-span rooms, an in-house hammam and a great rooftop terrace. This is the kind of place people tend to come back to, and part of the reason is perhaps the owner, the laid-back and cool Mohammed.

Sherazade
3 derb Jemaa, rue Riad Zitoun el Kedim; tel: 0524-429 305; www.hotelsherazade.com; $–$$; map p.139 D1
A deservedly popular small hotel (22 rooms), in two traditional riads with tiled and plant-filled courtyards and good rooftop terraces. Some rooms have air conditioning and some shared facilities, but most are en suite.

SOUTHERN MEDINA

Dar Fakir
16 derb Abou el Fadal, off Riad Zitoun el Jedid; tel: 0524-441 100; www.darfakir.com; $$$; map p.139 C1
From the same owner Nourdine Fakir, who runs the most trendy venues in town, including Villa Rosa and Nikki Beach *(see p.86)*, this small riad, just eight rooms, caters for the club-

Below: one of Dar Fakir's romantic bedrooms.

Above: atmospheric rooftop dining at La Sultana.

bing generation. The simple but stylish rooms are set around a great courtyard strewn with cushions. The heady incense burns non-stop, and the Buddha Bar lounging music adds to the chilled atmosphere.

La Sultana
403 rue de la Kasbah, Kasbah; tel: 0524-388 088; www.lasultanamarrakesh.com; $$$$; map p.136 B2
Ornate luxury hotel with a good location near the Saadian Tombs. A complex of four riads offers 21 spacious rooms, an attractive heated pool, and a well-equipped spa with an open-air Jacuzzi on its roof. A little over-the-top for many people's taste, but the very definition of oriental chic for others.

Relais and Châteaux Villa des Orangers
6 rue Sidi Mimoun; tel: 0524-384 638; www.villadesorangers.com; $$$$; map p.136 B3
Established hotel that successfully incorporates modern comforts (large, sleek beds and luxuriously appointed bathrooms) in a traditional but tasteful setting with antique furniture, open fires in winter, a good-sized pool and excellent restaurant. One of the city's top addresses, and not far from the Jemaa el Fna.

Riad Assakina
14 derb Alaati Allah, Hay Salaam; tel: 0524-380 552; http://riadassakina.com; $$$–$$$$; map p.137 D3
A large and spacious riad in the Mellah, overlooking the Bahia Palace. The rooms, overlooking the bright courtyard with swimming pool, are tastefully decorated in a contemporary Moroccan style with warm colours. In the afternoon complimentary Moroccan tea and sweets are served on the terrace for guests.

Riad Kaiss
65 derb Jedid, off rue Riad Zitoun el Kedim; tel: 0524-440 141; www.riadkaiss.com; $$$$; map p.137 C4
Sumptuous riad with just eight rooms around a peaceful tree-filled courtyard, which feels very much like a home away from home. The breezy colourful rooms are decorated in a mixed Moroccan-Mediterranean style, all with *tadelakht* en suite bathrooms.

Right: ornate opulence at La Sultana.

EASTERN MEDINA

Riad Akka
65 derb Lahbib Magni, off rue Riad Zitoun el Jedid; tel: 0524-375 767; www.riad-akka.com; $$$; map p.139 E1
Akka is what the last oasis before the caravan reaches the Sahara is called, and this small guesthouse with just five rooms truly is in an oasis in this hectic city. Designed by the owner, a French interior designer, this sleek riad successfully mixes a contemporary style with the rich traditional Moroccan heritage, but the overall effect is always sensuous. Freshly prepared meals can be ordered in advance.

Riyad Al Moussika
17 derb Cherkaoui, off rue Douar Graoua; tel: 0524-389 067; www.riyad-al-moussika.ma; $$$$; map p.139 E1
This traditional-style luxurious riad, five minutes' walk from the place Jemaa El Fna, was one of the residences of the former Pasha of Marrakesh, Thami el Glaoui *(see p.12)*. Six spacious double bedrooms are centred around a courtyard with a small pool and an Andalusian-style garden. Prices include airport transfers, access to the in-house hammam, breakfast, tea and a delicious lunch cooked by the resident Chef.

MOUASSINE QUARTER

Dar Attajmil
23 rue el Ksour, Quartier Ksour; tel: 0524-426 966; www.darattajmil.com; $$$; map p.138 B3
Another small guesthouse, with just four rooms, run by the friendly Italian Lucrezia, who has given every attention to details. The rooms are decorated in Marrakchi sand and terracotta hues with the best of local furnishings. The tiny in-house hammam is in a little turret on the terrace, and offers spa treatments as well.

Maison MKhotel
14 derb Sebaai, Quartier Ksour; tel: 0524-376 173; www.maisonmk.com; $$$$; map p.138 B3
If money is no object, then this is one of the newest and chic-est places in town, where everything is specially designed in a contemporary Moroccan style, with loads of gorgeous Arabic calligraphy.

The London-based Moroccan artist Hassan Hajjaj has made his name with his colourful pop-artworks of cool veiled Moroccan girls, framed in sweet wrappers, and other works. His riad in Marrakesh, **Riad Yima** (52 derb Arjane, Rahba Kedima; tel: 0524-391 987; www.riadyima.com, www.hassanhajjaj.com; $$–$$$; map p.139 D3), has a little shop-cum-gallery with his work and a few very colourful rooms decorated with his artworks and his furniture.

Every whim can be satisfied, with fabulous fairy-tale rooms, gourmet cooking and a seriously good spa.

Riad el Fenn
2 derb Moulay Abdallah ben Hezzian, Bab el Ksour; tel: 0524-441 210; www.riadelfenn.com; $$$$; map p.138 B3
This is one of the medina's most chic and exclusive riads, with contemporary Brit art on the walls and secluded areas for lounging. Facilities include a screening room (used in the city's International Film Festival) and an 18m-(60ft-) long putting green, as well as a superb pool and hammam.

Riad Tarabel
8 derb Sraghna, Dar el Bacha; tel: 0524-391 706; www.riadtarabel.com; $$$; map p.134 B1
One of the more recent arrivals, this airy and bright riad has a rather Mediterranean feel, and the large rooms are partly decorated with contemporary Moroccan furnishings as well as some family heirlooms from a French château. Charming and very peaceful.

Above: charming finishing touches at Riad Tarabel.

NORTHERN MEDINA

Dar Saria
46 derb Ouyaha, Sidi Abdelaziz; tel: 0661-444 358/0668-515 420; www.darsaria.com; $$; map p.134 B1
Set in an old *caid* (local chieftain's house), with 16 ornamental pillars surrounding the courtyard, are just three bright and airy rooms decorated sparingly but very effectively with Moroccan and West African textiles and crafts. Great atmosphere and delicious dinners cooked by the house cook.

Hotel and Ryads Naoura Barrière
rue Djebel Akhdar, Bab Doukkala; tel: 0524-459 000; www.naoura-barriere.com; $$$$; map p.134 A2

Prices given are for a standard double room with bathroom, in high season, including breakfast, service and taxes. Note that rates can often be significantly lower if booked online or through a travel agent, or in low season.

$ under 600Dh
$$ 600–1,100Dh
$$$ 1,100–1,600Dh
$$$$ over 1,600Dh

Talk of the town, the luxury French chain of hotels and casinos Lucien Barrière has just opened a large hotel for the medina, with 86 suites in several riads, several gourmet restaurants, including a Fouquet's of Paris fame, and a state-of-the-art spa.

La Maison Arabe
1 derb Assebhe, Bab Doukkala; tel: 0524-387 010; www.lamaisonarabe.com; $$$$; map p.133 E3
This hotel near Bab Doukkala started out as a restaurant, and its well-regarded cookery courses are part of its success. The standard rooms are good value, especially in low season, while the superior rooms have fireplaces and terraces. There's no on-site pool, but a shuttle bus takes guests to one 10 minutes away. Rates include afternoon tea as well as breakfast.

Riad Dyor
1 derb Driba Jdida, Sidi ben Slimane; tel: 0524-375 980; www.ryaddyor.com; $$$$; map p.134 B3
Fabulous small boutique hotel with plunge pool and hammam, owned and designed by an Ibiza-based designer couple. The eight stunning, elegant and spacious rooms are designed in a modern Moorish style, and breakfast is served up on the roof terrace.

Despite the large number of hotels in Marrakesh, the best ones fill up fast, so it is essential to book a room in advance, especially during peak periods such as Easter and Christmas. Room prices in Marrakesh are higher than anywhere else in the country, but they do usually include a good breakfast. If you are travelling with friends or in a small group, it is worth trying to book a whole riad, as many of them don't have more than four or five rooms.

Riad Farnatchi
2 derb el Farnatchi; tel: 0524-384 910; www.riadfarnatchi.com; $$$$; map p.134 C1
Five small riads in the oldest part of Marrakesh were put together and restored as a private holiday home of a retired award-winning British hotelier, but it was too good only to be used a few weeks a year. This feels like a beautiful opulent home, run like clockwork by the knowledgeable Lynn, who can just about make your every wish come true.

Riad Tizwa
Derb Gueraba, 26 rue Dar el Bacha; tel: 0668-190 872; www.riadtizwa.com; $$; map p.134 B2
This beautifully proportioned riad has six bedrooms over three floors, set around an open courtyard. The rooms, large and cubic, are painted white and decorated with splashes of colour, for a playful contemporary feel. Good value.

Tchai'kana
25 derb el Ferrane, Azbest; tel: 0524-284 587; www.tchaikana.com; $$–$$$; map p.139 E4
Tchai'kana means the place where you drink tea, and the splendid courtyard of this very friendly guesthouse is the perfect place for an afternoon cup or pre-dinner glass. The very spacious rooms reflect the owners' love of travel, with plenty of objects brought back from elsewhere. Delightful and tranquil place, offering excellent value.

Tlaata wa-Sitteen
63 derb el Ferrane, Riad Laarous; 0524-383 026/0661-246 887; www.tlaatawa-sitteen.com; $–$$; map p.134 B2
A definite favourite, this small riad is a far cry from slick, über-designed riads elsewhere in the medina. This very friendly guesthouse has the feel of a 1970s hippie hang-out. It is run by young Moroccans, who often organise an impromptu couscous

Below: a shady courtyard at Jnane Tamsna.

Above: a tranquil room at Tchai'kana.

for guests and friends, or join in for breakfast. Recommended. The same owners have opened another similar guesthouse with gallery nearby, **Dar Najma** (18 derb el Ferrane; Riad Laarous; tel: 0524-375 610/0661-246 887; www.darnajma.com; $$), also know as 'La Maison des Artistes'.

GUÉLIZ

Bab Hotel

Corner of blvd Mansour el Dahabi and rue Mohammed el Beqal; tel: 0524-435 250; www.babhotelmarrakesh.com; $$$; map p.132 B4

The hip Moroccan fashion designer Fadila el Gadi has opened her own funky hotel in Guéliz, said to mark the beginning of the return of trendy hotels to the New Town (Ville Nouvelle). The hotel has spacious, bright rooms that attract a younger crowd. The boutique sells Fadila's great clothes, such as kaftans and other traditional Moroccan garments, with a contemporary twist or with a touch of colour.

Hôtel Toulousain

44 rue Tariq ibn Ziad; tel: 0524-430 033; www.geocities.com/hotel_toulousain; $; map p.134 C4

A great budget hangout, run by a friendly Moroccan-American family, in an upmarket neighbourhood. The rooms are basic but well kept, set around some shady courtyards. It was a favourite with Beat Generation writers and artists like Brion Gysin and William Burroughs *(see p.17)*.

Jnane Tamsna

Hay Mohammadi, Douar Abiad, Palmeraie; tel: 0524-329 423; www.jnanetamsna.com; $$$$

Set in beautiful grounds designed by the ethnobotanist owner Gary Martin, this luxurious complex is comprised of spacious rooms and suites in four separate large villas, beautifully designed by his wife, the French-Senegalese designer Meryanne Loum-Martin. The hotel has several pools, an opulent salon where pre-dinner drinks are served, tennis courts and well-tended perfumed gardens, which supply organic produce for the kitchen.

SEE ALSO GARDENS, P.64

Prices given are for a standard double room with bathroom, in high season, including breakfast, service and taxes. Note that rates can often be significantly lower if booked online or through a travel agent, or in low season.

$ under 600Dh
$$ 600–1,100Dh
$$$ 1,100–1,600Dh
$$$$ over 1,600Dh

Les Deux Tours

Douar Abiad; tel: 0524-329 525; www.les-deuxtours.com; $$$$

A plush garden hotel in the Palmeraie, with a good pool and hammam. Recently refurbished, it is a favourite among the fashion crowd and those

Below: the open courtyard at Riad Tizwa *(left)* and enjoying the hammam at Riad Farnatchi *(right)*.

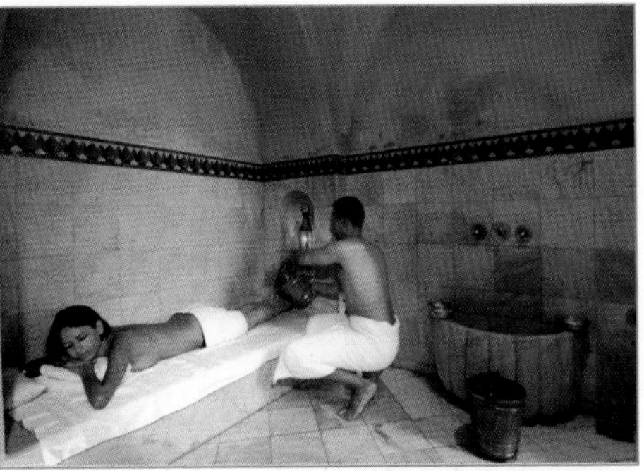

Right: the Kasbah du Toubkal is in a stunning location.

looking for peace and tranquillity, and more affordable than some of the private villas nearby.

HIVERNAGE

Es Saadi Hotel & Resort

Avenue el Qadissia; tel: 0524-448 811; www.essaadi.com; $$$–$$$$; map p.133 D1

The long-established, family-run es-Saadi has seen many illustrious guests hang out by its wonderful pool in the mature gardens. The hotel recently opened a more expensive, opulent wing, hoping to attract the international film stars attending the Marrakesh Film Festival.

La Mamounia

Avenue Bab Jedid; tel: 0524-444 409; www.mamounia.com; $$$$; map p.133 E1

This former palace, which was turned into a hotel in 1923, was putting the finishing touches to a massive refurbishment funded by the king at the time this book went to press. A preview of the new-look hotel showed that it will definitely restore its reputation as the premier place to stay in the city, full of old-school charm, a cross between a grand palace in Fez and the Orient Express. Its gardens, fabulous new Moroccan restaurant in a specially built riad, casino and piano bar will be open to non-residents. It should reopen by Oct 2009.

SEE ALSO GARDENS, P.64

> Many riad owners in Marrakech now arrange a day trip for their guests to the **Kasbah du Toubkal** *(see p.22 and right)*. Lunch on the rooftop terrace can be arranged in advance, followed by a walk in the beautiful surroundings. The Kasbah has another ecolodge about a day's walk away, for hikers who like their views with comforts. *See also Sports, p.119.*

OURIKA VALLEY

Beldi Country Club

6km (4 miles) south of Marrakesh, Route du Barrage, Cherifia; tel: 0524-383 950; www.beldicountryclub.com; $$$

Newly opened rustic mudbrick bungalows have been built to look like a Berber village, set in a great garden, with access to the already well-established Beldi Country Club, which boasts large pools, a rose garden, a restaurant and a spa.

SEE ALSO GARDENS, P.65; SPORTS, P.116

TOUBKAL PARK

Dar Adrar

Imlil, (60km/40 miles from Marrakesh); 0668-760 165/0670-726 809; www.daradrar.com; $

This is a simple but delightful guesthouse, perched on top of the village, run by one of the most expert mountain guides in the area, Mohammed Aztat. He can also arrange hikes in the Atlas.

SEE ALSO SPORTS, P.119

Domaine de la Roseraie

Ouirgane; tel: 0524-439 128; www.laroseraiehotel.com; $$$

Long-established mountain retreat (40 rooms and four suites, the latter with their own fireplaces) set in the midst of lovely mature gardens. There is a good restaurant, plus three pools and a hammam, and horseriding and trekking with mules can be arranged.

Kasbah du Toubkal

Imlil (60km/40 miles from Mar-

Below: a calm and simple room at La Pause.

Left: the Villa Persane at Es Saadi Hotel & Resort.

Above: La Pause can arrange cross golf for guests.

rakesh); tel: 0524-485 611; www.kasbahdutoubkal.com; $–$$$$
Superb converted kasbah with eco-friendly credentials, run by the local villagers. The Kasbah has the most stunning views over the Toubkal massif, and if you read the guest book, many a guest has had quite a spiritual awakening here. Offers a range of lodging options, from inexpensive dormitory accommodation to a luxury apartment.
SEE ALSO RESTAURANTS, P.106; SPORTS, P.119

La Bergerie
Ouirgane; tel: 0524-485 716; www.labergerie-maroc.ma; $$
A stone lodge in traditional Berber style situated in outstanding countryside. Offers simple but comfortable rooms (some with fireplace), cosy restaurant and bar, and an outdoor pool in summer.

TIZI-N-TICHKA

I Rocha
Douar Tisselday, Ighrem N'Oudal; tel: 0667-737 002; www.irocha.com; $–$$
Delightful guesthouse, with simple but lovingly decorated rooms, using textiles and furnishings collected on trips across Morocco. Geologist Ahmed was born in the village nearby, and Catherine has lived in the country for many years. Together they offer the warmest welcome, a passionate encounter with the local culture, interesting walks and delicious French-Moroccan meals supervised by Catherine, who is an excellent cook.

La Pause
Douar Lmih Laroussième, Agafay; tel: 0661-306 494; www.lapause-marrakesh.com; $$
Rustic rooms in mudbrick with a simple but warm and comfortable decor. This is the perfect place to come for a respite from Marrakesh city life, even for the afternoon or evening, but it is better for a longer stay. The hotel organises dinners by the fire, or sessions of cross golf, mountain biking, walking and horse riding to discover its amazing surroundings with the High Atlas peaks as a back drop.
SEE ALSO SPORTS, P.118

ESSAOUIRA

Hôtel Beau Rivage
145 place Moulay Hassan; tel/fax: 0524-475 925; www.essaouiranet.com/beaurivage; $
Refurbished classic Essaouira budget hotel, as central as it gets, overlooking the place Moulay Hassan. Rooms are squeaky clean and comfortable, and breakfast is served on the roof terrace.

Villa de l'Ô
3 rue Mohammed ben Messouad; tel: 0524-476 375; www.villadelo.com; $$$–$$$$
The new kid on the block, this stunning 18th-century riad has recently opened as a boutique hotel, with sumptuous rooms decorated in an elegant, vaguely old colonial style.

Prices given are for a standard double room with bathroom, in high season, including breakfast, service and taxes. Note that rates can often be significantly lower if booked online or through a travel agent, or in low season.

$ under 600Dh
$$ 600–1,100Dh
$$$ 1,100–1,600Dh
$$$$ over 1,600Dh

Architecture

Marrakesh and its surrounding areas are home to a rich mix of architectural styles. As the Berbers lived in the mountains and deserts, their buildings had to protect them both from the harsh conditions outside and from raiding intruders. Most famous are the kasbahs, from where the ruling families controlled the caravan routes through the Atlas Mountains. The Arabs brought their own architecture, a rich mixture with Persian, Byzantine and Andalusian elements. Meanwhile, European Art Deco influence is felt in the Ville Nouvelle. These listings describe prominent Marrakchi architectural features and buildings.

BAB

A door, but also a city gate.

Bab Agnaou

Rue Oqba ben Nafaa, Southern Medina; map p.136 B2

Most Marrakesh gates are in mudbrick or *pisé*, but the Bab Agnaou is carved from blue Guéliz stone.

SEE ALSO MONUMENTS, P.75

FONDOUK

A large courtyard complex with artisans' workshops on the ground floor and rented rooms above. Some foundouks have been turned into hotels, while a few are still used as workshops and warehouses, mainly in Mouassine and near Ben Youssef Medersa (*see opposite*).

HAMMAM

A communal bathhouse, also known as a Turkish bath, with a series of cold, tepid and hot steam rooms. The bathhouse was often next to a mosque as they shared an ablution fountain, or next to a bakery, where bread was baked over the fires used to heat the water.

Above: a tile detail at a Marrakchi riad.

SEE ALSO PAMPERING, P.88–9

KASBAH

A fortified castle or citadel within the city where the ruler was protected from the outside by thick walls. The ksar, ksour in plural, is a fortified village, designed to protect people from raids by neighbouring tribes. These are mostly built from *pisé* or mudbrick, as this material is easily available and protects from the summer heat.

The French built **Guéliz** in the 1930s and filled it with Art Deco architecture. One of the oldest buildings is the old tourist office, built 1918, on the junction of rue de la Liberté and avenue Mohammed V. Walk the streets around the avenue Mohammed V for some wonderful Art Deco and Mauresque (Moorish-influenced) villas.

Aït Benhaddou Kasbah

Aït Benhaddou, 22km (14 miles) off the Tizi-n-Tichka; free but tip the custodian

The most impressive kasbah of them all.

SEE ALSO FILM, P.56; KASBAHS AND PALACES, P.69

Marrakesh Kasbah

Southern Medina; map p.136 B2–C1

Much of the kasbah houses the royal palace.

Glaoui Kasbah of Telouet

Telouet, off the Tizi-n-Tichka; admission by donation

Fabulous kasbah built by the infamous Glaoui family.

SEE ALSO KASBAHS AND PALACES, P.69

Left: distinctive Moroccan mosque design elements.

Koutoubia Mosque

Avenue Mohammed V; closed to non-Muslims but gardens 8am–8pm; map p.138 A/B1

This 12th-century minaret was the model for most Moroccan minarets.

SEE RELIGIONS AND RELIGIOUS SITES, P.94

RIAD

A courtyard house in the medina, or also a garden, involving decorative elements such as *zellij*, *tadelakht* and *mashrabiyya*.

SEE ALSO RIADS, P.108–9

ZAOUIA

Sufi centre, where spiritual practices take place, around the tomb of the holy founder of the community, or the *Sidi*.

SEE RELIGIONS AND RELIGIOUS SITES, P.95–6

Below: the Almoravid-built Koubba el Ba'adiyin.

KOUBBA

The domed tomb of a Muslim holy man or sometimes woman, also called a *marabout*. In the countryside this is usually a whitewashed mudbrick structure, in cities a chamber with a green pyramid-shaped roof. People visit these shrines in the hope of receiving a *baraka* (blessing), or during the *moussem*.

SEE ALSO BERBER CULTURE, P.41; RELIGIONS AND RELIGIOUS SITES, P.97

Koubba Ba'adiyin

Place ben Youssef; admission charge; daily Apr–Sept 9am–7pm, Oct–Mar 9am–6pm; map p.134 C1

Not a shrine, but a domed ablution hall.

SEE ALSO MONUMENTS, P.76

Koubba Lalla Zohra

Koutoubia Gardens, avenue Mohammed V; free; map p.138 B1

Lalla Zohra was the daughter of a freed slave, who is believed to have been a woman by day and a dove at night.

SEE ALSO MONUMENTS, P.74

MEDERSA

A religious college where the Quran and Islamic sciences are taught.

Ben Youssef Medersa

Place ben Youssef; admission charge; daily Apr–Sept 9am–7pm, Oct–Mar 9am–6pm; map p.134 C1

This 12th-century *medersa* has the finest *zellij* and carved plaster work.

SEE ALSO RELIGIONS AND RELIGIOUS SITES, P.94; RIADS, P.108

MEDINA

Arabic for city, and in Marrakesh, as elsewhere, it refers to the old city as opposed to the colonial New Town (Guéliz).

MOSQUE

The house of prayer for Muslims. It usually has a courtyard, prayer room, ablution fountain and a minaret, the tower from which the muezzin calls the *adhan* (call to prayer). In Morocco most mosques are closed to non-Muslims.

Berber Culture

The Berbers are the original inhabitants of Morocco, and North Africa, more widely. Their name is often said to come from the Greek for 'barbarian', but it is more likely to have come from the Arabic *bambara*, meaning 'a mix of unintelligible noises'. Berbers call themselves *Amazigh*. Contrary to the romantic image that portrays Berbers as nomads who cross the desert on camel back, their main activities are agriculture, which they painstakingly carry out in mountains and valleys, and above all trade – they were the first to open the caravan routes from North to West Africa.

HISTORY

Morocco's Berber tribes, long established in the Rif and Atlas mountains, mostly converted to Islam after the Arab general Uqba ben Nafi conquered Morocco in AD682 (before allegedly riding his horse into the surf of the Atlantic Ocean to celebrate the fact that he had no more land to take). Until then, most Berbers worshipped their own pantheon of gods, and were surrounded by a few small Jewish and Christian communities. In the centuries that followed, one Berber dynasty after another ruled Moroccan lands, until 1549, when the Arabic Saadians seized power. They were followed by the Alaouites, another Arabic dynasty who continue to rule today. Meanwhile, the Berber tribes of the Atlas Mountains have continued to live in their traditional ways, never successfully conquered by any incoming powers.

Valuing the strength and richness of their oral tradition, Berbers have always passed on songs to the next generation. Traditional Berber music can be heard at *moussems*, or saints' celebrations *(see opposite)*, and at the Marrakesh Popular Arts Festival *(see Festivals and Events, p.55)*. The most famous Berber band, the Masters of the Joujouka, inspired the Rolling Stones and Led Zeppelin, as well as the Beat writers like William S. Burroughs. To hear the sounds, visit the excellent website www.azawan.com.

LANGUAGE

About 40 percent of the population now acknowledges Berber identity, while most others are of mixed Berber-Arab descent. In recent years Berbers have been fighting to have their language and culture recognised. King Mohammed VI has been keen to confirm their rights and has agreed to allow Berber to be taught in schools again (it was forbidden under his father) and to have Berber programmes on television.

Above: a Berber farmer.

Arabic is Morocco's official language, and most people speak *darija*, the Moroccan dialect. While Arabic is a Semitic language, Berber linguistically belongs to the Afro-Asiatic group. There are three main Berber dialects in Morocco: Tachelhit, Tamazigh and Tarifit, all called *shilha* in Arabic. Tachelhit or Chleuh is spoken in the Souss Valley in southwest Morocco, Tamazigh is spoken in the Middle Atlas and valleys of the High Atlas, and Tarifit or Rifia in the Rif of northern Morocco. The

Left: many Berbers still live in mountain villages.

Berber women have always made **rugs** and **carpets**, mixing colours from different plants and minerals found in the Atlas Mountains. Rugs were not just furnishings, but also a way of expressing the life and traditions of the tribe. Carpets were traditionally made as part of a dowry, but now the sale of a carpet is seen as a good addition to household income.

Berber languages have been mainly oral, but there are now attempts to develop written forms. The Berber alphabet, probably derived from the ancient Punic script, has existed for around 2,500 years.

MARKETS

The Arabs mostly settled in the Moroccan cities, so their trade occurs mostly in the souks, where different streets are dedicated to particular trades. Berbers are more spread out, living in small villages in the mountains and valleys, and their trade happens mostly when they all travel and get together in the weekly markets, also called souks, in the main town of the region.

Asni

47km (30 miles) south of Marrakesh on Tizi-n-Test

One of the largest markets in the region, with textiles, home wares, cattle and food, held on Saturdays. It now also draws some bus loads of tourists from Marrakesh, so get there early.

Rahba Kedima

Medina, Marrakesh; daily 9am–7pm; map p.139 D3

This is the central spice market. In the middle of the square, Berber women sell their handmade wares: knitted or straw hats, baskets, toys, and herbs collected in the countryside.

SEE ALSO SOUKS, P.114

Tnine Ourika

33km (20 miles) from Marrakesh

The small town of Tnine has a good weekly Berber souk on Mondays.

MOUSSEMS

Until Arabs brought Islam to Morocco in the 7th century, most Berbers were polytheists. This explains why Berbers are attached to their saints, a practice officially discouraged in Islam. The countryside is dotted with *koubbas*, in which a holy man or *marabout* is buried. Every year a *moussem* is held in celebration of the *marabout* at which people from different villages come together to feast and trade. *Moussems* are also a way of hanging on to old traditions, as they are an opportunity for performances of Berber music, poetry and dances.

Dakka Marrakchia

In several neighbourhoods in the medina; February

A tribute to the Sabatou Rijal, the seven saints of Marrakesh.

SEE ALSO FESTIVALS AND EVENTS, P.54; RELIGIONS AND RELIGIOUS SITES, P.95

Moussem of Setti Fatma

Setti Fatma; August

Moussem of the local saint, with a large fair, music and dancing.

SEE ALSO FESTIVALS AND EVENTS, P.55

Below: Berber children.

Cafés

The Jemaa el Fna and the avenue Mohammed V are lined with café terraces, but until recently there were surprisingly few in the medina. Times are changing though, and as the medina becomes a chic place to hang out, the number of cafés is growing steadily. Moroccans love taking their coffee alone or chatting about the day's events with friends in a café. Traditionally cafés were *masculin pluriel*, men and only men, but that has also changed in Marrakesh, and you will find women almost everywhere. Most cafés only serve juices, mint tea, coffee and cold drinks, although a few now also serve alcohol. *For bars, see Nightlife, p.84–7.*

JEMAA EL FNA

Aqua

68 Jemaa el Fna; tel: 0524-381 324; 8am–11pm; map p.139 C2

The most modern of the cafés around the square, with the same good views as most and the same mediocre food – so just go for drinks and sweets – but there is a buzzier atmosphere and candles at night. No alcohol.

Café de France

Northeast corner of place Jemaa el Fna; 8am–11pm; map p.139 D2

The café 'par excellence' on the square, looking a bit more tired every year, but still good for a mint tea on the terrace, with views over the city and the High Atlas, or a juice and coffee on the ground floor terrace while absorbing the full array of activity on the square. No alcohol.

In the courtyard of the beautiful Palace Dar M'Nebhi, now the **Musée de Marrakech** *(see Museums and Galleries, p.80)*, is a tranquil café where you can while away the afternoon, sipping a cooling mint tea away from the bustle of the souks or read the books you bought in the bookshop. A perfect retreat.

Terrasses de l'Alhambra

Northeast corner of place Jemaa el Fna; tel: 0524-427 570; 8am–11pm; map p.139 D2

The main meeting place on the square, with air con, perfect to cool down after a heated shopping experience. Good place for breakfast, too, with the best coffee on the square. No alcohol.

SEE ALSO RESTAURANTS, P.99

EASTERN MEDINA

Café des Epices

Rahba Kedima; tel: 0524-391 770; www.cafedesepices.net; daily 10am–11pm; map p.139 D3

This is a favourite café in the medina, relaxed and friendly, just the place to while away the afternoon with a mint tea or two, listening to Moroccan or African music, and climbing up to the rooftop terrace for the sunset. Light lunches and sandwiches are served all day long. No alcohol.

Above: a healthy salad at Café du Livre.

MOUASSINE QUARTER

Bougainvillea

33 rue el Mouassine; tel: 0524-441 111; daily 11am–10pm; map p.138 C4

A temporary retreat from shopping is on offer in this courtyard café-restaurant, as well as freshly squeezed juices, teas, coffee and a selection of

Left: patio eating, Marrakesh-style.

cakes. No alcohol.
SEE ALSO RESTAURANTS, P.100

Dar Cherifa – Café Littéraire
8 derb Cherfa Lakbir, off rue Mouassine; tel: 0524-426 463; daily noon–7pm; map p.138 C3
This literary café in a gorgeous 16th-century riad, with beautifully bleached woodwork, is a haven of tranquillity. Rose petals float in the fountain, contemporary art is on show and a great mint tea or saffron coffee is served with sweets. No alcohol.

Terrasse des Epices
15 Souk Cherifia, Sidi Abdelaziz, Dar el Bacha; tel: 0524-375 904/0676-046 767; www.terrassedesepices.com; daily 10am–midnight; map p.139 C4
A great place for a relaxed mint tea in a shady corner during the heat of the afternoon, or for hanging out late afternoon and evening, listening to cool music and having a few drinks. Free WiFi, temporary exhibitions and good food to boot.
SEE ALSO RESTAURANTS, P.101

GUÉLIZ

Café du Livre
44 rue Tareq ibn Ziad; tel: 0524-432 149; www.cafedulivre.com; Mon–Sat 9.30am–9pm; map p.132 C4
Bright and airy café with a selection of fresh juices and teas, delicious cakes and sandwiches, and a good bookshop with books on Morocco, new and second-hand fiction and free WiFi.
SEE ALSO LITERATURE, P.73, RESTAURANTS, P.103

Café Les Négociants
Place Abdelmoumen, avenue Mohammed V; tel: 0524-435 782; daily 6am–11pm; map p.132 B4
A Parisian style café terrace that serves a good breakfast and light lunches, but mostly is a place to have a coffee and watch the world go by.

Grand Café de la Poste
Corner of boulevard Mansour ed Dahbi and avenue Imam Malik; tel: 0524-433 731; www.grancafedelaposte.com; daily 8am–1am; map p.132 C3
The grand colonial-style terrace, hidden behind the post office, is the best place to meet in Guéliz for a coffee in the afternoon, for a light fusion lunch, or for a drink before dinner or clubbing.
SEE ALSO RESTAURANTS, P.103

ESSAOUIRA

Taros
Place Moulay Hassan; tel: 0524-476 407; www.taroscafe.com; Mon–Sat 11am–4pm, 6pm–midnight
Spread over several floors of a tall house that overlooks the harbour and main square, is this pleasant café with a nice library to browse in. The rooftop is the place to be at sunset or later at night, for an aperitif or a cold beer. Tapas and light lunches are available, as well as a good selection of crafts in the boutique on the first floor.

Below: while away some time at the Café des Epices.

Children

Moroccans dote on children, and everywhere children are welcomed, held, kissed and given sweets. Children usually love Marrakesh, although they may be a little overwhelmed at first. The snake charmers, acrobats, musicians and the whole whirlwind of the Jemaa el Fna will stir their imaginations, and wandering around the pedestrian souks, with only hurried donkey carts to worry about, is a bit like moving through an exotic fairy tale, with plenty of little cheap treats on hand. If the going gets tough, head for one of the city's parks or cool down in a swimming pool.

ACTIVITIES

Jnane Tamsna

Hay Mohammadi, Douar Abiad, Palmeraie; tel: 0524-329 423; www.jnanetamsna.com

The Jnane Tamsna organises botanical workshops for children from five years old, learning to recognise plants and herbs in the garden designed by ethno-botanist Gary Martin and making medical and cosmetic potions with it, collecting fruits and vegetables, learning how to grow them and cooking in the kitchen with the Moroccan chef.

SEE ALSO ACCOMMODATION, P.35; GARDENS, P.64

Le Bowling

Palmeraie Golf Palace, Circuit de la Palmeraie; tel: 0524-301 010; daily noon–10pm

This air-conditioned six-lane bowling alley is a good place to avoid the afternoon heat.

Below: try out some horse riding in the Atlas Mountains.

Les Cavaliers de l'Atlas

Palmeraie; tel: 0672-845 579; www.lescavaliersdelatlas.com

Reputedly with some of the city's best horses, these stables organise horse riding for kids and adults by the hour, half- or full day, including a meal with a Berber family or a picnic. Longer excursions on horse back are also possible.

SEE ALSO SPORTS, P.118

ESSENTIALS

Nappies and formula milk are widely available, usually in grocers' shops rather than pharmacies. However, to be sure of getting your usual brand you should bring these items with you. Pull-ups (trainer pants) are rarely available. Most of the larger hotels offer babysitting services.

PLAYGROUNDS AND GARDENS

Cyber Parc Moulay Abdeslam

Near Bab Nkob, avenue Mohammed V; daily 9am–7pm; free; map p.133 E2

A stone's throw from the

Left: dressed for the desert.

> Check when staying in a riad that the place is safe for children; the plunge pools and stairs can be dangerous and the stylish decor a hazard with curious little hands around. In fact, unless you rent the whole house, a stay in a riad is not recommended for small children, as the noise echoes through the courtyard into the other rooms. Choosing a hotel with a larger swimming pool and a garden is usually a better option with children, so they have space to run around, and can be entertained during the heat of the day.

Jemaa el Fna, this is the perfect place to escape from the busy square.
SEE ALSO GARDENS, P.62

Jnane el Harti
Avenue du Président Kennedy, Guéliz; free; map p.132 C3
Small park with a good children's playground and fountains.
SEE ALSO GARDENS, P.64

Oasiria
4km (2½ miles), route du Barrage; tel: 0524-380 438; www.ilove-marrakesh.com/oasiria; daily 10am–6pm, closed in winter; admission charge; free shuttle bus from Marrakesh
North Africa's largest water park with a wave pool, lagoons, water slides and a beach.

Tansift Garden
Palmeraie; tel: 0524-308 786; daily 8am–10pm
Kids can take a ride on a camel (or dromedary) in the Palmeraie.

RESTAURANTS

Many restaurants in Marrakesh cater for the clubbing set, and are therefore not very family-friendly. With bigger children it is always a good idea to order a cosy dinner in your riad, which means good food, and the kids can go to bed or to their room when they want. These restaurants are recommended for families:

Catanzaro
42 rue Tariq ibn Ziyad; tel: 0524-433 731; Mon–Sat noon–2.30pm, 7.30–11pm; $$; map p.132 C4
Excellent pizza and pasta for families.
SEE ALSO RESTAURANTS, P.103

Chez Chegrouni
Place Jemaa el Fnaa; tel: 0665-474 615; daily 8am–11pm; $–$$; map p.139 D2
Moroccan comfort food for the whole family, with a view over the square activities as entertainment.
SEE ALSO RESTAURANTS, P.98

Jemaa el Fna food stalls
Place Jemaa el Fna; daily 6–11pm; $; map p.139 C2
Kids will love choosing food from the stalls.
SEE ALSO RESTAURANTS, P.98

Oliveri
9 boulevard el Mansour ed Dahabi; tel: 0524-448 913; daily 7am–10pm; $; map p.132 B4
Simply the best ice cream in Marrakesh.
SEE ALSO RESTAURANTS, P.104

SIGHTS

Jemaa el Fna
Map p.138–9 C2
Watching the snake charmers, acrobats and musicians in the place **Jemaa el Fna** is fascinating, but avoid the henna tattoos, as the chemicals used can give an allergic reaction.
SEE ALSO SQUARES, P.120

Rakhba Kedima
Map p.139 D3
Kids love walking in the **souks** and holding the chameleons in the spice shops of the Rakhba Kedima. The souks are pedestrian, but watch out for donkey carts pushing through the crowds.
SEE ALSO SOUKS, P.114

Environment

The houses in the medina are being restored, but many green areas of what was North Africa's model garden city are now built over or have been abandoned. The population within the ramparts has grown dramatically from some 60,000 people in 1910 to well over 245,000 inhabitants today and building has taken precedence. The Palmeraie, created in the 11th century when the Almoravids chose to make Marrakesh their capital, was always an important part of the city's heritage. However, in recent decades even the Palmeraie has come under threat both from the building boom and a killer virus that has wiped out many of its palms.

RE-GREENING THE MEDINA

The garden city of North Africa, watered by the *khettaras (see opposite)*, was once a model of urban ecology, but has now lost many of its courtyard gardens and orchards. The city's political leaders have recognised the importance of recreating these gardens and, together with organisations such as the Global Diversity Foundation *(see p.62)*, have undertaken projects to re-green the medina's public spaces. The medina's local and foreign residents have also been encouraged to replant their gardens with traditional plants, such as citrus trees, mulberries, figs and grapevines. Another interesting project is the Ibn Abi Sofra school garden, where children learn about this heritage, and are fed at the same time.

Below: cracked, dry ground caused by drought.

PROTECTING THE PALMERAIE

The Palmeraie, created in the 11th century, has seen a continuous degradation in recent years, due to the fast expansion of Marrakesh, droughts, lack of upkeep and a virus that attacks date palms. Apart from date palms, the Palmeraie also harbours some 250 plant species and 111 animal species, including 64 different kinds of birds. The situation has recently become so critical that the Mohammed VI Foundation for the Protection of the Environment (www.fm6e.org) has created a 10-year plan to safeguard and regenerate the Palmeraie. Over 400,000 palm trees will be planted, a municipal nursery will be set up to provide plants for the beautification of Marrakesh, and an oasis museum with garden will be created to educate school children about the importance of the ancient traditional system of the oasis garden.

> Consider 'offsetting' the CO2 from your journey to and around Marrakesh through visiting the website **www.climatecare.org** and other websites, which use 'carbon calculators', allowing you to offset the level of greenhouse gases you are responsible for with a financial contribution to a sustainable travel scheme that reduces global warming.

Left: mopeds in the Medina's narrow streets worsen the air quality.

The Khettara System

After a succession of droughts, and with a fast-expanding population as well as a massive increase in tourists and tourist facilities, the water reserves of both Morocco and Marrakesh are at an all-time low. According to the Centre for Environmental Systems Research, the per capita water availability for Moroccans is less than half the level recommended by the World Health Organisation.

One of the solutions is perhaps to look back to the past. Since the 12th century the gardens of Marrakesh were efficiently watered by a sophisticated system of *khettaras*, underground water channels that brought the water directly from the mountains, a similar system to the *qanat* of ancient Persia. After working perfectly for many centuries, many of these *khettaras* have now fallen into disrepair.

GREEN PROJECTS

Dar Taliba School Garden

Village of el Hanchane, close to Imlil; admission by permission of the director; free but donations appreciated

Dar Taliba girls' school is a project of the Global Diversity Foundation *(see p.62)*.

SEE ALSO GARDENS, P.65

Diversity Excursions

Palmeraie; tel: 0524-329 423; www.diversity-excursions.co.uk

Half-day and full-day excursions in Marrakesh, the Atlas Mountains and to the Atlantic coast, to gain an insight into local culture and ecology with local expert guides.

Inside Morocco Travel

Riad Bledna, Palmeraie; tel: 0661-182 090; www.riadbledna.com

Eco-friendly tours and inside information in and around Marrakesh.

Jnane Tamsna

Hay Mohammadi, Douar Abiad, Palmeraie; tel: 0524-329 423; www.jnanetamsna.com

Eco-aware guesthouse that supports the re-greening projects in the medina, literacy programs and fair trade, and holds botanical workshops.

SEE ALSO ACCOMMODATION, P.35; GARDENS, P.64

Kasbah du Toubkal

Imlil (60km/40 miles from Marrakesh); tel: 0524-485 611; www.kasbahdutoubkal.com

Award winning ecolodge.

SEE ALSO ACCOMMODATION, P.36

Below: the Skoura oasis.

Essentials

For years, Marrakesh was notorious for the hassle visitors could expect from touts and hustlers, but with the advent of the king's tourist police, who keep a strict eye on goings-on in the medina, this problem is mostly gone. Likewise, violent crime is rare; keep an eye on your bags, especially in the Jemaa el Fna, and your visit should be pretty hassle-free. Marrakesh is an Islamic city and visitors should be conscious to behave with equivalent respect – dressing appropriately, in particular, will make your experience of Marrakesh that much more relaxed, especially if you are a woman.

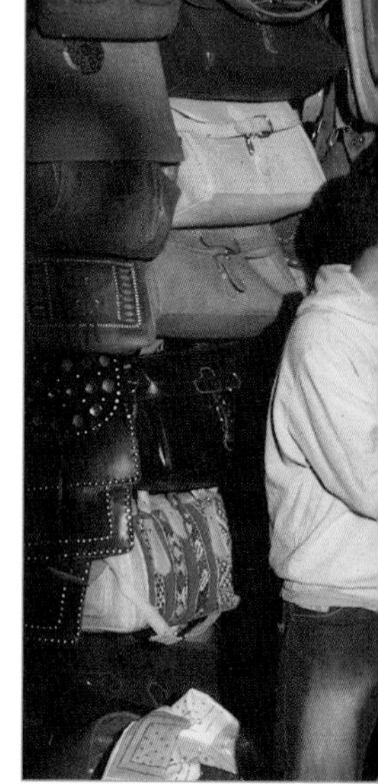

ADMISSION CHARGES

These are very low all over Morocco, usually 10Dh for an adult and quite often free for children. The Majorelle Garden and the Ben Youssef Medersa have higher charges, but these are still inexpensive by European standards.

AGE RESTRICTIONS

You must be over 21 to hire a car in Morocco, and over 16 to buy alcohol.

Above: veiled women shopping for dinner.

BUDGETING

Accommodation: An average price for a double room in a reasonable-quality hotel/riad will cost around 1,000Dh, perhaps a little less in midsummer, but you can stay in a clean but basic hotel for 300Dh or less.

Eating Out: A three-course meal for two with Moroccan wine in a mid-range restaurant will cost about 400–600Dh; a coffee about 20Dh; and a beer 30–60Dh, depending on the venue. You can eat in a good but basic grill restaurant for about 100–150Dh for two.

Transport: The cost of hiring a small car is around 500Dh per day; a 4WD is around 1,500Dh a day. Cars are best booked through an international car rental in advance, however, local ones are cheaper. Hiring a grand taxi and driver for the day costs around 600–800Dh, depending on distance, often more if organised through your hotel.

BUSINESS HOURS

The working week is from Monday to Friday. Many businesses close for a few hours around 11.30am–2.30pm on Fridays for Friday prayers. In Ramadan there is a different timetable, with business opening up a bit later in the morning and closing earlier in the afternoon.

Banks: 8.30am–4.30pm, many offices close on Friday afternoon and Saturday, but in tourist areas they remain open.

Left: busy Marrakesh life in the souks.

> **Clothing**
> In summer you will need light cottons or linens; in winter be sure to take both light clothes for daytime and warm clothing (including a coat) for the evening. Also remember that Morocco is an Islamic country: you should not wear revealing clothes on the streets. In the evenings smart casual is acceptable for most venues. You won't get into some of the more exclusive hotels, including **La Mamounia** *(see Accommodation, p.36)*, wearing jeans or shorts.

Post office: Mon–Fri 8.30am–4.30pm, Sat 9am–noon.
Restaurants: noon–3pm and 7–11pm daily, although many in tourist areas are open continually throughout the day.
Shops: Mon–Sat 9am–12.30pm and 2.30–8pm, but in tourist areas the shops are open daily throughout the day. Note that some shops may close on Friday afternoon, as it is the Muslim holy day.

CLIMATE

The best times to be in Marrakesh are late autumn and early spring. Winter is usually bright and sunny, and sometimes warm enough to swim, but it can also be damp and cold, especially at night, when temperatures can drop to below freezing. Midsummer is usually too hot for comfort, as temperatures average 33°C (91°F) and top 40°C (104°F). Summer visitors will need a hotel with air conditioning and preferably a pool. In the High Atlas the summer is the perfect time to plan a hike. During the month of April there is always the chance of a sandstorm coming from the desert.

CONSULATES AND EMBASSIES

For general information on Moroccan embassies in your home country, see: www.maec.gov.ma.
Most embassies in Morocco are in Rabat, usually open Mon–Fri 9am–noon.

Canada
13 rue Jaafar as Sadiq, Agdal, Rabat; tel: 0537-687 400
Also looks after Australian and Irish citizens, who don't have an embassy in Morocco.

United Kingdom
Embassy: 28 avenue SAR Sidi Mohammed, Rabat; tel: 0537-633 333; http://ukinmorocco.fco.gov.uk
Consulate-General in Casablanca: tel: 0522-857 400; email: british.consulate2@menara.ma
British Honorary Consulate in Marrakesh: Résidence Taib; 55 blvd Zerktouni, Guéliz; tel: 0524-420 846; email: matthew.virr@fconet.fco.gov.uk

United States
Embassy: 2 avenue de Marrakesh, Rabat; tel: 0537-762 265; http://rabat.usembassy.gov
Consulate in Casablanca: 8 blvd Moulay Youssef; tel: 0522-264 550; email: acscasablanca@state.gov

CRIME

Crime is not particularly common, but you should take the usual precautions: use a safe in your hotel; don't carry too much cash on you; keep an eye on bags and valuables; and don't leave belongings visible in a parked car. At night, be sure to park your car in a guarded car park. The streets of the medina are safe at night, but if you are worried about returning to your riad after dark, call ahead so someone can come and fetch from the taxi drop-off point.

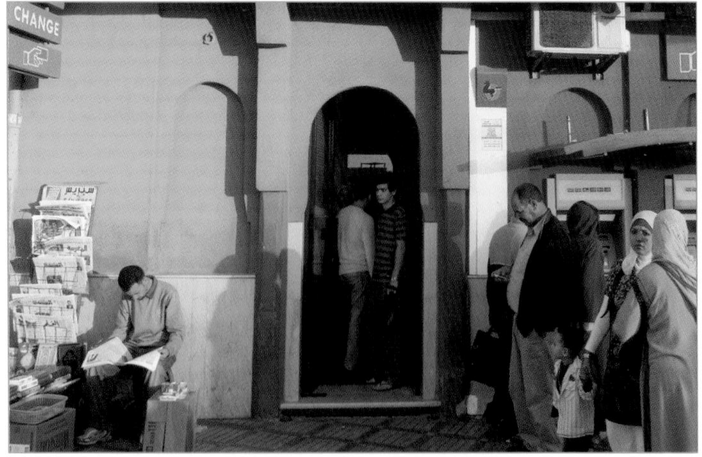

Above: newspapers for sale outside a busy bank.

If you are the victim of crime, you will need to report it to the police and obtain an official report to present to your insurer upon your return.

It is highly inadvisable to buy, carry or use hashish. There are many Westerners languishing in Moroccan prisons for drug offences.

Brigade Touristique (Tourist Police)
Based in rue Sidi Mimoun, on the north side of the Jemaa el Fna; tel: 0524-384 601; 24hrs.

CUSTOMS

The airport Duty Free shop is open to incoming as well as departing passengers. Passengers can import 1l of alcohol (wine or spirits); 200 cigarettes or 50 cigarillos or 25 cigars; 150ml perfume or 250 eau de toilette; and gifts up to a value of 2,000Dh. You may not import or export dirhams: all local currency must be exchanged in Morocco.

DISABLED TRAVELLERS

Disabled access is not good in Marrakesh. High kerbs in the New Town and uneven surfaces in the medina make wheelchair use difficult, and most of the museums occupy old palaces or riads with maze-like layouts and lots of steps. In the riad guesthouses wheelchair access could be possible in ground-floor rooms, but it might be hard to access the bathroom: check with riad owners. A larger hotel with a lift is a better bet. Even when restaurants are accessible, the toilets are rarely so. That said, Moroccans are always quick to assist wherever they can.

ELECTRICITY

The electricity supply is rated 220 volts in all but the very oldest hotels. Plugs are the round two-pin Continental type, so bring an adaptor if you want to use UK or US appliances.

ETIQUETTE

In the interests of tourism, Marrakchis are fairly tolerant of the behaviour of foreigners, but it is polite to be respectful of Morocco's Muslim culture and avoid wearing revealing clothes in the medina or indulging in overt displays of physical affection (although holding hands is usually fine). During Ramadan try to avoid eating on the streets in daylight hours.

Non-Muslims cannot enter working mosques in Morocco.

Below: a local pharmacy.

Emergency Numbers
Ambulance **15**
Fire **16**
Police **19**
Tourist Police **0524-384 601**

GAY TRAVELLERS

Homosexuality is officially illegal, and can incur a prison sentence of three months to three years. In practice, however, it is quite common, although few men involved would admit to being gay. Even though Moroccan men often hold hands or are quite physical with each other in a platonic way, public displays of affection are seriously frowned upon, particularly from homosexual couples, but also heterosexuals *(see Etiquette, opposite)*.

Marrakesh is more gay-friendly than most towns, and gay couples are welcome in most of the foreign-owned riads. It is important to approach gay encounters with Moroccans with some caution; it could be a set-up or there may be an economic motive. Lesbians shouldn't have any trouble: many Moroccans still refuse to believe that there is such a thing.

GOVERNMENT

Morocco is a constitutional monarchy, with a parliament and government. The king, HM Mohammed VI, retains substantial powers, including the appointment of key ministers. The administrative region *(wilaya)* of Marrakesh is governed by the *wali* (governor), who is also appointed by the king.

HEALTH

No vaccinations are required for entry into Morocco unless you have come from a yellow fever, cholera or smallpox zone.

All medical care must be paid for, so be sure to take out adequate health insurance before you travel.

If you need to see a doctor or dentist, staff in your hotel or riad can help you find an English-speaking practitioner. Failing that, contact your embassy or consulate.

Stomach upsets are commonplace. To help avoid them, decline food that has been left standing or reheated, peel fruit and avoid buying ice cream from itinerant vendors. If you are struck down, drink plenty of water and take a diarrhoea remedy (available at pharmacies).

Polyclinique du Sud
Rue de Yougoslavie, Guéliz; tel: 0524-447 999; 24hrs
Emergency medical and dental care at private hospital.

Pharmacie
Jemaa el Fna (tel: 0524-430 415); 9am–midnight
Handily located in the centre of town, with convenient late and long hours.

HOLIDAYS

These Muslim holidays follow the Hegira lunar calendar and are therefore movable. The holidays are earlier by 11 days each year (12 in a leap year). Exact dates depend on the sighting of the new moon.
Mouloud (Prophet Mohammed's birthday): 22 Aug 2009, 11 Aug 2010.
Aid el Fitr (four-day feast at the end of Ramadan): 20 Sep 2009, 9 Sep 2010.
Aid el Adha (feast of Abraham's sacrifice of a lamb instead of his son): 30 Nov 2009, 19 Nov 2010.
Ras es Sana (Muslim New Year): 31 Dec 2009, 20 Dec 2010.
SEE ALSO FESTIVALS AND EVENTS, P.55

Below: banks are easily found in the new town; there are a few in the medina *(see p.53)*.

Above: commercial signage painted on a wall in the medina.

Useful Websites

www.tourism-in-morocco.com
The official site of the Moroccan National Tourist Board.

www.maroc.net
Moroccan news and culture.

www.ilove-marrakesh.com
General information and listings about what's on in Marrakesh, as well as riad rental.

INTERNET CAFES

There are numerous internet cafés, and some of the *téléboutiques* also offer internet access. The Cyber park on avenue Mohammed V has internet booths scattered around as well as an indoor internet station. Internet access costs around 10Dh an hour; many of the better hotels and bars offer WiFi.

MAPS

A free and up-to-date map is distributed by the tourist office *(see opposite)*, but its coverage of the souk area is sketchy.

In addition to the map in the back of this book, the best available maps are Insight FlexiMap Marrakesh, published by APA Publications, and Marrakesh and Essaouira published by Editions Laure Kane.

MEDIA AND LOCAL PAPERS

PUBLICATIONS

There is a range of daily and weekly publications for sale in French and Arabic. The two main publications in French are the socialist *Libération* and the slightly more liberal *L'Opinion*. Weeklies include *Le Journal* and the outspoken *TelQuel*. *Le Monde* is widely available, as are some English newspapers, but the latter will be at least a day old.

For listings of upcoming events consult the monthly *Couleurs Marrakech*, available at newsstands.

RADIO

You can pick up the BBC's World Service on short wave 12095 or 9410 kHz from 6am–9.30pm and 4–9.05pm.

TELEVISION

Most hotels provide CNN and BBC World satellite channels. Morocco has two state-run TV channels, 2M and TVM, in French and Arabic.

MONEY

Moroccan dirhams (Dh) may not be imported or exported, which means that they cannot be obtained in advance of your trip. On departure you can change unspent dirhams back into hard currency in the airport, if you can show exchange receipts totalling twice the amount you want to change back, as well as your flight boarding card.

The dirham is a reasonably stable currency. Recent exchange rates have hovered around 12Dh to £1 sterling, 11Dh to €1, and 8.5Dh to $1. Rates vary between banks, so shop around.

Left: satellite dishes dot the roofs of the Old Town.

ATMS

ATMs are the easiest way of obtaining cash, although your bank may charge you a handling fee as well as interest if you are using a credit card (you can often use debit cards bearing the Cirrus logo, but don't rely on this alone). ATMs are plentiful in the New Town and there are a couple of Banque Populaire ATMs at the top of rue Bab de Agnaou off the Jemaa el Fna. The daily limit on withdrawals is currently 2,000Dh.

Above: armed with the essentials, you can get on with enjoying your holiday.

CREDIT CARDS

MasterCard and Visa are accepted in most hotels, petrol stations and the more expensive shops and restaurants. Other cards are less widely accepted.

POST

The main post office (PTT) is on place du 16 Novembre in Guéliz. Stamps are available from *tabacs* (tobacconists).

Below: the city's main tourist office, in Guéliz.

TELEPHONES

Phone booths, mainly run by Maroc Telecom, are plentiful. They are operated with phone cards (10Dh, 20Dh, 50Dh and 100Dh) that are sold at tobacconists. In addition you will find *téléboutiques* where you can use coins and get change from the attendant.

To make an international call, dial 00 for an international line, followed by the country code (44 for the UK). Remember to drop the initial zero of the area code you are dialling.

TIME ZONE

Morocco keeps to Greenwich Mean Time all year round. It is one hour behind UK time during summer and the same time as the UK in winter.

TIPPING

It is usual to tip porters, chambermaids, other hotel staff if they are particularly helpful, guides and waiting staff. There are no hard and fast rules for the amount: 10 percent would be considered generous.

TOURIST INFORMATION

Office National Marocain du Tourisme

Place Abdel Moumen Ben Ali, Guéliz; tel: 0524-436 179; Mon–Fri 8.30am–noon, 2.30–6.30pm, Sat 9am–noon, 3–6pm; map p.132 B4

The main tourist office is good for basic information.

VISA INFORMATION

Holders of British or American passports can enter Morocco for a stay of up to three months without a visa, if their passport is valid for at least six months after the planned departure date.

Most visitors from other countries do not require a visa to Morocco and can stay in the country for up to 90 days, except for holders of an Israeli or South African passport or many sub-Saharan nationals (for list check www.visitmorocco.com).

Festivals and Events

Every night is party time at the Jemaa el Fna, but since King Mohammed VI ascended the throne, he has been keen to organise new events to boast the city's year-round appeal. A few of these festivals are held annually, others seem to happen more sporadically. Always check with the tourist office. Some tourists avoid visiting during the month of Ramadan, but it can be a special experience in the medina, as after sundown the whole city gathers in the Jemaa el Fna, which is even more festive than usual. *See also Essentials, p.51.*

JAN–FEB

Marrakesh Marathon

End of Jan; tel: 0524-446 822; www.marathon-marrakesh.com

For the last 20 years, 5,000 runners from all over the world have been taking part in this marathon. The record for the run is held by the Moroccan top athlete, Abdelkader el Moaziz, who did it in 2h08m15s in 1994. The distance is 42,195km (26,220 miles) for the marathon and 21,097km (13,110 miles) for the half-marathon on a flat and rapid course around the city walls and Guéliz and through the Palmeraie.

Dakka Marrakchia Festival

Feb; Various neighbourhoods, medina

The Dakka Marrakchia Festival is organised by the 'Friends of the Palm Tree' Association, who want to preserve this traditional event. This festival of traditional music dates back to the time when the Saadian dynasty was in power in Morocco and pays tribute to the **Sabatou Rijal**, the seven spiritual saints of Marrakesh. Musicians from the seven districts in which the saints' shrines are located take part in the festival, and local shopkeepers, artists and others join in, filling the streets with traditional music, involving lots of drumming and chanting. This festival gives a glimpse into a long-standing Marrakchi tradition and offers the rare chance to hear some excellent and authentic traditional music.

SEE ALSO RELIGIONS AND RELIGIOUS SITES, P.95

Above: traditional music at the Marrakesh Popular Arts Festival.

MAR–APR

Marrakesh Festival of Magic

Mar; Royal Theater, Palais des Congrès and Jemaa el Fna

One of the world's largest festivals of magic, this festival gathers some of the best magicians in the world in Marrakesh.

Marathon des Sables

Ouarzate to Sahara Desert; Apr; www.saharamarathon.co.uk;

Held annually in aid of African charities, involving a six-day, 151-mile (243km) endurance race across the Moroccan Sahara Desert. It is considered the hardest foot race in the world, as every day consists of running the equivalent of a half-marathon or more. Competitors have to carry

Left: at the Gnaoua Festival.

Public Holidays
New Year's Day – 1 Jan
Independence Manifesto Day – 11 Jan
Labour Day – 1 May
Feast of the Throne – 30 July
Act of Allegiance – 14 Aug
Revolution Day and Birthday of the King – 20 Aug
Youth Day – 21 Aug
Anniversary of the Green March – 6 Nov
Independence Day – 18 Nov

everything they need for the duration (apart from a tent and water) on their backs in a rucksack, not to mention contend with the difficulty of running on uneven, stony ground, and up soft and steep sand dunes, with midday temperatures of up to 120°F (50°C).

Jardin'Art
Apr; www.jardinsdumaroc.com/festival
This festival is a celebration of Moroccan traditional and contemporary gardens, held in the Menara and several other locations, with an emphasis on the organic and ecological garden. Exhibitions, garden fair, demonstrations and shows.
SEE ALSO GARDENS, P.64

JULY–AUG

Marrakesh Popular Arts Festival
July; www.marrakeshfestival.com
Venues around the city, including the el Badi Palace and its courtyards, host traditional folk performances from all over the country, from Gnaoua trance-inducing music to Berber folk singers and dancers.

Moussem of Setti Fatma
Aug; Setti Fatma
Villagers and Berbers come from all over to Setti Fatma to celebrate the day of the local saint with a big *moussem*. This religious event is also a fun affair with a large souk, a fair, games and entertainment.

Gnaoua Festival
Essaouira; Aug; www.festival-gnaoua.net
Increasingly popular, the Gnaoua Festival, held on 10 different stages in Essaouira, attracts over 500,000 festival-goers. The original aim was to emphasise Gnaoua heritage in all its forms, but the festival now also features jazz and world music, particularly from West Africa. There are traditional Gnaoua *lilas*, or nights of exorcism, in the Gnaoua Zaouia every evening at midnight.

NOV–DEC

Marrakesh International Film Festival
www.festival-marrakesh.com
King Mohammed VI's favourite festival, attended by many Hollywood stars.
SEE ALSO FILM, P.57

Below: hardy competitors in the Marathon des Sables.

Film

Just about any Hollywood film in need of an ancient, biblical or Middle Eastern set is filmed in Morocco. King Mohammed VI loves movies and has made the Marrakesh Film Festival into a well-regarded international event, while relentlessly promoting the country as the place to film blockbusters. The gorgeous nature of Morocco's south has often overshadowed the performances in more recent films, but there are a few classics, too, that have been filmed locally. Moroccans themselves prefer to watch Bollywood productions, but local cinema production, with a little help from Europe, is slowly gaining a foothold in the country.

MOROCCAN FILMS

In recent years young Moroccan directors have hit the international film circuit, but being mostly French co-productions, their films are little known here in the UK.

Much talked about in Morocco, the film *Les Yeux Secs (Cry No More)* by Narjiss Nejjar won a prize at the Paris and Marrakesh film festivals in 2003. It tells the story of a former prostitute returning to her village to save her daughter from repeating her mistakes.

Jilali Ferhati's *Mémoire en Détention (Memories in Detention)* gives a very realistic account of an ex-prisoner trying to find the relations of a friend who loses his memory in prison.

In 2005, the Cannes Film Festival showed Leila Marrakchi's *Marock*, the tender love story between a Jewish boy and a Muslim girl.

CLASSIC FILMS

Alfred Hitchcock's *The Man Who Knew Too Much* was partly filmed in Marrakesh, with scenes set in the Jemaa el Fna.

Above: Orson Welles takes on the tragic Moor.

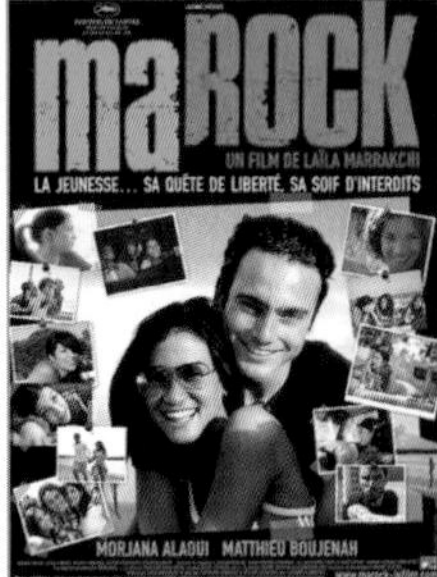

Above: the more recent, highly-successful *Marock*.

Orson Welles shot *Othello* in 1948 in Essaouira, then still known as Mogador, because he wanted to return Shakespeare's Moor to his homeland. The director's financial troubles necessitated some serious improvisation, with local actors taking the roles of international stars and the tailors in the Mellah making suits of armour from sardine cans. Welles was later to reflect that his time in Mogador was 'one of the happiest times I've ever known – despite all the struggle'.

In *Hideous Kinky* the UK director Gillies MacKinnon journeys back to the hippie Mecca that Marrakesh was in the early 1970s.

SEE ALSO LITERATURE, P.72

BLOCKBUSTERS

The fortified village of **Aït Benhaddou** *(see Kasbahs and Palaces, p.69)* is one of the most spectacular kasbahs in the south of Morocco, and is in such good condition because many Hollywood movies

Left: *Hideous Kinky*, based on Esther Freud's novel, embodies the Marrakesh of popular fantasy.

Marrakesh International Film Festival (Nov–Dec; www.festival-marrakesh.com) Movies are shown in cinemas around town and on large screens in el Badi Palace *(see p.9)* and the Jemaa el Fna *(see p.6). See also Festivals and Events, p.55*

were filmed here: *Lawrence of Arabia* (1962), *Jesus of Nazareth* (1977), *The Jewel of the Nile* (1985), *The Living Daylights* (1987), *The Sheltering Sky* (1990), *Kundun* (1997), *The Mummy* (1999), *Gladiator* (2000), *Alexander* (2004) and, more recently, *Babel* (2006) and *Prisoners of the Sun* (2009). Many films are filmed at the **Atlas Film Studios** in Ouazarzate, which can be visited.

More than a third of all films shown in Morocco are **Bollywood** productions, dubbed in *darija* (Moroccan dialect), and subtitled in French. The Moroccans in local cinemas appreciate the sugary love stories mixed with over-the-top action, and sing along to the songs in Hindi. When the Indian movie star Rani Mukherjee attended the premiére of the blockbuster *Chalte Chalte* in Casablanca, the crowds went wild. It is said that cinema owners only show films with happy endings as the cinema-goers get too upset and rowdy if things go the other way.

CINEMAS

Cinema Eden

Derb Debachi, near rue des Banques, just off the Jemaa el Fna; shows at 3pm, 6pm, 9pm; map p.139 D2

Expect either a Bollywood film or a Jackie Chan karate affair, or both, all dubbed in Arabic except for the songs, and a loud and interactive all-male crowd. A good place to experience the *couleur locale*, as Juan Goytisolo wrote in his story about the cinema, where he describes it as the 'holy of holies'.

SEE ALSO LITERATURE, P.73

Institut Français

Route de Targa, Guéliz; tel: 0524-384 601; www.ifm.ma

The Institut offers French language courses as well as a good programme of French and Moroccan films and concerts.

Le Colisée

Boulevard Mohammed Zerktouni, near rue Mohammed el Beqal, Guéliz; tel: 0524-448 893; daily shows at 3pm, 7pm, 9.30pm; map p.x132 B4

Generally regarded as the best and most comfortable cinema in town, attracting a crowd of locals and expats, both men and women.

Below: a Moroccan scene in *The Man Who Knew Too Much*.

Food and Drink

The boom in tourism and the arrival of a cosmopolitan crowd has encourged the creation of a rich and varied restaurant scene in Marrakesh. Gone are the days when dining out here was a choice between French classics in an old-fashioned restaurant in Guéliz or a *couscous royale* in a cavernous and half-empty palace. Nowadays it seems just as easy to find a plate of sushi or a carpaccio as to encounter a good couscous. Although most visitors find that the variety of Moroccan food keeps their palate amused, it is now also possible to also enjoy first-rate Italian, Spanish, Japanese, Indian and modern European food in über-stylish settings.

Right: classic mint tea service, a Moroccan staple.

MOROCCAN CUISINE

In Moroccan homes cooking is traditionally done by the women, with men taking care of the tea. A meal involves many dishes, needing complicated and lengthy preparations, so a meal is considered an act of love. The old adage to eat where locals eat doesn't really work when it comes to Moroccan food. Ask a local for a good Moroccan restaurant in the medina, and apart from the street food on the Jemaa el Fna, he'll probably not know what to answer. The only place to eat for Moroccans is at home. If they do go out to a restaurant, it will most likely be to eat something different.

If you are not lucky enough to be invited to a home, then there are several options to sample something close to the real thing. Several riads in the medina, including **Le Tobsil**, **Dar Yaqout** and **Dar Moha** *(see p.100)* offer a *diffa* or feast with a gourmet set menu, including several salads, a soup, a *pastilla*, couscous or tajine and dessert, which come with magnificent exotic surroundings, luxurious seating and music. The food is good, albeit expensive by Moroccan standards, but most people can only do it once, finding it hard to get beyond the third course.

A lighter option is to order dinner in your riad. Prepared by the woman in the kitchen, it is usually the closest you can get to home cooking. In good Moroccan restaurants like **Al Fassia** *(see p.103)* specialities such as roast shoulder of lamb need to be ordered 24 hours in advance. Those taken with the strong flavours of Moroccan dishes can take up one of the cookery classes available at hotels and riads.

Left: tajines offer up tasty blends of flavours.

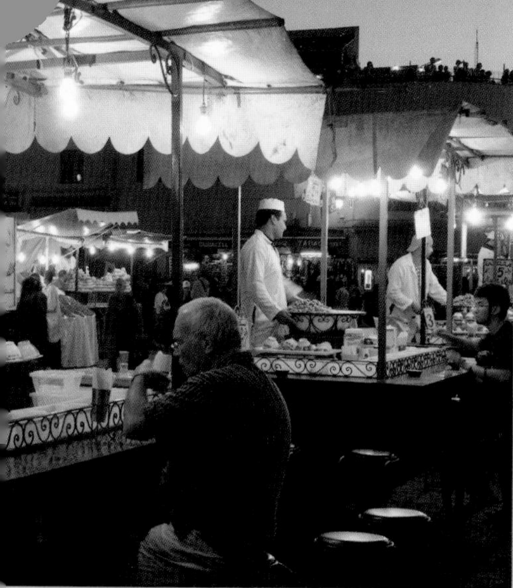

Left: the famous food stalls on the Jemaa el Fna.

Tajines – tasty stews served in distinctive earthenware pots with conical lids – come in many delicious guises, and are where many of the subtleties and surprises of Moroccan cuisine are found. They frequently pair sweet and savoury, or savoury and sour, with knockout results. Typical combinations are beef with quince, lamb with prunes and chicken with a sweet tomato jam. One of the most common tajines is chicken with preserved lemons and olives *(djej m'qalli)*.

COUSCOUS AND TAJINES

In restaurants the once ubiquitous couscous has lost out to the highly versatile tajine in the popularity stakes, but it remains a favourite in Moroccan homes, especially on Friday lunchtimes, when it is traditionally served after prayers at the Friday Mosque. The national dish of North Africa, it has Berber origins, and the name comes from the Berber word *seksou*. North African women traditionally make their own couscous, by rolling two parts of semolina with one part of flour, some salt water and a little oil, until it's grain-sized. Then it is dried on the rooftops, and then it can be stored for a while.

Unlike the pre-cooked stuff available in Western supermarkets, real couscous is steamed above a reduced broth of meat, vegetables and spices, with which it is then served. Traditionally seven vegetables are used: turnips, carrots, potatoes, pumpkin, tomatoes, courgettes and chickpeas, and on the coast meat is often replaced with fish.

THE MOROCCAN MENU

bessara Thick soup of fava beans, olive oil and spices
briouats Deep-fried filo pastry filled with lamb and herbs or cheese
brochettes Grilled skewers of lamb, chicken, beef or liver
harira Hearty soup of mutton, tomatoes, chickpeas and cumin, traditionally eaten with dates to break the Ramadan fast
harissa Spicy red pepper sauce served with the couscous

In wealthy families, food was – and often still is – traditionally cooked by a *dada*, often a woman descended from African slaves. The *dada* cooks a treat and looks after the children. Some of the best *dadas* are paid good money to cook at special occasions. At **Al Fassia** in Guéliz *(see p.103)*, the all-women staff are dressed like *dadas*.

hhubz Bread, either French baguette or a flat round loaf, is highly respected by Moroccans who consider it a gift of God.
kefta Meatballs flavoured with coriander and cumin
laban Fermented milk traditionally served with couscous
mechoui Spit-roasted lamb for special occasions
merguez Spicy lamb sausages
pastilla Sweet pigeon pie topped with a dusting of sugar.
tanjia Marrakchia Lamb stew slow-cooked in an urn-shaped earthenware pot

DESSERT

A meal usually ends with fresh fruit in season, particularly melon, watermelon, or slices of orange sprinkled with cinnamon. Sweet *pastilla au lait* consists of layers of filo pastry with a light orange blossom-flavoured *crème anglaise*.

Mint tea is served with a selection of sweet pastries made with almonds, nuts and honey. The finest is the *corne de gazelle* (gazelle horn), a crusty pastry stuffed with fine almond paste.

MEAL TIMES

Breakfast (8–9am)
Continental style with *café au lait* (milky coffee), *baguette* (French bread) and croissant, or Moroccan with fresh orange juice, flat Moroccan bread, *amlou* (crushed almonds with honey and argan oil), *beghrir* (Moroccan pancake) with honey and freshly baked *rghaif* (flat buttery pastry).

Lunch (1–4pm)
The most important meal in the day, with salads, a couscous, tajine (stew) or *mechoui* (roast lamb), followed by mint tea, sweets and most probably a nap.

Dinner (8–11pm)
After the sunset *paseo* (walk), locals will eat a soup or lunch leftovers at home, a snack at Jemaa el Fna, or go out for a pizza or a bite with drinks.

A fragrant syrupy green **tea** with mint has become Morocco's national drink, but it wasn't always so. Peppermint *(Mentha piperita)* was always plentiful here, but green tea only arrived in 1720, when England's King George I offered the Sultan of Morocco a box of Chinese green tea as a gift. The sultan couldn't drink it as it tasted too bitter, so he had it mixed with sugar and fragrant mint. The green tea of choice is still the inexpensive Chinese Gunpowder tea, which was rolled especially to preserve its freshness for the long journeys from China to Africa.

DRINKS

Mineral water and fizzy drinks are available everywhere. The orange juice sellers on the Jemaa el Fna squeeze oranges fresh all day long. A tall glass is about 15Dh, but make sure it's freshly squeezed and no water or sugar is added, as this can cause sickness. Fresh apple, pear, carrot, banana, *lait d'amande* (almond) and even avocado juices are all avail-

Below: olives, dried fruit and sweet pastries make good foodie gifts and are easy to find.

Above: argan oil is highly prized and unique to southwestern Morocco.

able in season. Moroccan coffee comes very strong and black; if you want it with milk, ask for a *noss noss* or a *café au lait*. Milk with some coffee is called *café cassé*. The most popular drink is *thé à la menthe*, or green tea with mint *(see box, opposite)*.

BEERS AND WINES

Until fairly recently it was impossible to buy alcohol in the medina, but recently a few bars have opened, **Terrasse des Epices** and **Kosybar** *(see p.85)* being among the best. The national brews are Flag, Stork, Heineken and the more expensive Casablanca, all lager-type bottled beers.

Moroccan wine, mainly produced around Meknes, has come a long way in recent years. The best reds are Cuvée du Président, Médaillon, Domaine de Sahari, Ksar, Guerrouane and Siroua. Good whites are Val d'Argan, Valpierre and Chaud-Soleil, while among the rosé the Président and Guerrouane are most recommended. For the past few years, a French winemaker from Châteauneuf du Pape has been producing a very good wine near Essaouira, the Val d'Argan red, rosé and white.

FOODIE SOUVENIRS

Buy spices from the spice market at **Rahba Kedima** or the spice market in Essaouira, including cumin, saffron, black pepper, dried verbena and *ras el-hanout*, a mixture of 27 spices used on special occasions, particularly in stews. Just off the north side of the Jemaa el Fnaa is the dried fruit and nuts souk, for nuts and delicious dates.

Argan oil *(see p.89)*, which has a delicate, nutty flavour, can be bought both in Marrakesh and Essaouira, where it is produced in women's co-operatives like **Coopérative Amal** (tel: 0524-788 141; www.targanine.com; Mon–Fri 8am–7pm), winner of a Slow Food award.

A selection of Moroccan sweets makes a good souvenir or gift to take home: check out the patisseries in rue de la Liberté in Guéliz. Investigate the **Marché Central** on rue Ibn Toumert (behind Plaza Marrakesh) in Guéliz for jars of olives and preserved lemons.

SEE ALSO SOUKS, P.114

Ramadan may be the month of fasting, but the daily breaking of the fast at sundown is eagerly anticipated and several special dishes are served during this time. The most important is *harira (see The Moroccan Menu, p.59)*; almost everyone ends their fast with a bowlful, sometimes accompanied by dates and milk, and followed by *shebakkia*, knots of deep-fried pastry dipped in honey or syrup and sprinkled with sesame seeds. If you want to try *harira* outside Ramadan, several of the food stalls on Jemaa el Fna *(see Restaurants, p.98)* serve it.

Gardens

The word *agdal* is Berber for both a closed garden and the grazing land up in the mountains. The *agdal* as grazing land was all-important to the shepherds and, as their survival depended on it, they always respected and looked after these lands. More than just spaces for animals, they were also important meeting places. The city version of the *agdal* can in many ways be seen as the idealisation of these grazing lands, reflecting the idea of an idyllic paradise. Marrakesh was developed as a garden city, and although many of the gardens have disappeared or are hidden behind walls, there are still a few gardens open to the public.

THE IDEA OF THE MOORISH GARDEN

The Moorish garden usually has orange trees, flowers and a water feature, all of which are intended to provide calm, shade, perfume, beauty and pleasure. The enclosed garden is important in Islamic culture. As an earthly version of the paradise described in the Quran, it is a place of reflection, a place where heaven meets earth and where humans meet God.

Water was, and is, an important element in the Moorish garden, which occurs mostly in hot and dry climates. The sound of a fountain adds to the tranquillity and sense of luxury of the garden, but it also has a practical use, as it is used to irrigate the rest of the garden. In Marrakesh, water was brought from the Atlas Mountains by an intricate system of *khettaras* (underground water channels).

SEE ALSO ENVIRONMENT, P.47

Global Diversity Foundation (www.globaldiversity.org.uk) has a 'Regreening the Medina' project, which includes replanting the daliyas (grapevine arbours) of the Souk el Loghzel and planting a fruit orchard and vegetable garden for the Ibn Abi Sofra primary school, in order to encourage traditional farming knowledge and new agricultural practices among young city children. The Foundation organises trips exploring the cultural and ecological heritage of Marrakesh and surroundings, guided by local experts (www.diversity-excursions.co.uk).

JEMAA EL FNAA

Cyber Parc Moulay Abdeslam

Near Bab Nkob, avenue Mohammed V; daily 9am–7pm; free; map p.133 E2

The Cyber park, formerly the garden of the 18th-century Alaouite prince and poet Moulay Abdel Salam, was brought into the 21st century by the Mohammed VI Foundation for the Protection of the Environment and now boasts free WiFi booths, a central internet café and contemporary gardens featuring typical local vegetation, including olive groves, date palms, fruit trees, wild grasses and water features. This is a favourite meeting place for young lovers and families in the late afternoon.

Right: the Koutoubia Gardens are the perfect place to relax from the bustle of the Jemaa el Fna and admire the mosque's minaret.

Left: the colourful Majorelle Garden.

Children in Marrakesh still sing this **nursery rhyme**, which is more than 800 years old, about a garden that no longer exists. The garden, which was named after the saint Saliha, was located near Bab Aghmat. Today part of the Agdal Gardens is still named after Lalla Saliha.
'Oh salty grasshopper, where have you been walking?
In the garden of Saliha.
What have you eaten and what did you drink?
Just an apple and it smelled so good...'

Koutoubia Gardens
Avenue Mohammed V; daily 8am–8pm; free; map p.138 A1
These beautifully restored gardens are the best place from which to admire the perfect craftsmanship of the minaret and to hear the *adhan*, the call to prayer.

SOUTHERN MEDINA

Agdal Gardens
South of Royal Palace and Kasbah; Fri and Sun, closed if the king is in residence; free; map p.137 D1
Originally spread over 500 hectares (1,250 acres), the Agdal was about the same size as the entire medina. Laid out in 1156 by the Almohads, the gardens are centred around the **Sahraj el Hana** (Tank of Health). The pool became infamous as the place where the 19th-century Sultan Mohammed IV drowned while rowing his son. It is now surrounded by orchards, a palm grove and several ornamental pavilions.

GUÉLIZ

Majorelle Garden and Museum
Avenue Yaqoub el Mansour; tel: 0524-301 852; www.jardinmajorelle.com; daily Oct–May 8am–5pm, June–Sept 8am–6pm; admission charge to garden, further charge for Islamic Museum
Created in the 1930s by Jacques Majorelle, the gardens were restored by the late French fashion designer Yves Saint Laurent and his partner Pierre Bergé, who also owns the villa next door. The painter Jacques Majorelle was inspired by the light and colours of Marrakesh. He laid out the exotic garden around his studio, with cactuses collected from around the world, majestic palms, bougainvillea and a wonderful bamboo forest. The bright green of the plants is reflected in the many water pools, and set off perfectly against the electric-cobalt-blue walls of

Below: in the Cyber park, a popular meeting place.

his studio *(see box, p.81)*. This studio now houses an **Islamic Museum**; some of Majorelle's paintings are also on show. A small garden café serves a good breakfast, and salads and snacks for lunch.
SEE ALSO MUSEUMS AND GALLERIES, P.81

Jnane el Harti
Avenue du Président Kennedy; free; map p.132 C3
Originally laid out by the French in the colonial period, the small park is now a popular place for families to take a late afternoon stroll and has a good children's playground and fountains.

Jnane Tamsna
Hay Mohammadi, Douar Abiad, Palmeraie; tel: 0524-329 423; www.jnanetamsna.com; free
The perfumed garden of the **Jnane Tamsna** guesthouse was designed by the owner, ethno-botanist Gary Martin, and planted with vegetation that suits the land and doesn't need excessive watering, including orange trees, pomegranates and rosemary. The organic vegetables are used in the kitchen. The guesthouse also organises workshops about gardening and promotes the use of herbs in medicine and cosmetics for adults and children.
SEE ALSO ACCOMMODATION, P.35

Palmeraie
Once the Palmeraie spread over more than 13,000 hectares (32,500 acres) with around 150,000 palm trees, all watered by the *khettaras* (underground water channels), but a lot has changed in recent years. Water is now provided by artesian wells, the date palms are dying from a virus, like elsewhere in North Africa, and much land has been used to build luxury hotels and villas. Less exotic than it used to be, the Palmeraie is still a peaceful place for an afternoon cycle or stroll.
SEE ALSO ENVIRONMENT, P.47

HIVERNAGE

Menara
Avenue de la Menara; tel: 0524-439 580; daily 5.30am–6.30pm; free but admission charge to pavilion
The Menara is a large olive grove, laid out by the Almohads during the 12th century, with a central pool, 200m (650ft) long and 150m (500ft) wide, for the irrigation of the city's gardens. It is a popular picnic spot for Marrakchi families, and at night the pool is lit for the **Marvels and Reflections** show (Mar–Dec Mon–Sat 10pm, Apr–May, Aug daily 10pm; 250–400Dh), which features music, dancers and acrobats.

The mature gardens of **La Mamounia** hotel inspired Winston Churchill to start painting; he described it to his friend Franklin D. Roosevelt as 'the loveliest spot in the world'. The Saadian prince Moulay Mamoun established it as his pleasure garden, the Arset el Mamoun, in the 18th century. The gardens have more or less kept their traditional design with orange and olive groves, rose beds, and some of the most majestic palm trees in town. If you are not staying in the hotel, go for a drink or a meal at the hotel and then stroll through the gardens. *See also Accommodation, p.36.*

Left: camels and palm trees in the Palmeraie.

OURIKA VALLEY

Beldi Country Club

6km (4 miles) south of Marrakesh, route du Barrage, Cherifia; tel: 0524-383 950; www.beldicountryclub.com; admission charge; daily 10am–10pm

'Beldi' means 'from the countryside', and everything is done to keep the gardens, restaurant and mudbrick guesthouse as rural and simple as possible, offering the perfect retreat close to Marrakesh. The splendid gardens include a magnificent *roseraie* or rose garden with 12,000 rose bushes, a large olive grove and orchards. The garden is open to visitors, who pay a fixed fee for a day by the beautiful swimming pools in the garden with lunch. There is also a full-service spa using aromatic oils.

SEE ALSO ACCOMMODATION, P.36; SPORTS, P.116

Jardins Bioaromatiques de l'Ourika (Nectarôme)

Km34, Tnine-l'Ourika; tel: 0661-340 049; www.nectarome.com; daily Oct–Feb 9am–5pm, Mar–Sept 9am–7pm; admission charge

In these gardens, 50 different aromatic and medicinal plants are grown for the production of the organic Nectarôme essential oils and bath products. The delightful gardens can be visited on your own or on a guided tour, which can include a lunch from the garden. Nectarôme also runs workshops involving the many uses of plants.

Jardin du Safran

Km34, Tnine-l'Ourika; tel: 0522-484 476; www.safran-ourika.com; daily 8.30am–6pm; admission charge

More a farm than a garden, this is where the purple flowers of the *Crocus sativus* are grown for saffron. The plants, originally from Kashmir and Nepal, only flower about 20 days a year, more or less the three first weeks of November. It takes 140 flowers to produce 1g of saffron. Guided tours are on offer, explaining the whole process of saffron production, an important ingredient in Moroccan cuisine.

TOUBKAL PARK

Dar Taliba School Garden

Village of el Hanchane, close to Imlil; admission by permission of the director; free, but donations much appreciated

The garden at the Dar Taliba girls' school is a project of the Global Diversity Foundation. The aim is to increase educational opportunities for the girls in the village, so that they can play a larger role in the community's development. At the same time the garden feeds the pupils, and aims to preserve Berber knowledge of plants.

SEE ALSO ENVIRONMENT, P.47

Morocco has different kinds of garden. The *arset* is an orchard garden, with vegetable beds in the shade of fruit trees (citrus, figs, quince, pomegranate, etc), which are themselves shaded by date palms, watered traditionally by *khettaras*. A *riad* is the interior courtyard garden, protected by the walls of the house. The *agdal* is a protected conserved area, ranging from pastures to urban gardens with a central basin. A *jnane* is a general term for garden, with a special connotation of 'paradise garden', sometimes related to the *bustan*, a garden of relaxation and reflection, with ornamental and fragrant plants. *See also Riads, p.108–9.*

Below: in the Nectarôme.

History

12TH C BC
Phoenician sailors establish a series of trading posts along Morocco's coast, including Karikon Telichos (modern-day Essaouira).

AD682
Arabs invade Morocco under the command of the Umayyad Oqba ibn Na, introducing Islam to the region. Until then the Berbers were mainly polytheists, as well as some Jews and a few Christians.

MID-8TH C
Berbers convert to Islam, but revolt against the Ummayad rulers and cut them off from Morocco and Spain.

1062
Beginning of the reign of the Almoravids, a pious Saharan Berber dynasty, led by Youssef ben Tachfine, who establishes Marra Kouch (Marrakesh) as his new capital.

1126–7
Worried about the surrounding Berber tribes, Youssef ben Tachfine surrounds his capital with 16km (10 miles) of 5m- (16ft-) high city walls, and establishes a palm grove near the city, the Palmeraie.

1147
The Almohad dynasty, also Berber but from the High Atlas, seizes power. They destroy most of the Almoravid monuments, to replace them with their own: the Koutoubia Mosque in Marrakesh, the Giralda in Seville and the Tour Hassan in Rabat.

1184
The city's golden age under the Almohad ruler Yaqoub el Mansour, with a flourishing of arts and science.

1230
The Almohad Sultan el Mamoun accepts 12,000 Christian cavalry from King Ferdinand of Castile and Leon to retake Marrakesh from dissidents. A Catholic church is built in the city for foreign mercenaries.

1248
Another Berber dynasty, the Merenids, rise up from the Sahara and conquer Fès.

1269
The Merenids conquer Marrakesh, and build a medersa next to the Ben Youssef Mosque. But with Fès the capital, Marrakesh goes into decline.

1492
Fall of Muslim Spain.

1551
The Saadians re-establish Marrakesh as the capital of an empire that stretches from the Niger to the Mediterranean.

1578–1603
The great Saadian ruler Ahmed el Mansour builds the el Badi Palace, restores the Ben Youssef Medersa and establishes the Mellah.

1668
The Alaouite dynasty, of which the current King Mohammed VI is a descendant, comes to power.

1672
The Alaouite ruler Moulay Ismail moves the capital to Meknes, and the city once again falls into decline for several centuries.

1866

El Bahia Palace is built.

1894–1908

Sultan Abdelaziz leaves Morocco bankrupt and wide open to European encroachment.

1912

The Treaty of Fès. Morocco is carved up between France and Spain. In Marrakesh, General Lyautey, the first Resident General, establishes the Ville Nouvelle or New Town, known as Guéliz.

1920S

Thami el Glaoui, Pasha of Marrakesh, connives with the French, pacifying rebellious tribes in exchange for power and privileges.

1923

La Mamounia hotel opens.

1953

El Glaoui and 300 allies convene in Marrakesh to draw up a proposal to replace the legitimate monarch (Sultan Mohammed Ben Youssef, later Mohammed V) with the elderly Ben Arafa. The sultan and his family are exiled to Madagascar.

1955

Mohammed V is restored to the throne.

1956

France grants Independence. Mohammed V changes his title of 'sultan' to 'king'.

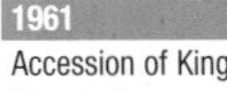

1961

Accession of King Hassan II.

1963–77

King Hassan survives the first of five different plots against him, the most serious of which are led by the army.

1969

The album *Marrakesh Express*, inspired by the night train from Tangier to Marrakesh, is released by Crosby, Stills & Nash. By now, Marrakesh is a well-established stop on the hippie trail.

1975

The Green March: 350,000 unarmed Moroccans claim the Spanish (Western) Sahara for Morocco.

1999

King Hassan II dies. His son and successor, Mohammed VI, embarks on a programme of increased democratisation.

2001

Marrakesh's International Film Festival is inaugurated.

2006

Second terminal opens at Marrakesh-Menara airport; La Mamounia hotel closes for refurbishment.

2010

Deadline for the king's Vision Morocco 2010, where he hopes to see 10 million visitors a year, the culmination of an ambitious plan to increase tourism.

Kasbahs and Palaces

Powerful kings built lavish palaces on a vast scale in Marrakesh, but few remain as they were generally razed to the ground by the following dynasty, who often deplored the worldliness and excess on display. Their palaces tended to be in the kasbah quarter, surrounded by high walls, which formed a city within the city. In the countryside, local chieftains outside the cities built kasbahs too; here this meant fortified mudbrick structures, to protect their commercial interests, as well as their families, from outside attacks.

SOUTHERN MEDINA

El Badi Palace

Bab Berrima; daily 8.30–11.45am, 2.30–5.45pm; admission charge; map p.136 C2

Recognisable from the many storks' nests is Ahmed el Mansour's palace. It was built by the best craftsmen of the time, using the finest materials. The walls and ceilings were covered with Timbuktu gold, the sunken gardens were filled with perfumed flowers, the central pool was 90m (295ft) long and had an island in the middle. The palace took 25 years to be built, and was only just finished before el Mansour's death in 1603.

Ninety years later, Moulay Ismail razed the palace to the ground, and took 12 years to strip it. A lot of imagination is needed to reconstruct what was one of the most splendid palaces ever built. The central courtyard is vast, with five basins and four sunken gardens, now planted with orange trees. The gardens would have been typical Moorish gardens planted with orange trees, cypresses, palms, olive trees and perfumed flowers. On the western side was the Koubba el Hamsiniya (Pavilion of 50 Columns) and, opposite it, the Crystal Pavilion. To the north was the Green Pavilion, and to the south the Koubba Khaysuran, named after the sultan's favourite wife. At the northeastern corner, the staircase in the corner gives access to the rooftop terrace. In an annexe in the southeastern corner is the splendid Koutoubia Minbar.

SEE ALSO MUSEUMS AND GALLERIES, P.79

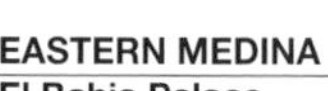

EASTERN MEDINA

El Bahia Palace

Corner of rue Riad Zitoun el Jedid and place des Ferblantiers; Sat–Thur 8.45–11.45am, 2.45–5.45pm, Fri 8.45–11.30am, 3–5.45pm; admission charge; map p.137 D3

Grand vizier Si Moussa started building this charming palace in the 1860s, and his son Ba Ahmed, who was regent for the child-sul-

Left: the impressive Glaoui Kasbah of Telouet, set in dramatic scenery.

Left: the evocative Aït Benhaddou Kasbah.

In the 12th century, Sultan Yaqoub el Mansour was the first to build the kasbah or walled citadel in the southern part of the medina. The vast walled space encircled palaces, barracks and the royal mosque. Successive rulers all added to the splendour of the imperial city. Today the kasbah still holds the royal palace and the house King Mohammed VI uses when he is in town (closed to visitors).

tan Abdelaziz, finished it. The Bahia palace was vast, spread over 8 hectares (20 acres), with a series of courtyards, gardens, pavilions and 150 rooms. Sultan Abdelaziz is said to have become so jealous of his vizier's fortunes that when Ba Ahmed died, he forced his family to leave and stripped the palace bare. The infamous warlord Madani Glaoui lived here from 1908 until 1911, when it became the residence of the French Resident General under the French Protectorate. Only part of the palace can be visited, as some of it is still used by the royal family and their staff. King Mohammed VI threw a lavish party here for the rapper P. Diddy a few years ago.

MOUASSINE QUARTER

Dar el Bacha

Rue Dar el Bacha; closed at the time of writing; map p.138 B4

This is the palace of the cruel Pasha of Marrakesh, T'Hami el Glaoui, who ruled over Marrakesh and the Atlas for the French. Lavish parties for international leaders such as Churchill and Roosevelt and many movie stars were held here, all happily ignoring the fact that the wealth was obtained by corruption and prostitution. Hours after he died in 1956, the building was plundered with a vengeance, but it has now been restored, and rumour has it that it will re-open as a Museum of Islamic Arts.

TIZI-N-TICHKA

Aït Benhaddou Kasbah

Aït Benhaddou, 22km (14 miles) off the Tizi-n-Tichka; free, but tip the custodian

A familiar sight now, as this well-preserved kasbah has been used often as a background for Hollywood movies. The mudbrick fortress, now declared a Unesco World Heritage Site, was started in the 11th century as an Almoravid caravanserai. Now it's a series of kasbahs, a confusing but superb warren of walls with a formal gateway by the riverbank. In recent years most inhabitants have moved to the new village across the river, but a few are still around to show visitors their traditional homes for a small tip. From the top there are wonderful views over the stunning surroundings of this most impressive of kasbahs.

SEE ALSO FILM, P.56

Glaoui Kasbah of Telouet

Telouet, off the Tizi-n-Tichka; admission by donation

Several generations of Glaoui built mudbrick kasbahs here, but the most prominent white kasbah was built in stone by T'hami el Glaoui between 1934 and 1955. The kasbah is crumbling fast, but still an atmospheric place, and the guardian leads visitors through the maze of corridors and large, opulent reception rooms. All the furniture has gone, but these rooms need to be imagined decorated with the finest rugs and textiles. The older kasbah is on the edge of the village, but very little is left standing.

Language

The official language in Morocco is Arabic. Moroccans speak *darija*, their own dialect, but written communication is in standard, modern Arabic. The Berbers speak various dialects of their own, Tamazigh in the Middle and High Atlas valleys, and Chleuh in the High Atlas. Although most Berbers now speak and understand Arabic, few Arabs understand Berber. French is widely spoken and understood, although fluency is not as widespread as it once was. In tourist areas, you will be surprised by youngsters speaking several languages. Here are some helpful phrases in Moroccan-dialect Arabic and French.

USEFUL PHRASES

Hello *Márhaba, la bes* Bonjour
reply *Bikheer?* Bonjour
Greetings (formal) *Es-Salám aláykum* (lit. Peace be upon you)
reply *Waláykum es-salam* (And to you peace)
Welcome *Márhaba* Soyez le bienvenu
Good morning *Sabáh el-kháyr* Bonjour
Good evening *Mesá el-kháyr* Bonsoir
Goodbye *Bessaláma* Au revoir
How are you? *La bes/Káyf hálak (to m)/Káyf hálik (to f)?* Ça va?
Fine, thank you *Bikheer el-hámdu li-lláh* Ça va, merci
Please *'Afak, 'afik, 'afakum (to m, f, pl)* S'il vous plaît
Thank you (very much) *Shúkran (bezzef)* Merci (beaucoup)
Thanks be to God *El-hámdu li-lláh*
Yes *Eeyeh/náam* Oui
No *La* Non
If God wills *Insha'allah?* Si Dieu le veut
What is your name? *Asmeetek?* C'est quoi votre nom?
My name is... *Esmee...* Je m'appelle
Where are you from? *Mneen enta/enti/entum? (to m/f/pl)* Vous êtes d'où?
I am from England/ United States *Ana min Inglaterra/Amrika* Je suis anglais(e) /américain(e)
Do you speak English/ French? *Wash kat'ref negleezeeya/faranseeya?* Vous parlez anglais/ français?

Below: signage is usually bilingual, Arabic and French.

Above: Arabic carvings on a Marrakesh building.

I do not understand *Mafhemtsh* Je ne comprends pas
I understand *Fhemt* Je comprends
What does this mean? *Ash kat'anee hadhee?* Qu'est-ce que ça veut dire?
Never mind *Ma'alésh* Pas de problème
It is forbidden *Mamnú'* C'est interdit

TIME

What time is it? *Shal fessa'a?* Il est quelle heure?
When? *Emta/Fuqash?* Quand?
Today *Elyaum* Aujourd'hui
Tomorrow *Ghedda* Demain
Yesterday *Lbareh* Hier
Morning *Fi-ssbah* Le matin

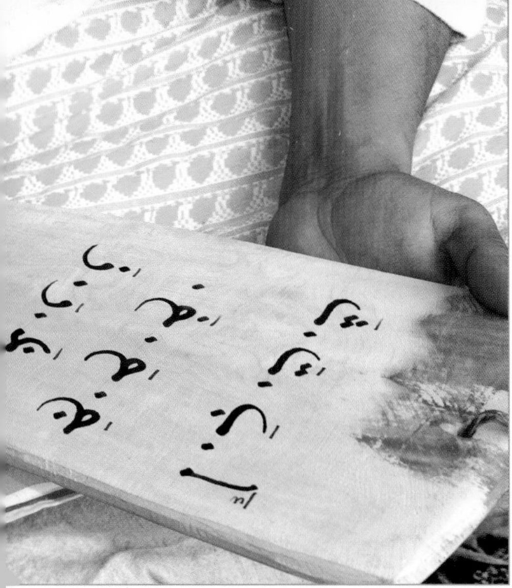

Left: writing Arabic letters.

ACCOMMODATION

How much does a room cost per night? *Bash halkayn gbayt i wahed leyla?* La chambre est à combien la nuit?
I would like a room... *Bgheet shee beet...* Je voudrais une chambre...
for one person *dyal wahed* pour une personne
for two people *dyal jooj* double
with a bathroom *belhammam* avec salle de bain
shower *dúsh* douche
air con *kleemateezaseeyun* clim (climatisation)

EMERGENCIES

Help *'Teqnee!* Au secours!
doctor *tbeeb* médecin
hospital *mustáshfa* hôpital
pharmacy *saidalíya* pharmacie
I am sick *Ana mreed/mreeda (f)* Je suis malade
diarrhoea *ishál* la diarrhée
medine *dawa* un médicament
police *esshúrta* la police
lawyer *muhámmi* un avocat

Numbers

0 *sifr* zéro
1 *wahed* un/une
2 *jooj* deux
3 *tlata* trois
4 *reb'a* quatre
5 *khamsa* cinq
6 *setta* six
7 *sab'a* sept
8 *tmenya* huit
9 *tes'ood* neuf
10 *ashra* dix
20 *ishreen* vingt
30 *tlaateen* trente
100 *miya* cent
1,000 *alf* mille

Afternoon/evening *Fil-sheeya* L'après-midi/le soir
Quickly *Bizerba* Vite
Slowly *Bishweeya* Lentement
On time *Fi-lweqt* A l'heure

EATING/DRINKING

coffee/tea *áhwa/shái* café/thé
with milk *wa hleb* au lait
with/without sugar *wa/bla sukur* avec/sans sucre
with mint *b'na'na'* à la menthe
orange juice *aseer limoun* un jus d'orange
mineral water *mái ma'adaniya* une eau minérale
wine *sh'rab* du vin
beer *béera* une bière
I am a vegetarian *Ana nabbáti (for m)/nabbatiya (for f)* Je suis végétarien(ne)
the bill please *el-hsáb 'afek* L'addition, s'il vous plaît

SHOPPING

market *souk* le marché
money *flóos* de l'argent
I want to change money *Bgheet nserref floos* Je veux changer de l'argent
How much is it? *Bshhal?* C'est combien?
It's too expensive *Ghalee bezzaf* C'est trop cher
I like this *Ajebni* Ça me plaît
I do not like this *Ma'jebatneesh* Cela ne me plaît pas
big/small *kebeer/sagheer* grand/petit
open/closed *mehlool/mesdoud* ouvert/fermé

TRANSPORT

Where..? *Feen?* Où?
How do I get to...? *Keefeesh ghaadee nuwsul l...?* Comment peut-on aller à...?
taxi *ettaks* le taxi
train station *lagaar* la gare
bus station *mehetta dyal uttubisaat* la gare routière
airport *elmataar* l'aéroport
to *li/íla* à
from *min* de
right *leemen* à droite
left *leeser* à gauche
How far..? *Bsshal ba'yd?* Est-ce que c'est loin...?

Literature

Every night in the Jemaa el Fna, storytellers retell the tales of old heroes, of desperate love and of the glorious city of Marrakesh. Morocco has a long tradition of poetry and stories, passed on orally for the simple reason that for years most people could not read. The colourful city where events and facts are often stranger than fiction has inspired foreign writers too, who have tried to grasp the strangeness and magic. The Beat generation authors of the 1950s and 1960s were fascinated by the old stories, and added a few of their own. Some ventured to Marrakesh on their travels and, in the process, influenced a generation of Moroccan authors.

MOROCCAN AUTHORS

In *Moroccan Folk Tales,* Jilali el Koudia tells the classic tales recounted for generations by storytellers.

Mohammed Choukri's *For Bread Alone* and Mohammed Mrabet's *Love with a Few Hairs*, were directly influenced by the Beat movement, including the writers' friend Paul Bowles, who translated the books into English. The best-known Moroccan author is Fès-born Tahar Ben Jelloun, also a psychotherapist, who now lives in France. His most famous book is *The Sand Child*, about a girl in Marrakesh brought up as a boy by her father. His book *The Sacred Night* won the most prestigious literary price in France, the Prix Goncourt.

Recently, with less censorship and more openness under King Mohammed VI, several quite individual novels have been published in Morocco, among them *Welcome to Paradise* by Mahi Binebine and Laila Lalami's *Hope and other Dangerous Pursuits*, both of which are concerned with the dreams and problems of emigration.

FURTHER READING

FICTION

This Blinding Absence of Light
Tahar Ben Jelloun
Based on the true story of a political prisoner who managed to survive incarceration in an underground prison in the High Atlas. He could neither stand nor see for 20 years.

The Sheltering Sky
Paul Bowles
Not really about Marrakesh, but nobody captures the mysteries of Morocco better than Paul Bowles.
SEE ALSO FILM, P.57

Hideous Kinky
Esther Freud
Amusing novel based on the author's experience of living in Marrakesh with her sister and hippie mother in the 1960s.
SEE ALSO FILM, P.56

HISTORY AND SOCIETY

Morocco
Marvine Howe
This is an engrossing examination of contemporary Morocco and Mohammed

Left: the most influential book in Morocco: the Quran.

Left: at the excellent Café du Livre.

One of the best foreign writers to have lived and written in Morocco was **Paul Bowles**, who died in Tangier in 1999, aged 88. He arrived in Tangier after WWII, and soon gathered around him an interesting circle of both local writers like Mohammed Mrabet and Larbi Layashi, whose work he translated into English, as well as visitors such as Brion Gysin, Allen Ginsberg and William Burroughs. He was fascinated by and recorded a lot of Moroccan folk music. His book *The Sheltering Sky* was filmed by Bernardo Bertolucci.

VI's reign so far by an ex-foreign correspondent.

Lords of the Atlas
Gavin Maxwell
Compelling story of the Glaouis, who colluded with the French to pacify southern Morocco during the protectorate.

The Conquest of Morocco
Douglas Porch
Highly readable history of Morocco in the pre-colonial period.

TRAVEL LITERATURE

Voices of Marrakesh
Elias Canetti
Lyrical impressions of the city by Nobel Prize-winner.

Cinema Eden
Juan Goytisolo
A few stories about Marrakesh and other Moroccan places by this Spanish writer fascinated by rituals, traditions and, above all, stories.

A Year in Marrakesh
Peter Mayne
Engaging account of the author's stay in Marrakesh during the early 1950s.

Marrakesh The Red City, The City Through Writers' Eyes
ed. **Barnaby Rogerson**
The most delightful collection of the best snippets of history, stories and anecdotes that fully capture the magic of the city.

The Caliph's House
Taher Shah
The brilliant story of a London writer who falls in love with a house in Casablanca and then decides to do it up and move there, for anyone thinking of doing the same in Marrakesh.

BOOKSHOPS

ACR Librairie d'Art
55 boulevard Mohammed Zerktouni, Guéliz; tel: 0524-446 792; Mon–Sat 10am–1.30pm, 3.30–7.30pm; map p.132 B4
A good place to find glossy coffee-table books on Morocco, its gardens, architecture and crafts in English and French.

Café du Livre
44 rue Tareq ibn Ziad, Guéliz; tel: 0524-432 149; www.cafedulivre.com; Mon–Sat 9.30am–9pm; map p.132 C4
Excellent bookshop with new and used books of fiction, books on Morocco and North Africa, free WiFi and a great café-restaurant. Occasional readings by visiting writers.
SEE ALSO CAFES, P.43; RESTAURANTS, P.103

Below: reading materials for sale in the Mouassine quarter.

Monuments

Marrakesh may not have many traditional monuments, but the 11th-century medina itself is a sight to behold – it was recognised as a World Heritage Site by Unesco in 1985. Getting lost in the Old City, you come across tombs, saints' shrines and fondouks. Many of the city's buildings are hidden behind high walls, a feature in themselves. Some of the sights you can visit and walk into, others, including shrines, are only open to Muslims. Some structures have now been turned into museums. See also *Architecture, p.38*; *Kasbahs and Palaces, p.68*; *Museums and Galleries, p.78*; and *Religions and Religious Sites, p.92*.

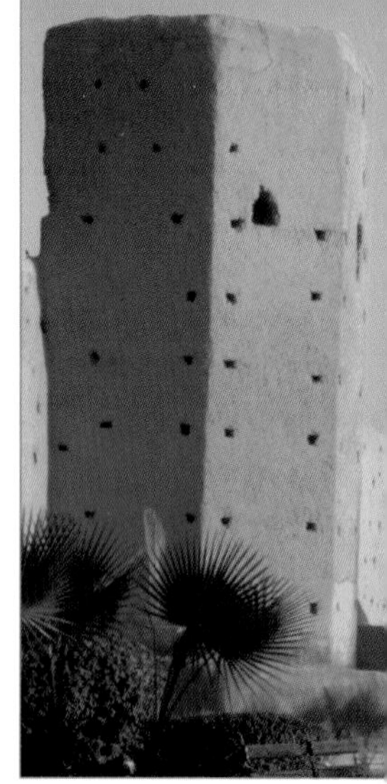

JEMAA EL FNA

Koubba Lalla Zohra

Koutoubia Gardens, avenue Mohammed V; free; map p.138 B1

On the plaza in the Koutoubia Gardens is a small white-domed *koubba* or tomb of Lalla Zohra, daughter of a freed slave, who, it is said, was a woman by day and could be seen hovering over the shrine as a white dove at night.

Marrakesh City Walls: Ramparts and Gates

Around the old medina

Surrounding the medina of Marrakesh are the *pisé* (sun-dried clay) ramparts, built by the Almoravids in 1126, to protect the city against the threat of the Berbers from Tin Mal. The walls have been repaired and expanded since then; they are now 16km (10 miles) long, nearly 10m (30ft) high and have 200 towers and 20 gates. Until relatively recently, it made for a great bike or horse-drawn carriage *(calèche)* ride to follow the walls around the entire medina, but heavy traffic on the road makes it less fun, so gates and city walls are now better explored from inside the medina. The most elaborate of all is the Bab Agnaou *(see right)*, the entrance to the kasbah enclosure. There

Below: the Bab Agnaou, the official gateway into the medina.

Left: the city walls of Marrakesh's medina.

South of the Koutoubia rose gardens, across avenue Houmane el Fetouaki, on place Youssef ben Tachfine, behind a wall is the tomb of the city's founder, Youssef ben Tachfine, open to the sky and off limits for the public.

The restored **Saadian Tombs** are one of the city's major attractions, popular with loads of tour buses, so go early in the morning or late in the afternoon to avoid the crowds.

is a large junk market near Bab el Khemis *(see Shopping, p.110)*, and the leather tanneries.

SOUTHERN MEDINA

Bab Agnaou

Rue Oqba ben Nafaa; map p.136 B2

The ramparts' official gate was built by Yaqoub el Mansour in 1185 and is beautifully carved from the blue Guéliz stone, rather than the standard mudbrick. Some say that *agnaou* is the Berber word for 'a ram without horns', referring to the fact that the gate lost its two towers; more likely is that the name comes from 'Gnaoua', the Guinean soldiers who guarded the palace. Next to the Bab Agnaou is the Bab er Rob, the official entrance into the rest of the city.

SEE ALSO ARCHITECTURE, P.38

Saadian Tombs

Behind the Kasbah Mosque; daily 8.30–11.45am, 2.30–5.45pm; admission charge; map p.136 B2

The 16th-century Saadians, originally an Arab family from the Souss Valley, chose the garden of the royal kasbah mosque to bury their sultans and their families. The *shorfa* of Marrakesh, the direct descendants of Prophet Mohammed, were already interred here, and the first Saadian to be buried here in 1557 was the founder of the dynasty, Sultan Mohammed esh Sheikh. The more elaborate tombs belong to his son, the great conqueror Ahmed el Mansour, and family.

The enclosed garden cemetery was originally only accessible through the mosque, and the Saadian tombs escaped destruction by later dynasties. The tombs disappeared in the overgrown garden until the French Resident

Below: in the Saadian Tombs.

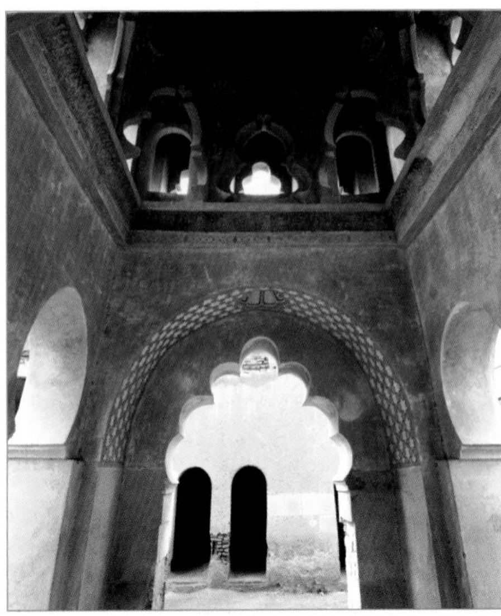

Above: inside the Almoravid Koubba el Ba'adiyin.

Perhaps Marrakesh's greatest monument is the Old City itself. Founded in 1070, the medina was, until about 100 years ago, entirely enclosed by miles of mud-brick walls and pierced by about 20 gates. Inside the walls, the medina was further divided by interior walls into different districts: the protected kasbah in the south was home to the royal palaces, next to it was the Mellah for the Jews, and then there were also the souks and other residential quarters. It remains Marrakesh's biggest attraction, and even though it has been seriously spruced up in recent years, it retains much of its magic and medieval character. Each quarter is traditionally a cluster of riads or courtyard houses surrounding a mosque, a school, a bakery and a hammam. The medina's main squares are the Jemaa el Fna and Rahba Kedima. *See also Squares, p.120–121.*

General Lyautey found them after he had the area surveyed by air in 1917.

The prayer hall with a fine mihrab is connected to the Hall of the Twelve Columns. In the middle of it is the tomb of Ahmed el Mansour, who died from the plague in 1603, his son Zaidan to his right and his grandson Mohammed esh-Sheikh II to his left. The rich gilded cedarwood decoration of the dome is beautifully set off by the mosaic.

Thirty-three other Saadian princes are buried in this hall, and more in the Hall of the Three Niches to the right.

The more modest second *koubba* in the middle of the garden contains the tomb of Ahmed el Mansour's mother, the venerated Lalla Messaouda, and his father, Mohammed esh Sheikh.

MOUASSINE QUARTER

Mouassine Fountain

Rue Mouassine; map p.139 C4

This ornate fountain with carved wooden details, near the Mouassine Mosque, is a remnant from a previous way of life. At the beginning of the 20th century, the medina had about 80 of these fountains and the water was used for cooking, bathing and watering the gardens.

NORTHERN MEDINA

Koubba Ba'adiyin

Place ben Youssef; daily Apr–Sept 9am–7pm, Oct–Mar 9am–6pm; admission charge combined with ticket to Medersa and Musée de Marrakesh; map p.134 C1

This small two-storey domed structure is important because this is where the Almoravids tested for the first time many ideas that were used ever after in Moroccan architecture. It was once probably the ablution pavillion of the 12th-century Almoravid Ben Youssef Mosque. Have a good look and you will find the scalloped and horseshoe arches, the ziggurat-style merlons and fine arabesque patterns that are now very familiar, especially after a few days wandering around Marrakesh.

ESSAOUIRA

Skala du Port

Harbour; daily 8.30am–noon, 2.30–6pm; admission charge

The Porte de la Marine is the Marine Gate, fronting the L-shaped Skala du

Right and below: visit the ramparts of the Skala du Port and the Skala de la Ville for stunning views over the harbour and Atlantic Ocean.

Port. This sea bastion with cannons protected the harbour. From the top there are superb views over the medina, the sea and the Ile de Mogador, just off the mainland. The harbour is a constant hub of activity; don't be put off by the guards outside the towers of the Skala du Port, everyone can walk in.

Skala de la Ville
Rue de la Skala; free
The Skala de la Ville is an impressive 200m- (656ft-) long sea bastion with 18th-century bronze cannons, where lovers come to watch the sun set over the Atlantic Ocean. The old ammunition warehouses underneath have been turned into workshops where the city's famous thuya wood is carved into boxes, salad bowls and furniture.

Museums and Galleries

Marrakesh has only a few museums, but they are worth visiting, as they give insight into different aspects of the city. A large museum of Islamic Art is rumoured to be planned in the Dar el Bacha, but no date is fixed at the time of writing. The interest in Middle Eastern and North African contemporary art is rising, and some internationally recognised Moroccan artists are making their mark. The number of galleries is increasing too, most of them in Guéliz. Meanwhile, Essaouira is known for its Gnaoua folk art.

CONTEMPORARY MOROCCAN ARTISTS

Hassan Hajjaj (www.hassanhajjaj.com) is a London-based Moroccan artist who draws inspiration for his pop art from everyday life in Marrakesh, and in particular mixes the urban youth culture and the old world together. Hajjaj calls his photographs 'souk with a twist'.

The Marrakchi **Larbi Cherkaoui** is an artist who was formally trained as a calligrapher, but his work is boisterous and bold, sometimes spread over several canvases, and using local pigments.

Hicham Benohoud, a local photographer and arts teacher, made a great series of surrealist pictures called 'Class Photos', where he asked a pupil to interrupt his work at a random moment and pose for him, while the others continued their work.

Ymane Fakhir is a photographer interested in ordinary situations which through their strongly scripted nature call up associations with the theatre.

Above: at the Musée de Marrakech *(see p.80)*.

Essaouira is famous for its folk-art Gnaoua painters, who were not formally trained. Once the Gnaoua were travelling trance doctors; now they paint their dreams in their own very particular style. The first gallery to support them was **Galerie Frédéric Damgaard** *(see p.81)*.

Above: the courtyard at the Dar Bellarj *(see p.80)*.

EASTERN MEDINA

Dar Si Said Museum

Rue Kennaria; off rue Riad Zitoun el Jedid; tel: 0524-389 192; daily 9am–noon, 3–6pm; admission charge; map p.139 E1

This delightful small palace, built by Si Said, the younger brother of Ba Ahmed who built the imposing **el Bahia Palace** *(see Kasbahs and Palaces, p.68)* next door, houses an important collection of

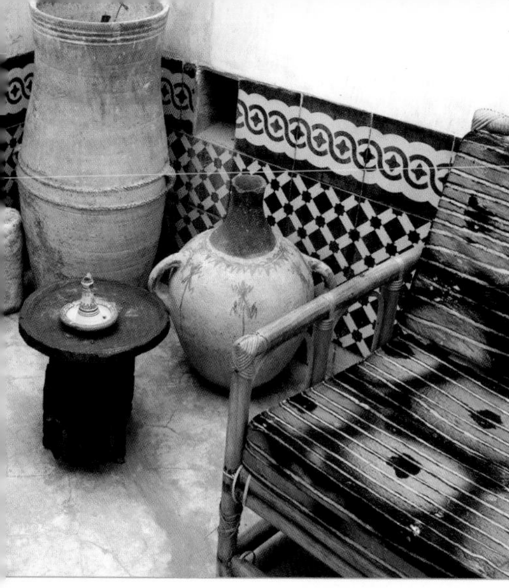

Left: African finds in the Maison Tiskiwin.

decorative arts and crafts from the south of Morocco. Both the beautiful house with its ornate painted ceilings and fine woodwork and the excellent collection are reasons to visit. Ancient wooden doors rescued from kasbahs and old medina houses are stacked up in the entrance. The oldest item in the collection is a fine 10th-century marble fountain basin brought to Marrakesh from Cordoba.

An old ferris wheel like the one near the garden was present at every *moussem* or saint's festival until at least the 1970s, to the delight of the medina and village kids. Other rooms show the variety of Moroccan jewellery, with filigree silver from the Jbel Siroua and fibulae from Tiznit, as well as a rich carpet collection, showing the style differences between Berber and Arab carpets. Berber carpets or *hanbels* are more colourful and use mainly geometric patterns, while the carpets made by the Arab tribes are traditionally narrow to fit their tents, in dark reds and purples.

Maison Tiskiwin

8 derb el Bahia, off rue Riad Zitoun el Jedid; tel: 0524-389 192; daily 9.30am–12.30pm, 3–5.30pm; admission charge; map p.137 C3

A special pavilion has been built in **el Badi Palace** to house the 12th-century **minbar** (stepped pulpit) of the Koutoubia Mosque, a marvel of medieval Islamic art. It was built for an Almoravid mosque in Cordoba, but brought to Marrakesh by the Almohad rulers for their new Koutoubia Mosque. The *minbar* was restored by a US-led team in 1996 and moved to its own pavilion in el Badi Palace. This masterpiece was composed of 1.3 million pieces of carved wood and intricate marquetry, with some pieces tinier than a grain of rice, all carved by the greatest artisans. *See also Kasbahs and Palaces, p.68.*

The Dutch anthropologist Bert Flint, a long-time resident of Marrakesh, has been fascinated by the connection between Marrakesh and sub-Saharan Africa, particularly Timbuktu, for many years. He is convinced that the influence of Africa in Morocco is much stronger is than the Arab influence. For decades, he has collected tribal art and textiles, and here in his private house, visitors are taken on a fascinating journey along the old trade routes between Marrakesh and Timbuktu.

The objects, pottery, beautiful jewellery and textiles belong to the different tribes one encounters en route, and all is well explained, particularly the connection between the two cities. This is a fascinating museum, very far away from the noise and bustle of the souks. The journey ends in Timbuktu and in Flint's peaceful courtyard filled with birdsong.

Riad Yima

52 derb Arjane, Rahba Kedima; tel: 0524-391 987; www.riadyima.com, www.hassanhajjaj.com; free; map p.139 D3

This colourful guesthouse run by London-based artist Hassan Hajjaj has a small shop-cum-gallery selling his work, and the rooms are entirely decorated by him.

SEE ALSO ACCOMMODATION, P.33

MOUASSINE QUARTER

Ministerio del Gusto

22 derb Azouz el Mouassine, near Villa Flore, off rue Sidi el Yamani; tel: 0524-426 455;

www.ministeriodelgusto.com; Mon–Sat 9.30am–noon, 4–7pm; free; map p.138 B4
In a West African-inspired interior is the ever changing gallery-cum-shop of designer Fabrizio Bizzari and Alessandro Lippini, a former style editor for Italian *Vogue*.
SEE ALSO SHOPPING, P.113

Riad el Fenn
2 derb Moulay Abdallah ben Hezzian, Bab el Ksour; tel: 0524-441 210; www.riadelfenn.com; free; map p.138 B3
This luxury riad has a good collection of contemporary art.
SEE ALSO ACCOMMODATION, P.33

NORTHERN MEDINA

Dar Bellarj
9 Toulalat Zaouiat Lahdar, near the Medersa ben Youssef; tel: 0524-444 555; daily 9am–1.30pm, 2.30–6pm; admission charge; map p.134 C2
The Dar Bellarj Foundation restored this former fondouk *(see Architecture, p.38)* that long served as a stork hospital. It is a cultural centre now for the medina, with story-telling, film screenings, exhibitions and concerts, and it has a lovely, peaceful courtyard to escape from the bustle of the souks.

Musée de Marrakech
Marrakesh Museum; place ben Youssef; tel: 0524-441 893; www.museedemarrakesh.ma; daily 9am–6.30pm; admission charge combined ticket with Medersa and Koubba; map p.139 D4
One of the finest 19th-century palaces in Marrakesh, the palace of defence minister and ambassador Mehdi M'Nebhi was bought and restored by Omar Benjelloun. A passionate collector of traditional Islamic arts, he also restored the nearby **Ben Youssef Medersa** *(see Religions and Religious Sites, p.94)* and **Koubba Ba'adiyin** *(see Monuments, p.76)* to their former glory. The museum shows temporary exhibitions of traditional and contemporary Moroccan arts. Just past the entrance is a tranquil courtyard with fountains, a pleasant café and a good bookshop. The interior has excellent examples of stuccowork and *zellij* tiling, and the galleries are housed in the original hammam (bathhouse) and *douira* (kitchen).

GUÉLIZ

Galerie Bleue
119 avenue Mohammed V; tel: 066-192 129; daily 10am–1pm, 4–8pm; free; map p.132 B4
The well-established Galerie Bleue specialises in contemporary figurative Moroccan art. The owner Abdelkader Chekkouri doesn't like abstract art, and promotes both internationally renowned and younger Moroccan artists such as Roman Lazaref and Aziz Benja.

Galerie Ré
Résidence el Andalous III, corner of rue de la Mosquée and rue Ibn Toumert; tel: 0524-432 258; www.galeriere.com; daily Mon–Sat 10am–1pm, 3–8pm; free; map p.133 C4
Lucien Viola's contemporary art gallery is in a modern space in the Ville Nouvelle, dedicated to young Moroccan and Mediterranean artists.

Matisse Art Gallery
43 passage Ghandouri, off 61 rue de Yougoslavie; tel: 0524-448 326; www.matisse-art-gallery.com; Mon–Sat 9am–1pm, 3.30–8pm; free; map p.132 B4
This marble-fronted gallery displays contem-

Jacques Majorelle painted the exterior of his studio, which now houses the **Musée Islamique**, an electric cobalt blue *(see picture, left)*. It is now named Majorelle blue, which gives an even more exotic touch to the greenery of the garden. Some say it was inspired by the archetypal French blue workman's jacket, others claim he was inspired by the blue used in some Berber homes in the south. *See also Gardens, p.63.*

porary Moroccan artworks such as Hassan Hajjaj, Farid Belkahia's henna paintings and Mahi Binebine, as well as Orientalist paintings.

Musée Islamique
Majorelle Garden; avenue Yaqoub el Mansour; tel: 0524-301 852; www.jardinmajorelle.com; daily, Oct–May 8am–5pm, June–Sept 8am–6pm; admission charge to garden, extra for Islamic Museum
The French artist Jacques Majorelle created this exotic garden around his electric-blue studio. The building now houses a small Islamic Museum, with a collection of his paintings, and Yves Saint Laurent's superb collection of Moroccan crafts, including great silver Berber jewellery, robust carved doors and fine textiles. The small boutique sells books, contemporary jewellery and fine Moroccan crafts.
SEE ALSO GARDENS, P.63

ESSAOUIRA

Galerie Frédéric Damgaard
Rue Oqba ben Nafi; tel: 0524-784 446; www.galeriedamgaard.com; daily 9am–1pm, 3–7pm
The city's most important gallery, Galerie Frédéric Damgaard, the first to be interested in the Essaouiran Gnaoua painters, has the widest and most interesting collection, including works by one of the masters, Mohammed Tabal.

Musée Sidi Mohammed ben Abdallah
Derb Laalouj; tel: 0524-475 300; Wed–Mon 8.30am–6pm; admission charge
This small museum, in a pasha's 19th-century town house, has a great collection of the region's traditional crafts and decorative arts since antiquity. On the ground floor is a collection of Roman and Phoenician objects found in the Bay of Essaouira. On the first floor are some wonderful examples of the inlaid woodwork and the silver Arab and Jewish jewellery the city was famous for. The museum also has a beautiful collection of Arabo-Andalusian and Berber musical instruments made in the local woods.

Below: Gnaoua artworks in Galerie Frédéric Damgaard.

Music, Dance and Theatre

You hear music all the time in Marrakesh, but it's not that easy to find a Western-style gig. Any night on the Jemaa el Fna, however, there are performances of Gnaoua music and dancing, and many Moroccan restaurants in the medina have live music to go with dinner, either Arab-Andalusian or Gnaoua trance, or occasionally a belly dancer. What little theatre there is is in Moroccan dialect or French, but the new Théâtre Royal is hoping to attract international shows. The best time to see performances of traditional arts is during the festivals or *moussems*.

MOROCCAN MUSIC

The classical music of the cities, and the one that accompanies most classy dinners or celebrations, is Arab-Andalusian. The music Arabs brought with them from Spain and Persia is comprised of melancholic love songs and complex instrumental music. *Chaabi* music is on full blast in most shops and cars: this is Morocco's version of pop.

Berber music is very different. In the villages, music is sung and danced by the whole village together at celebrations, with only drums and flute. There are *imdyazn*, professional musicians who travel around in small groups in the mountains during the summer months, accompanied by a poet, who improvises poems about the events.

Orthodox Islam only tolerates music that sings Allah's praises, and this includes the *adhan* or call to prayer, chanting of the Quran and the music of the Sufi brotherhoods, who use music as a means to get closer to God.

The Gnaoua claim to be the descendants of Prophet Mohammed's revered first muezzin, the Ethiopian Bilal. Their music is used to exorcise evil spirits from the ill.

Below: local musicians.

Listen to a variety of Moroccan music and the Moroccan top 10 on the Moroccan website (in French) www.maroc.net/newrc.

SEE ALSO BERBER CULTURE, P.40; FESTIVALS AND EVENTS, P.55

MUSIC VENUES

Institut Français

Route de la Targa, on the outskirts of Guéliz; tel: 0524-446 930; www.ifm.ma

Occasional concerts of Moroccan or French music.

Kechmara

1bis–3 rue de la Liberté, Guéliz; tel: 0524-422 532; www.kechmara.ma; Mon–Sat noon–midnight; map p.132 B4

Popular restaurant and bar, packed on Wednesdays and Fridays at 7.30pm when there is good live music.

SEE ALSO NIGHTLIFE, P.85; RESTAURANTS, P.104

Kosybar

47 place des Ferblantiers, Southern Medina; tel: 0524-380 324; daily noon–midnight; map p.137 C3

Left: a belly-dancing extravaganza at Le Comptoir.

Above: a poster advertising the Gnaoua Festival.

The trendy piano bar has jazz live music on weekend evenings.
SEE ALSO NIGHTLIFE, P.85; RESTAURANTS, P.100

Montecristo
20 rue ibn Aïcha, Guéliz; tel: 0524-439 031; www.montecristomarrakech.com; daily from 10.30pm
Daily live performances of two Latino bands in the pub.

Palais Jad Mahal
10 rue Haroun Errachid, Fontaine Mamounia, Hivernage; tel: 0524-430 457; daily 7.30pm–3am; map p.133 D1
This over-the-top oriental folly has a live cover band (rock and pop) from midnight every night in its cocktail bar – if you enjoy live music and a sexy atmosphere, this makes for a great evening out. No live music on Mondays.

Taros
Place Moulay Hassan, Essaouira; tel: 0524-476 407; www.taroscafe.com; Mon–Sat 11am–4pm, 6pm–midnight
Live music every night on the rooftop terrace.
SEE ALSO CAFÉS, P.43

DANCE VENUES

Le Comptoir
Rue Echouhada, Hivernage; tel: 0524-437 702; www.comptoirdarna.com; daily dinner only; daily 8pm–1am; $$$–$$$$; map p.133 D1
The best belly dancers perform at 9pm every night.
SEE ALSO NIGHTLIFE, P.85; RESTAURANTS, P.105

Marvels and Reflections
Menara Gardens, avenue de la Menara, Hivernage; Mon–Sat 10pm in Apr, May and Aug; map p.132 A1
Show that presents the history of Morocco through dance, music and fireworks in the Menara Gardens.
SEE ALSO GARDENS, P.64

THEATRE VENUE

Théâtre Royal
Corner of avenue de France and avenue Mohammed VI, Hivernage; tel: 0524-431 516; daily 8.30am–7pm; map p.132 B3
Designed by one of Morocco's leading architects, Charles Boccara, in 2001, this 800-seat opera is linked by a stunning courtyard to the 1,200-seat open-air theatre. The theatre is only sporadically used during festivals, but temporary exhibitions of local and visiting artists fill up its exhibition hall.

On the Jemaa el Fna, in riad restaurants or at the Essaouira Festival you can see the exotic-looking Gnaoua musicians in their red robes, with shell-encrusted caps, spinning tassels and loud castanets. They may be performing for tourists, but they are still following in a long African tradition. Descendants of black slaves who came on the trans-Saharan caravans, they are traditionally wandering healers who travel in groups. They hold a *lila*, a night of exorcism, where with the help of trance-inducing music, they take possession of the spirits of someone who is ill or possessed. For good Gnaoua music look out for the CD *Marrakech Undermoon: the Black Album* (www.kamarstudios.com) available in Marrakesh.

Nightlife

The city no longer sleeps, and with the arrival of Pacha a few years ago, Marrakesh has acquired an Ibiza-like reputation for nightlife. Trendy new clubs in Hivernage and bars in Guéliz pop up all the time. For daytime partying there are day clubs and beaches too. A siesta during the heat of the day may become a necessity, as nightclubs only get going around midnight. Admissions range from 150–400Dh, and include a drink, but pretty girls and the smartly dressed sometimes get in for free. Very often bars will double up as restaurants, and some cafés now serve alcoholic drinks alongside mint tea, so *see also Cafés, p.42*, and *Restaurants, p.98*.

BARS

Bab

Bab Hotel, corner boulevard Mansour ed Dahbi and rue Mohammed el Beqal, Guéliz; tel: 0524-435 250; www.babhotelmarrakesh.com; map p.132 B4

The recently-opened bar attracts all the trendy young things in town.

SEE ALSO RESTAURANTS, P.103

Bar du Grand Tazi

Corner of avenue el Mouahidine and rue de Bab Agnaou, Jemaa el Fna; daily 7pm–1am; map p.136 B3

Great old-fashioned bar that gets quite raucous as the evening goes on, popular with male locals and travellers in search for a cheap cold beer.

As alcohol is prohibited in Islam, alcoholic drinks are usually served behind walls away from the public eye. The traditional bars are very raucous, places where men come and drink after work with the sole purpose of getting drunk. Many of the bars frequented by both men and women tend to be either in hotels or in restaurants. Alcohol used to be forbidden in the medina until recently, but it is slowly making its way in, and there are now a few bars.

Bar L'Escale

Rue Mauretanie, off avenue Mohammed V, Guéliz; daily 5–11pm; map p.132 C3

One of the rare relaxed places where beers can be taken out to the pavement tables, but very much a men-only establishment.

Bo&Zin

Douar Lahna, route de l'Ourika, 3.5km (2 miles); tel: 0524-388 012; http://bo-zin.com; daily 8pm–1am or later

This stylish restaurant hosts many parties and has regular guest DJs playing. The bar really gets going after midnight, particularly at weekends, and the whole place has a very Ibizan vibe. There are Thai, French and Moroccan menu options, and it is open seven nights a week. Popular outdoor dining and bar with fabulous bamboo and cactus garden in summer.

SEE ALSO RESTAURANTS, P.105

Above: the cosy Kosybar.

Café Arabe

184 rue Mouassine, Mouassine Quarter; tel: 0524-429 728; www.cafearabe.com; daily 10am–midnight; map p.138 C4

Another atmospheric medina rooftop and *zellij*-clad courtyard where you can cool down with a beer or relax with some Moroccan wine. Avoid the food, though, as it is pretty mediocre.

Grand Café de la Poste

Corner of boulevard Mansour

Left: spectacle and hedonism at Teatro *(see p.87)*.

Eddahbi and avenue Imam Malik, Guéliz; tel: 0524-433 038; www.grandcafedelaposte.com; daily 8am–11pm; map p.132 C3
The upstairs bar lounge has a DJ every evening; it is *the* meeting place in town, and is an ideal spot for a relaxed drink before or after dinner.
SEE ALSO RESTAURANTS, P.103

Kechmara
1bis–3 rue de la Liberté, Guéliz; tel: 0524-422 532; www.kechmara.ma; Mon–Sat noon–midnight; map p.132 C4
Popular bar with live music on Wednesdays and Fridays at 7.30pm.
SEE ALSO MUSIC, DANCE AND THEATRE, P.82; RESTAURANTS, P.104

Kosybar
47 place des Ferblantiers, Southern Medina; tel: 0524-380 324; daily noon–midnight; map p.137 C3
Perfect place for a sundown or late-night drink on the roof terrace with great views over the medina.
SEE ALSO MUSIC, DANCE AND THEATRE, P.82; RESTAURANTS, P.100

L'Abyssin
Palais Rhoul, Dar Tounsi, route de Fès, Palmeraie; tel: 0524-328 584; www.palaisrhoul.com; Tue 8–11pm, Wed–Sun noon–3.30pm, 8–11pm
Super-cool lounge bar in canvas pavilions in the glorious garden of the chic Palais Rhoul hotel, serving tasty Mediterranean morsels to accompany your cocktail.

Le Comptoir
Rue Echouhada, Hivernage; tel: 0524-437 702; www.comptoirdarna.com; daily 8pm–1am; map p.133 D1
The best late night DJ bar in town, consistently good – you can enjoy a cocktail there after dinner in the bar upstairs with cabaret and great oriental tunes.
SEE ALSO MUSIC, DANCE AND THEATRE, P.83; RESTAURANTS, P.105

Raidd Bar
Rue Oum Er Bia, Guéliz; tel: 0524-432 007; www.raiddbarmarrakesh.com; daily 6pm–1am; map p.133 D3
New and very popular bar with a pre-clubbing atmosphere and in-house DJs – popular with the young Moroccan crowd and deep house music lovers.

Terrasse des Epices
15 Souk Cherifia, Dar el Bacha, Mouassine Quarter; tel: 0524-375 904/0676-046 767;

Below: the highly rated and stylish Le Comptoir.

Above: Villa Rosa.

www.terrassedesepices.com; daily 10am–midnight; map p.139 C4

The coolest rooftop to hang out on in the medina, with great music, excellent food and good-looking Marrakchi waiters.

SEE ALSO RESTAURANTS, P.101

Villa Rosa

64 avenue Hassan II, Guéliz; tel: 0524-449 635; daily 7.30pm–midnight; map p.132 B3

One of the places to meet for a drink before moving on to dinner next door, the bar is packed at weekends.

SEE ALSO RESTAURANTS, P.104

Yellow Submarine

82 avenue Hassan II, Guéliz; tel: 0672-569 864; daily 7.30pm–1am; map p.132 B3

Known as the 'Sub', this is a 1970s psychedelic-themed restaurant and bar, with pictures of The Beatles on the wall, and in-house DJs spinning a nostalgic mix of sixties, seventies, eighties and nineties disco and rock.

CASINOS

Casino de Marrakesh

Hotel Es Saadi and Casino, avenue el Kadissia, Hivernage; tel: 0524-448 811; www.essaadi.com; Sun–Thur 7pm–4am, Fri–Sat 7pm–5am; map p.133 D1

Grand casino, as well established as the hotel, where the rich and famous hang out.

SEE ALSO ACCOMMODATION, P.36

Grand Casino de la Mamounia

Avenue Bab Jedid, Hivernage; tel: 0524-444 570; www.grandcasinomamounia.com; Sun–Thur 9pm–4am, Fri–Sat 9pm–5am; map p.133 E1

Splendid Art Deco casino next door to the famous La Mamounia hotel, with 20 live games and more than 200 gambling machines.

SEE ALSO ACCOMMODATION, P.36

DAY CLUBS

Nikki Beach

Circuit de la Palmeraie, Guéliz; tel: 0663-519 992; www.nikkibeach.com; late Mar–Sept: daily noon–10pm

With an atmosphere of Ibiza meets St-Tropez, this is the hottest day club in town every summer, where light lunches, including sushi, and cocktails are served beside a huge swimming pool lined with large bed-style loungers. This is a see and be seen destination – dress to impress!

SEE ALSO SPORTS, P.116

Pacha Marrakesh

(see right)

This nightlife complex continues the party during the day, with DJs daily, by the poolside. Lunch and drinks are served to tables and large canopy sun-lounger beds.

Plage Rouge

Km10, route de l'Ourika; tel: 0524-378 086; www.ilove-marrakesh.com/laplagerouge; daily noon–1am

DJs spin their non-stop house music by the large pool in Marrakesh, surrounded by sun loungers, but children and families welcome. The party continues until well into the night.

SEE ALSO SPORTS, P.117

> Remember when going to the clubs out of town, like Pacha, that there is no night bus home. The only way back is by taxi, and it will be expensive, as taxi drivers realise you really don't have much choice.

GAY AND LESBIAN VENUES

Specifically gay and lesbian bars and clubs in Marrakesh are few to none, but most places are fairly tolerant towards gay clientele. Around the Jemaa el Fna and elsewhere in the medina, as well as out on the town at night, are many good-looking Moroccans who are out to make a bit of extra cash. Non-working locals may be uncomfortable at meeting in an obvious public place where relatives might see them, or where they may be picked up by *Brigade touristique* (the tourist police), who keep a watchful eye over goings-on. Sex between men is illegal; for Moroccans it doesn't really exist between women, but there haven't been any arrests in recent years.

The only place that is more obviously gay-friendly than the others is **Diamant Noir** *(see right)*, which has professionals hanging around of both sexes looking for some business. **Pacha** *(see right)* is so large that it has everything, and

Above: glamorous Nikki Beach.

gay people will feel comfortable mixing in.

NIGHTCLUBS

Cantobar

Corner of Moulay Hassan and avenue du Président Kennedy, Guéliz; tel: 0524-433 350; www.cantobar-marrakesh.com; daily 7.30pm–4am; free if you have dinner and drinks; map p.132 C2

Bar-restaurant-nightclub with popular karaoke nights on the stage for a relaxing night out.

Diamant Noir

Hotel Marrakesh, corner avenue Mohammed V and rue Oum Errabia, Guéliz; tel: 0524-434 351; daily 10pm–4am; admission charge; map p.133 D3

More old-fashioned and kitsch nightclub that attracts a less glitzy clientele with hip-hop and Marrakchi tunes. Very gay-friendly on weekend nights.

Pacha Marrakesh

Boulevard Mohammed VI, Hivernage; tel: 0524-388 405; www.pachamarrakesh.com; daily 8pm–5am; admission charge after 10pm

Enormous entertainment complex with several restaurants, lounges and a large clubbing area where the world's best DJs and home-grown talents turn the tables, mixing exotic Magrebi tunes with international music. The place looks stunning and is always busy, but best on Saturday nights when the Casablancans come into town just for clubbing.

Suite Club

Hotel Le Méridien N'Fis, avenue Mohammed VI, Guéliz; tel: 0524-420 700; www.suiteclub.ma; daily 10pm–3am; admission charge; map p.133 C1

Super chic nightclub with some of the best DJs in town; attracts a cosmopolitan crowd.

Teatro

Hotel Es Saadi and Casino, avenue el Quadissia, Hivernage; tel: 0524-448 811; www.essaadi.com; Sun–Thur 10pm–3am, Fri–Sat 10pm–4am; admission charge; map p.133 D1

Near Le Comptoir, this popular nightclub in an old theatre is a good late night destination for serious house music clubbers, packed on most nights. Saturday nights are 'white nights', with many clubbers dancing in their phosphorescent looking white clothes to techno, house and Moroccan pop music.

Below: the DJs join in with the dancing at Teatro.

Chez Ali in the Palmeraie (Route de Casablanca; tel: 0524-307 730; www.ilove-marrakesh.com/chezali) offers a dinner with folklore spectacle including traditional music, a fantasia or horsemanship show, folkloric dancing and magicians: good for a night out with kids to entertain, but all in all pretty touristy and a bit kitsch.

Pampering

Until not that long ago only wealthy Moroccans had a bathroom; everyone else went to the hammam (Turkish bathhouse). The hammam is all about deep cleansing, but there is more to it. It is a place to go and relax, to meet friends and chat, and for women in particular it's a way of getting out of the house and the daily routines. Marrakchis have long enjoyed all these pleasures, but the bathhouse has very much become part of the Marrakesh experience for stressed-out foreign visitors. If the hammam is too public for your liking, head for one of the many, ever more sumptuous, day or hotel spas, that are popping up everywhere in the city.

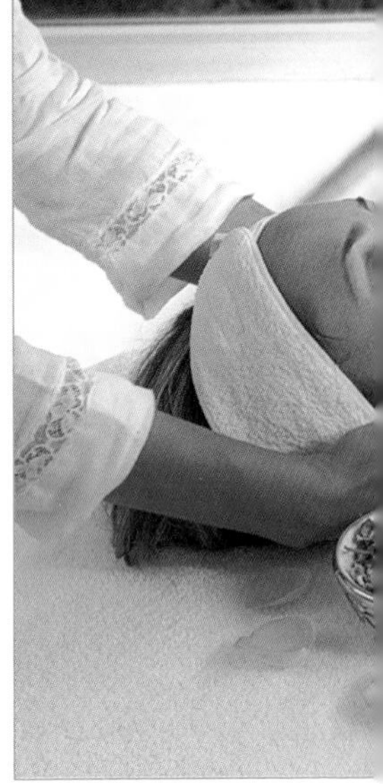

THE HAMMAM EXPERIENCE

Cleanliness is close to godliness in this part of the world. Muslims perform ritual ablutions, washing face, hands and feet with a jug and a bowl of water, before prayers, five times a day. Until recently most people went to their local hammam once or twice a week. Now with in-house bathrooms, they go less frequently but they still go, both for the deep-pore cleansing domestic showers don't really achieve and for the social gathering. Every neighbourhood had one, some attached to the local bakery in order to share its furnace, some attached to a mosque. The bathhouses have separate opening times for women and men. For women it is like going to a party where, with young children in tow, they can meet friends, gossip and joke, or even pick out a potential bride for a male member of the family. For men, it is more a place of rest and contemplation, where mental stress is relieved and the resident masseur sets to work on the knotty tensions in their back and shoulders.

Many luxury hotels have their own hammam, often a place of luxury and even decadence – a sumptuous spa with deep-blue pools, petal-strewn divans and state-of-the-art treatments that can rejuvenate even

Left: locals visiting Hammam Lalla Mira.

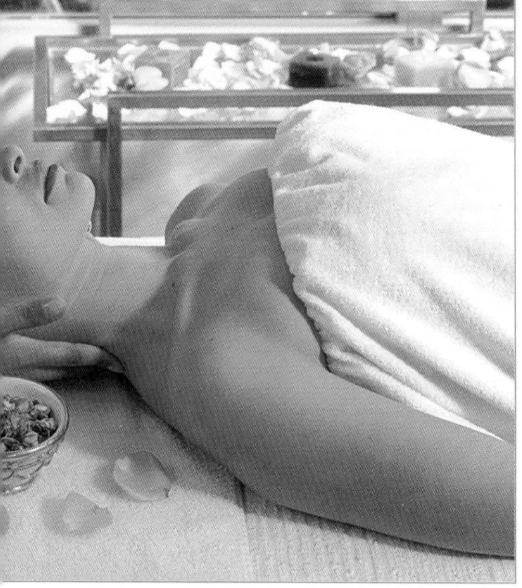

Left: luxuriant relaxation at L'Oriental Spa *(see p.90)*.

Above: essential oils at La Sultana *(see p.90)*.

the most work-worn customer.

HAMMAM ETIQUETTE

Going for the first time to the hammam can be intimidating if you don't know what to expect. There are no or different rules in the luxury hotel spas, but in the traditional hammam a certain modesty prevails: women keep their underwear on while men wrap themselves in a *fouta* (towel). You can leave your clothes in a locker or changing room, before you are led into a series of rooms of varying temperature and given a bucket for sluicing down. If you forget to take your own, locals are often happy to share soap (the traditional black kind) and other equipment; the masseur (a massage is sometimes included in the price) will find you at some point during your stay to give you a good *gommage* (exfoliation) and pummelling. It is usual to tip the various attendants a few dirhams.

TRADITIONAL HAMMAMS

Hammam Bab Doukkala

Next to the Bab Doukkala Mosque; daily, men 7am–1pm, women 1–9pm; map p.133 E3

This 16th-century hammam is not luxurious, but well-run, clean and functional.

Hammam el Bacha

20 rue Fatima Zohra, Mouassine Quarter; daily, men 7am–1pm, women 1–9pm; map p.133 E3

This huge hammam is the closest thing to a neighbourhood hammam experience; bring your own soap and loofah or buy them here.

Hammam Lalla Mira

14 rue d'Algérie, Essaouira; tel: 0524-475 046; http://base.lallamira.net; daily, men 7–10pm, women 9.30am–7pm

Part of the Lalla Mira guesthouse, but still public, this is the oldest traditional bath in Essaouira, and the first to be heated with solar thermal equipment.

Hammam Ziani

14 rue Riad Zitoun el Jedid; tel: 0524-375 378/0662-715 571; www.hammamziani.ma; daily 7am–10pm; map p.136 C3

Moroccan Cosmetics in the Spice Market

Argan Oil Locally produced oil of the argan nut, known for its anti-ageing and anti-oxidising properties.

Cochineal Little pottery saucers impregnated with cochineal are used as lip rouge.

Dadès Roses Dried roses are used to perfume rooms, and rose water refreshes the body.

Henna Green leaves, sometimes in powder, used to dye the hair, or for tattooing the hands and feet at celebrations.

Kohl Silvery antimony is ground into a powder, which at the same time gives a black outline to the eyes, and protects them from dust.

Loofah Loofah is the dried sponge-like fruit of a climbing vine related to the gourd, used as a scrub in bathhouses.

Savon noir Black soap used in the hammam.

Suek Walnut root or bark used as a toothbrush.

Near the el Bahia Palace is one of the most popular traditional hammams, well used to tourists staying in the riads in the kasbah area. Just go for a scrub or choose one of the several packages including a *gommage* or massage.

DAY SPAS

Les Bains de Marrakesh

2 derb Sedra, Bab Agnaou, Southern Medina; tel: 0524-381 428; lesbainsdemarrakesh.com; daily 9am–7pm; map p.136 B2

A more luxurious spa-hammam with a choice of treatments and massages using only natural products. Needs to be booked in advance.

Les Secrets de Marrakesh

62 rue de la Liberté, Guéliz; tel: 0524-434 848; Mon–Sat 10am–8.30pm; map p.132 C4

One of the best-run spas, popular with well-heeled Marrakchis, is Les Secrets de Marrakesh. Its relatively pricey treatments include a one-hour 'Sultans' Massage', a 'Better than Botox' facial and all manner of tempting wraps.

L'Univers de la Femme

22 rue Bab Agnaou; tel: 0524-441 296; Tue–Sun 9am–1pm, 3–8pm; map p.138 C1

A popular place for a wide variety of beauty treatments at affordable prices.

Parfumerie Jemaa el Fna

72 place Jemaa el Fna, next to the Café de France; tel: 0661-712 191; Tue–Sun 9am–1pm, 3–8pm; map p.139 D1

Not a hammam or spa, but a spotless, well-run beauty salon where you can get a top-to-toe makeover (massage with argan oil, facial, manicure and blow dry) for an all-in very low price, and good-quality henna tattoos.

HOTEL SPAS

Angsana Spa

Riad Aida, 59 derb Lamouagni, off rue Riad Zitoun el Jedid; tel: 0524-438 493; www.angsana.com/EN/Properties/Marrakesh; map p.139 D1

Several riads form this hotel part of the Banyan Tree chain, each with their own award-winning spa, where Asian healing and wellness blends with Moroccan traditions.

Hôtel Hivernage and Spa

Corner of avenue Echouhada and rue des Temples, Hivernage; tel: 0524-424 100; www.hivernage-hotel.com; daily 9am–9pm; map p.133 D1

The Hotel Hivernage is particularly noted for its spa, with everything from a traditional hammam to the most sophisticated beauty treatments.

La Sultana

403 rue de la Kasbah; tel: 0524-388 008; www.lasultanamarrakesh.com; daily 9am–8.30pm; map p.136 B2

Luxurious spa in this sumptuous hotel.

SEE ALSO ACCOMMODATION, P.32

L'Oriental Spa

Es Saadi Hotel, avenue el

Below: sheer opulence at the Spa Palais Rhoul.

Above: the ornate pool room at Angsana Spa.

Qadissia, Hivernage; tel: 0524-448 811; www.essaadi.com; daily 9am–9pm; map p.133 D1
The sumptuous spa beside the swimming pool has a traditional hammam providing *gommages* and hydrating massages with essential oils, a sauna, a gym and a spa area providing a selection of massages and beauty treatments.

Spa Palais Rhoul
Route de Fès, Dar Tounsi, Palmeraie; tel: 0524-329 494; www.palais-rhoul.com; daily 9am–9pm
One of the most opulent spas in Marrakesh, with a gorgeous hammam and a real old-school masseur who bends you over double, over his feet, to work your back.

BEAUTY PRODUCTS

La Savonnerie
Marché Central, rue Ibn Toumert, Guéliz; tel: 0668-517 479; Mon–Thur, Sat 9.30am–7pm, Fri, Sun 9.30am–2pm; map p.133 D4
Small shop selling delicious soaps with natural perfumes.

Les Parfums du Soleil
Rue Tarik ibn Ziyad, behind el Boustan Hotel, Guéliz; tel: 0524-422 627; www.lesparfumsdusoleil.com; Mon–Sat 10am–7pm; map p.132 C4
Perfumes made in Marrakesh, with local oils and plants.

Nectarôme
Tnine-l'Ourika, Ourika; tel: 0524-482 447; www.nectarome.com; daily 9am–6pm
Organic products and essential oils prepared with plants from the garden.
SEE ALSO GARDENS, P.65

Scènes de Lin
70 rue de la Liberté, Guéliz; tel: 0524-436 108; Mon–Sat 9.30am–12.30pm, 3.30–7.30pm; map p.132 C4
Chic store selling bed and bathroom linen, including natural bath products and lovely hammam towels.

The **argan tree** *Argania Spinosa* is endemic to the region south of Essaouira, the Haha Coast and the Souss Valley, now designated as a Biosphere Reserve by Unesco. Berber women collect the nuts fallen from the trees in autumn and feed them to their goats, whose digestive system dissolves the tough outer shell. The nuts are then again collected from the dung, shelled and roasted, and made into oil. The oil is known to reduce cholesterol, and with a high Vitamin E content it is used in anti-wrinkle creams. It has a nutty flavour and is also excellent in salads. The oil is widely available in Moroccan food stores and some specialist oil shops in Essaouira. *See also Food and Drink, p.61.*

Religions and Religious Sites

Nearly 99 percent of Moroccans are Muslim, and although Morocco is a relatively tolerant Muslim country, Islam is a fundamental influence on day-to-day life. The call to prayer wakes you in your riad, and echoes all day as you walk around. Officially Morocco follows the Sunni (orthodox) branch of Islam. However, there are also many thriving Sufi brotherhoods. The Jewish, and to a much lesser degree the Christian, community always played an important role, but their numbers have dwindled since independence in 1956.

BEFORE ISLAM

Islam only came to Morocco in the 7th century. Before that the Berbers, the original inhabitants of Morocco, were mostly polytheists who worshipped many gods. They worshipped, the sun, the moon, the god of war, the Atlas Mountains, rain and a whole pantheon of Greek, Roman and Egyptian gods. Some Berber tribes were Jewish, and a few had converted to Christianity. In AD682 the Arab general Uqba ben Nafi, from the Arabian Peninsula, conquered Morocco and reached the Atlantic. He was killed on his way back home, but still most Berbers converted to Islam within the next century.

SEE ALSO BERBER CULTURE, P.40

Because the Koutoubia Mosque is an active place of worship it is not possible to visit the interior of the mosque, but you can get a good glimpse walking around the exterior walls through the delightful rose gardens. The Koutoubia *minbar* is now housed in a pavillion in the el Badi Palace *(see p.9)*.

ISLAM

ISLAM IN MOROCCO

The presence of Islam in Moroccan culture cannot be underestimated; it provided an integral common custom and order throughout centuries of tribal disparity and warring dynasties and today, it continues to shape daily life and society.

Most Moroccans are guided by their faith, even the ones you meet drinking alcohol, forbidden in Islam, or flirting in a nightclub. In Marrakesh during

Left: the elaborate tiling in Zaouia Sidi Bel Abbès *(see p.96)*.

Left: there is a fairly even split between Marrakchi women who choose to wear a hijab and those who do not.

Ramadan *(see p.54, 61),* when Muslims abstain from drinking, eating, smoking and sex from sunrise to sunset, you will find some young men drinking and smoking on a terrace, but many establishments are closed during the day for the entire month. Many shopkeepers in the souks pray five times a day, and sometimes if you walk in while they are praying you have to wait a few minutes until they are finished. Most men go to the mosque for the Friday noon prayers, the most important prayer of the week. Mosques in Morocco are not open to non-Muslims.

THE FUNDAMENTALS OF ISLAM

Prophet Mohammed was born in Mecca, Saudi Arabia, in AD570, and he became a trader on the caravan routes. In 610, at the age of 40, he is said to have received his first revelation from God. Muslims believe that the Quran is the word of Allah or God, dictated to Prophet Mohammed by the archangel Gabriel. At first the *suras* (chapters) were memorised and orally transmitted, until 18 years after the Prophet's death they were written down. Prophet Mohammed organised the religious life of his community around the five pillars or requirements of Islam, which are still central to many Moroccans, as they are to all Muslims: affirmation that there is no other god but Allah and that Mohammed is his Messenger; prayer five times a day; the observance of Ramadan; the giving of alms to the poor; and making the hajj (pilgrimage) to Mecca at least once in a lifetime.

PRAYER

The muezzin calls *adhan*, the call to prayer, five times a day: at dawn, at noon, midway between noon and sunset, just after sunset, and when it's dark. He calls: 'God is great. I testify there is no god but Allah and Mohammed is his messenger. Come to prayer, come to security. God is great', with the addition in the early morning of: 'Prayer is better than sleep.' Muslims perform ritual ablutions before praying by washing their hands and feet with water, or with sand in the desert. They face Mecca when they pray.

Below: there is a law in place stating that no building can be built higher than the Koutoubia Mosque's *(see p.94)* minaret.

MOSQUES AND MEDERSAS

Ben Youssef Medersa

Place ben Youssef, Northern Medina; daily Apr–Sept 9am–7pm, Oct–Mar 9am–6pm; admission charge; map p.134 C1

The splendid Ben Youssef Medersa was founded in the 14th century by the Merenid sultan Abu Hassan. The Saadian Moulay Abdellah in the 16th century turned it into the country's largest *medersa* to rival the Bou Inania Medersa in Fès. *Medersas* were Quran schools where free lodgings were offered to the *tolba* (students). At its height, the monastic-style cells on the first floor of this *medersa* could house up to 900 students. It remained in use as a religious school until 1962. The courtyard is a large open space with a central marble basin, flanked by two galleries of pillars. At one end is the entrance to the prayer hall, where classes were held, with an octagonal domed roof supported by marble columns. The arched elaborate stuccowork on the mihrab, the niche that indicates the direction of Mecca, is beautiful. The perfect proportions and the balanced use of the different decorative elements like *zellij*, stucco and carved wood, make this *medersa* a prime example of Moorish architecture.

SEE ALSO ARCHITECTURE, P.39; RIADS, P.108

Right: visitors gather at the Ben Youssef Medersa.

Ben Youssef Mosque

Place ben Youssef, Northern Medina; closed to non-Muslims; map p.134 C1

The Ben Youssef Mosque, recognisable by its green tiled roof and minaret, was built by the Almoravid sultan Ali ben Youssef in the 12th century. The present mosque dates from the early 19th century.

Below: two men going to prayers at the mosque.

Kasbah Mosque

Bab Agnaou, Southern Medina; closed to non Muslims; map p.136 B2

This mosque, built by Sultan Yaqoub el Mansour (1184–99), is recognisable by its green tiled minaret, but the vast interior with five inner courtyards is mostly out of sight. The mosque was restored and expanded by several rulers, including the late King Hassan II.

Koutoubia Mosque

Avenue Mohammed V, Jemaa el Fna; mosque closed to non-Muslims, gardens 8am–8pm; free; map p.138 A1

A firm landmark on the Marrakesh skyline is the elegant 77m (252ft) -high minaret of the Koutoubia

Marrakesh has a small Christian community. They are served by the French colonial **Eglise des Sts Martyrs** (Rue el Imam Ali, Guéliz; tel: 0524-340 585; map p.133 C3) which has services at 6.30pm from Monday to Saturday, and at 10am on Sunday.

Mosque. A building rule brought in by the French states that no building in the medina should be higher than a palm tree, and no building in the Ville Nouvelle higher than the Koutoubia.

Ali ben Youssef built a mosque here on top of his father's mosque as well as a palace, but both buildings were destroyed when the Almohads captured the town in 1147; the remains can still be seen in the glassed-over plaza in the garden. The Almohad sultan Abdel Moumen started building a new mosque immediately, but it had to be destroyed as soon as it was completed for being wrongly aligned to Mecca. Nothing could stop the sultan, and he started building another mosque, the present one, with a large open courtyard surrounded by horseshoe arches. The minaret was finished by Sultan Yaqoub el Mansour, his grandson, who constructed other beautiful minarets: the Tour Hassan in Rabat, and the splendid Giralda in Seville. These minarets became the blueprint for most minarets in Morocco.

Each side of the Koutoubia minaret has a different decoration, increasingly richer and finer towards the top. The only surviving strip of the original turquoise green faience work is at the very top. The interior consists of six rooms, one above the other, surrounded by a ramp on which the muezzin climbed up five times a day to call for prayer. At first there were three balls at the top of the minaret made of pure gold, and it is said a fourth was added by Yaqoub el Mansour's wife, who melted all her gold jewellery down for it, after breaking her Ramadan fast by eating four grapes.

Mouassine Mosque

Rue Mouassine, Mouassine Quarter; closed to non-Muslims; map p.138 C4

The Mouassine Mosque was built by the Saadian sultan Abdullah el Ghalib in 1560, as was traditional, with a hammam, fountain and *medersa*. Most of the splendid mosque is hidden by outside buildings.

Tin Mal Mosque

Tin Mal, Tizi-n-Test; tel: 0662-725 612; daily 8.30am–noon, 3–5pm; free but tip for the guardian expected

On the Tizi-n-Test, 40km (25 miles) south of Ouirgane, is the village of Tin Mal, with the only mosque in the area than can be visited by non-Muslims. This splendid mosque is all that remains of the 12th-century Almohad city of Tin Mal. Built in 1156 for their spiritual leader Ibn Tumert, the kasbah-like mosque has an austere but gorgeous interior, well worth the little detour, and the views from the minaret are stunning.

SHRINES

Marrakesh has seven saints, each marked with a shrine *(see p.12)*. The *moussem* or celebration of

the Sabatou Rijal, also known as the Seven Men of Marrakesh, starts at the shrine of Sidi Ayyad and ends at the most important shrine, the Zaouia of Sidi Bel Abbès.
SEE ALSO FESTIVALS AND EVENTS, P.54

Zaouia Sidi Abd el Aziz
Rue Mouassine; closed to non-Muslims; map p.138 C4
Shrine of the 14th-century pious silk merchant from Fès, a follower of el Jazuli.

Zaouia Sidi Bel Abbès
Bab Targhzout; closed to non-Muslims; map p.134 B3
Born in Ceuta in 1145,this pious Sufi master established a community where Guéliz is now, and is said to have performed many miracles. The city's blind are fed at the zaouia every evening, and the storytellers start their stories by evoking this patron saint.

Zaouia Sidi ben Slimane el Jazuli
South of Bab Targhzout; closed to non-Muslims; map p.134 B2
This shrine with the green pyramid-shaped roof houses the tomb of one of the great Sufi mystics of Morocco *(see below)*.

Zaouia Sidi Qadi Ayad
Close to Bab Ailen; closed to non-Muslims; map p.135 E1
Shrine of a very pious Yemeni who became a judge in Granada before being exiled to Marrakesh, where he died in 1149.

Below: in the Jewish cemetery.

Zaouia Sidi el Ghazwani
Near the Mouassine Mosque; closed to non-Muslims; map p.132 C4
This holy man was banned from Marrakesh after he predicted the end of the Merenid dynasty, but he returned and died here in 1528.

Zaouia Sidi es Souheili
near Bab er Rob; closed to non-Muslims; map p.136 B2
A Spanish Sufi poet who died in Marrakesh in 1186. Students come to his shrine to strengthen their memory.

Zaouia Sidi Youssef ben Ali
Opposite Bab Aghmat; closed to non-Muslims; map p.137 E3
The shrine of the Yemeni Sufi master who died of leprosy in 1196.

SUFISM

Beside Orthodox Islam there has always been a tradition of Sufism, a mystical discipline *(see also box, opposite)*. It is believed that Prophet Mohammed's cousin and son-in-law Ali, was the first Sufi, who came up with the more mystical approach to Islam. Morocco's tolerant Islamic tradition is greatly due to the strong culture of Sufism practised by young and old, in all layers of society. In fact, Sufism is increasingly popular with Moroccan youth because of its more fluid interpretation of the Quran, its rejection of fanaticism and the importance of the principles of beauty and humanity, allowing its followers to enjoy arts, music and love without having to abandon their spiritual and religious obligations.

MARABOUTS

The historian Herodotus (484–*c.*425 BC) wrote that the ancient Berbers believed the spirits of their ancestors to be gods. They attached special importance to the tombs of brave or particularly righteous men from which they received a blessing. This worship of pious men still exists among the Berbers today, which is why the countryside is dotted with *koubbas (see p.39)*. Although the holy men or *marabouts*, also called Sidi (or Lalla for women), are often pious Muslims, this practice has nothing to with Orthodox Islam, which discourages idol worship. Moroccans go these *marabouts*, to receive a *baraka* or blessing, to ask for a fertility blessing, or to be cured of illnesses and broken hearts.

JEWISH MARRAKESH

Jews first came to Morocco on Phoenician ships, and their descendants form one of the oldest Jewish communities in the world. After the fall of Rome, the Jews converted many Berbers to their faith. Throughout history, Moroccan Jews held key positions in trade, jewellery and crafts. The 16th-century Saadian sultan Abdullah el Ghalib built a Mellah for the Jewish community, a secure and isolated quarter, a city within the city, adjacent to the royal palace. Jews were also very influential traders and bankers under the Saadians. They lived in the Mellah, separated and protected from the Muslim part of town, and always acted as an intermediary between the Christians and the Muslims. Jewish people always enjoyed a special protection from the ruler, even during WWII, but after 1948 many families emigrated to Israel or Europe. Today, only a handful of Jewish families remain in the Marrakesh Mellah, and many synagogues have been turned into shops.

Essaouira too once had an important Jewish community who lived in the local Mellah. Today the Marrakchi Mellah is a Muslim quarter, but information about existing synagogues is available from the Jewish Community Centre.

Fnaire, the most popular hip-hop band from Marrakesh, identifies itself as a blend of American rap with Moroccan Sufi tradition. Even *rai* music, Moroccan hip-hop and rap, drawes on Sufi poetry and values, though it sounds pretty Western. They rap about the primordial essence of the human body, the virtues of simplicity, and the healing powers of Sufi saints such as Sidi Ahmed Tijani, Sidi Boumediene and others. The spiritual powers of Moroccan music inspired bands like the Rolling Stones and Led Zeppelin.

Above: the Lazama Synagogue.

Jewish Community Centre

142 avenue Houmane el Fetouaki, Arset el Maach, Medina Marrakesh; tel: 0524-448 754; map p.136 B3

For any information on synagogues or Friday services.

Lazama Synagogue

36 derb Regraga; Mellah; Sun–Thur 9am–6pm, Fri 9am–1pm; admission by donation, tip the guardian; map p.137 C3

The Alzama was built at the turn of the 20th century, around a well-tended courtyard. Recently a gallery was added for women, and on the floor above the synagogue is a Talmud Torah School, soup kitchen and community centre.

Miara Jewish cemetery

Eastern side of the Mellah; Sun–Thur 7am–6pm, Fri 7am–3pm; admission by donation; map p.137 D3

Knock at the gate and the gatekeeper will let you in to see the atmospheric cemetery, where families have piled small pebbles of remembrance on the tombs of their loved ones.

Restaurants

The medina restaurants offering the *diffa* (feast) only do so for dinner, but there are increasingly more places in the medina that serve a light lunch. In the Ville Nouvelle there is a wider choice, with restaurants catering to a mixed crowd of tourists and local office workers. The growth of tourism, and general affluence, in Marrakesh has made the city an increasingly popular place to eat out, so it is advisable to make reservations at most of the restaurants listed. You can usually find a table available at lunchtime, but in the evening the city's more popular restaurants can be very crowded.

JEMAA EL FNA

Argana

Jemaa el Fna; tel: 0524-445 350; daily 6am–11pm; $–$$; map p.139 C2

This is a vast, no-nonsense café-restaurant overlooking 'La Place' which serves cheap Moroccan dishes as well as venturing into some basic Mediterranean specials, but what counts here is the view from the terrace. Perfect for a quick lunch, or as an escape from the heat of the square. No alcohol served.

Price guide for a three-course meal for one, excluding alcoholic drinks:
$$$$ over 500Dh
$$$ 300–500Dh
$$ 150–300Dh
$ below 150Dh

Chez Chegrouni

Jemaa el Fna; tel: 0665-474 615; daily 8am–11pm; $–$$; map p.139 D2

Next door to Le Marrakchi *(see opposite)*, Chez Chegrouni couldn't be more different. With tables on the terrace on the square, Chegrouni has been here for ever and doesn't do any frills. You write down your own order of tajine, couscous or omelette, but when it comes it is simply delicious. Some regulars rate the chicken tajine with preserved lemon and olives as the best, after their mother's, of course. No alcohol served.

Below: great views and a romantic ambiance at Le Marrakchi.

Food Stalls Jemaa el Fna

Jemaa el Fna; daily 6–11pm or later; $; map p.139 C2

For an authentic experience pull up a stool with the locals in the Jemaa el Fna square. At these highly animated outdoor eateries expect anything from a steaming tajine or stew to sheep's heads or snails in a spicy soup. Less adventurous diners may decide to stick to delicious *brochettes* (skewers), chips and salad. The food is great and the atmosphere is even better. *(See box, opposite, for menu decoder.)*

Hajj Mustapha

East side of Souk Ablueh; daily 6–9pm; $; map p.139 C2

Left: terrace dining at Le Tanjia *(see p.100)*.

DJ and often arranges live music performances.

Terrasses de l'Alhambra
Jemaa el Fna; tel: 0524-427 570; daily 8am–11pm; $–$$; map p.139 D2
More elegant than most on this square, the Alhambra café-terrace serves a proper espresso, home-made ice cream and a menu of light snacks and salads. The terrace is a favourite meeting place, but on a hot day the air-conditioned interior might be a more attractive proposition. No alcohol served.
SEE ALSO CAFÉS, P.42

Very cheap and simple eatery, but a good place to eat the real Marrakchi dish of *tangia*, lamb cooked slowly in an earthenware dish, traditionally in the ashes of the hammam or public bathhouse. This olive souk is east of the Terrasses de l'Alhambra, and although this particular stall is the cleanest, there are several others in the alley.

Le Marrakchi
Jemaa el Fna, 52 rue des Banques; tel: 0524-443 377; www.lemarrakchi.com; daily noon–1am; $$$; map p.139 D2
Perfectly located on the Jemaa el Fna, this upstairs dining room has the best views over the square and of the Koutoubia Mosque. This is a good place to come on your first night in Marrakesh, so you can venture into Moroccan cuisine for the first time while watching the frenetic energy of the square from above. Good value set menus or à la carte Moroccan food served every evening with oriental cabaret (belly dancers).

Street Food

Boubbouches Snail soup
Brochettes Skewers with meat or chicken
Calamars Frits Fried squid
Couscous Steamed semolina with stew
Harira Spicy chick pea soup with lamb
Hergma Calves' feet in a broth, considered a delicacy
Merguez Spicy lamb sausages
Tagine de poulet Chicken stew
Tangia Slow-cooked lamb in earthenware pot
Tête d'agneau Sheep's head

Narwama
30 rue el Koutoubia; tel: 0524-442 510; daily 8pm–1am; $$$; map p.138 B2
Set in a spectacular riad, the Narwarma has a good Thai chef preparing a mean Thai curry or sticky rice with mango; they also serve a good lamb tajine for those who can't live without, and a few Mediterranean dishes. The owner is an ex-

SOUTHERN MEDINA

La Maison du Couscous
53 rue Bab Agnaou; tel: 0524-382 092; daily 11.30am–10pm; $$; map p.138 C1
A good place for a properly prepared couscous, with a larger selection than most: try the couscous with prunes, chicken and caramelised onions for a change. The decor is perhaps a bit too slick and polished, the air con defi-

Below: Thai food is the speciality at Narwama.

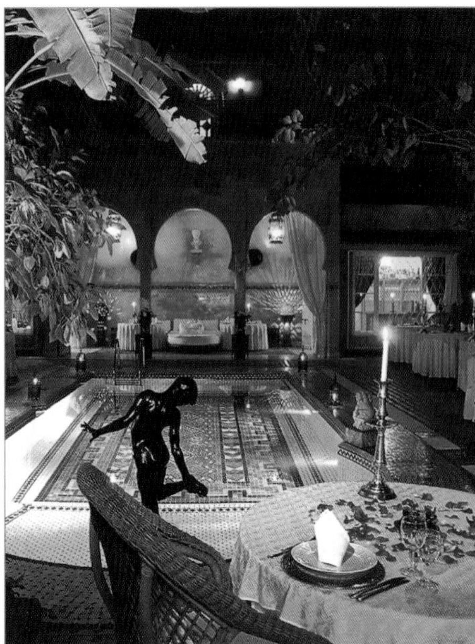

Above: Dar Moha boasts poolside dining.

nitely turned up too high, but the young guys running it are charming and the food is good.

Kosybar

47 place des Ferblantiers; tel: 0524-380 324; daily noon–midnight; $$$; map p.137 C3

This trendy venue is a popular meeting place for an evening or late night drink on the roof terrace with great views over the medina rooftops and the storks' nests on the Badia Palace. The large menu offers many Moroccan-Mediterranean dishes as well as good sushi prepared by a Japanese sushi chef. The owner, the son of a Moroccan winemaker, assures a good wine list, and at weekends there is live music in the piano bar.

SEE ALSO MUSIC, DANCE AND THEATRE, P.82; NIGHTLIFE, P.85

Le Tanjia

14 derb Jdid; tel: 0524-383 836; http://letanjia.blog.com; daily 10am–1am; $$$; map p.137 C3

Chic oriental brasserie at the edge of the Jewish Mellah, with a sumptuous contemporary Moroccan decor and palm trees, serving an elegant and rich Moroccan cuisine. Waterpipes and tea on the terrace in the afternoon.

Tatchibana

38 route de Bab Ksiba, Kasbah; tel: 0524-387 171; http://tatchibana.free.fr; Tue–Sun noon–11pm; $$–$$$; map p.136 B1

This Japanese restaurant is a testament to how cosmopolitan Marrakesh has become. In a peaceful setting, with lots of light, reflected on the white walls and pale wooden furniture, the Tatchibana serves excellent set menus and à la carte Japanese dishes.

MOUASSINE QUARTER

Bougainvillea

33 rue Mouassine, on the corner with rue Sidi el Yamani; tel: 0524-441 111 33; daily 11am–10pm; $$; map p.138 C4

Pleasant all-pink courtyard café-restaurant in the middle of the souks, perfect for a recharge during shopping, with salads and sandwiches, and fresh juices.

SEE ALSO CAFÉS, P.42

Dar Moha

81 rue Dar el Bacha; tel: 0524-386 400; www.darmoha.com; Tue–Sun noon–3pm, 7.30pm–midnight; $$$$; map p.138 B4

Dar Moha is one of the city's most celebrated restaurants. This 19th-century villa, with lovely garden and poolside dining options, serves set menus as well as à la carte Moroccan cuisine, prepared by inventive chef Mohammed Fedal. The choice set menus look and taste excellent, definitely Moroccan with a twist, but as elsewhere in town, the

To experience the full extent of Moroccan cuisine, head for one of the swish medina restaurants, like **Dar Yaqout** or **Le Tobsil** *(see right)*, for a *diffa*, a full-blown Moroccan feast, with an endless series of dishes served in an opulent riad setting, with live music and entertainment. These places serve a fixed-price set menu, usually including a variety of salads, tajines, *pastilla*, couscous, fruit and sweets. Just make sure you haven't eaten for a while before you go, and be sure to book ahead.

Price guide for a three-course meal for one, excluding alcoholic drinks:
$$$$ over 500Dh
$$$ 300–500Dh
$$ 150–300Dh
$ below 150Dh

service can be hit or miss. Reservations essential.

Dar Yaqout
79 rue Sidi Ahmed Soussi, Bab Doukkala; tel: 0524-382 929; Tue–Sun 7.30–11pm; $$$$; map p.134 A2
Ranked among Marrakesh's finest restaurants, this beautiful medina house, adorned with magnificent stucco and cedar ceilings, serves set menus to satisfy even the most discerning palate. Delicious *diffa* (feast) including salad selections, followed by tajines and couscous, are rounded off with superb Moroccan pastries. This is not just a meal, it's an experience.

La Maison Arabe
1 derb Assehbe, Bab Doukkala; tel: 0524-387 010; www.lamaisonarabe.com; daily noon–3pm, 7.30–11pm; $$$–$$$$; map p.134 A1
The Maison Arabe has long been renowned for its cooking, and offers some of the best cooking classes. The hotel has a famous Moroccan restaurant in a gorgeous Moorish setting, as well as the more colonial Saveurs d'Ailleurs restaurant serving the best of world cuisine.

Le Tobsil
22 derb Moulay Abdellah Ben Hassaien, Bab Ksour R'mila; tel: 0524-444 052; Wed–Mon 7.30–11pm; $$$$; map p.138 B2
Even the hard-to-please UK food critic AA Gill enjoyed Le Tobsil, a splendid restaurant secluded in a beautiful old medina riad. Gnaoua musicians and the candlelit atmosphere create a wonderfully exotic and romantic evening. The set menu is a *diffa* (feast) of five courses of delicious Moroccan staples, finished off with mint tea and sweets. Be sure to have a light lunch.

Terrasse des Epices
15 Souk Cherifia, Dar el Bacha; tel: 0524-375 904/0676-046 767; www.terrassedesepices.com; daily 10am–midnight; $$; map p.139 C4
Delightful lounge bar/restaurant/gallery with a laid-back, authentic Marrakchi feel to it. The large terrace overlooks the medina on all sides, and has shaded booths to get away from the midday heat, with WiFi and cool lounge music. The menu is uncomplicated but somehow features just what you want to have for lunch: a plate of grilled vegetables, the tajine of the day, or a fab dessert like prunes with fresh goat's cheese or apple confit with chocolat.
SEE ALSO CAFÉS, P.43

Villa Flore
4 derb Azzouz, Mouassine; tel: 0524-391 700; www.villa-flore.com; daily 12.30–3pm, 7.30–11pm; $$–$$$; map p.138 C4
Right in the heart of the souks, in an Art Deco riad guesthouse with tranquil courtyard, is this small but pleasant restaurant serving set menus of inventive, beautifully presented Moroccan dishes.

Below: romantic decor at Le Tanjia.

NORTHERN MEDINA

Le Foundouk

55 Souk el Fassi, Kaat Ben-nahid, near Ben Youssef Medersa; tel: 0524-378 190; www.foundouk.com; Tue–Sun noon–1am; $$$; map p.135 C1

Hidden in a maze of alley-ways and caravanserai in the northern medina, French-owned Le Foundouk is a very fashionable and atmospheric place, serving excellent French and Moroccan cuisine in a highly agreeable setting. Open throughout the day (until late), it is a marvellous place for lunch on the roof, but at night it is always packed to the rafters.

Le Pavillon

Derb Zaouia, Bab Doukkala; tel: 0524-387 040; daily 7pm–midnight; $$$; map p.134 A1

For refined French cuisine in the medina, there are few better options than Le Pavillon. Here you'll be served haute cuisine prepared by a Michelin-starred chef, in a sumptuous courtyard under the olive and fig trees, a true oasis of calm sheltered from the noise of the medina. It is located close to Dar el Pacha, and can be accessed by taxi.

Riad des Mers

411 derb Sidi Messaoud, Bab Jacout; tel: 0524-375 304; daily noon–3pm, 7–11pm; $$$; map p.134 A3

Riad des Mers, situated just inside Bab Jacout, is the only fish restaurant in the medina, and definitely the best place in the city to sample Morocco's ample choice of fresh fish and seafood. Tables arranged around a luminous courtyard create the perfect atmosphere in which to enjoy perfectly cooked seafood dishes.

Price guide for a three-course meal for one, excluding alcoholic drinks:
$$$$ over 500Dh
$$$ 300–500Dh
$$ 150–300Dh
$ below 150Dh

Below: tasty dishes and smart style at Le Foundouk.

GUÉLIZ

Al Fassia

55 boulevard Mohammed Zerktouni; tel: 0524-434 060; Wed–Sun noon–10.30pm; $$$; map p.132 B4

Arguably the most authentic Moroccan restaurant in Marrakesh, close to home cooking, run by an all-female crew, dressed like the traditional Moroccan *dada (see Food and Drink, p.59)*. The couscous is heavenly but there are many other delights, including chicken with caramelised pumpkin and *pastilla* or sweet pigeon pie. Specialities such as slow-roast lamb shoulder must be ordered in day in advance.

Amanjena

Amanjena Hotel, route de Ouarzazate; tel: 0524-403 353; daily noon–10pm; www.amanresorts.com; $$$$

For excellent Thai cuisine and a good look at the interior of one of the most extravagant hotels in Marrakesh, head for the restaurant at this hotel in the Amelkis Golf Complex. The restaurant is situated alongside the swimming pool. Booking essential.

Bab Restaurant

Bab Hotel, corner of blvd Mansour el Dahabi and rue Mohammed el Beqal; tel: 0524-435 250; www.babhotelmarrakesh.com; $$$; daily 8pm–midnight; map p.132 B4

Destination bar and restaurant at the chic Miami-styled boutique hotel Bab Marrakesh, with a fashionable crowd every evening and set to be very hip in summer with the development of their 'Soho House'-style swimming pool and decking bar. The menu has everything from oysters to club sandwiches and smoked haddock.

Brochette Grills

Rue ibn Aicha; daily noon–10pm; $

In the street between the Montecristo bar and the rue Casablanca (heralded by smoke and the smell of barbecued meat), a row of simple restaurants with pavement seating serve fresh cuts of meat barbecued in open kitchens. Just select the meat you want at the counter and take a seat. Cheap, fresh and very tasty.

Café du Livre

44 rue Tariq ibn Ziyad; tel: 0524-432 149; Mon–Sat 9.30am–9pm; $$; map p.132 C4

This café-cum-bookshop has become a favourite hangout for expats. The bookshop has a good selection of French but mainly English books, free WiFi access, and the peaceful adjoining café-restaurant serves an excellent breakfast served until 11.30am, while lunch is good Mediterranean sandwiches and salads.

SEE ALSO CAFÉS, P.43; LITERATURE, P.73

Catanzaro

42 rue Tariq ibn Ziad; tel: 0524-433 731; Mon–Sat noon–2.30pm, 7.30–11pm; $$; map p.132 C4

Catanzaro is arguably the best-known restaurant in Guéliz. Serving a wide range of moderately priced pizzas and pasta dishes, this expat hangout is very popular, and deservedly so. The food is old-fashioned Italian and comforting; it is a great place to take the kids, and the atmosphere makes the place a one-off.

Above: modern style at Kechmara *(see p.104)*.

Grand Café de La Poste

Corner of boulevard Mansour el Dahabi and avenue Imam Malik; tel: 0524-433 038; www.grandcafedelaposte.com; daily 8am–11pm; $$–$$$; map p.132 C3

Situated next to the main post office on place du 16 Novembre, this colonial style French brasserie-café occupies an old 1920s building. The number one meeting place for the fashionable Marrakesh set, it offers breakfast from 8am, light lunches, ice cream, cakes and pastries in the afternoon, and modern European choices for din-

> Moroccans tend to eat later, particularly in Marrakesh, than in Western Europe or America. Restaurant opening times resemble more those of Southern Europe, with lunch taken between 1pm and 3pm and dinner served from 8pm until around 11pm, or later.

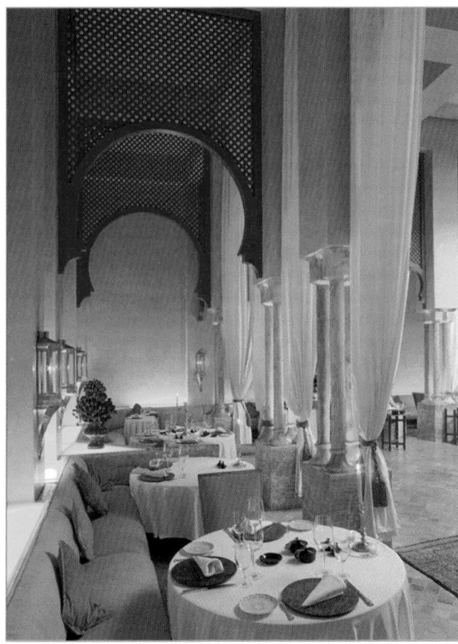

Left: grand dining at Amanjena *(see p.103)*.

ner. Its upstairs bar lounge has a DJ every evening and is an ideal spot for a relaxed drink before or after dinner.
SEE ALSO CAFÉS, P.43

Katsura
Rue Oum Errabia; tel: 0524-434 358; daily 7.30pm–midnight; $$$–$$$$; map p.133 D3
Hotspot popular with expats and pretty young things for its very contemporary Asian interior and excellent Thai food and sushi prepared by Asian chefs. No reservations taken.

Kechmara
1bis–3 rue de la Liberté; tel: 0524-422 532; www.kechmara.ma; Mon–Sat noon–midnight; $$$; map p.132 B4
Popular and happening laid-back restaurant, decorated with 1960s furniture, and serving a small menu with well-prepared, light Mediterranean dishes. Great rooftop terrace for an alfresco lunch in spring and summer, and live music at 7.30pm on Wednesdays and Fridays. Perfect place for a pre-dinner drink too.
SEE ALSO MUSIC, DANCE AND THEATRE, P.82; NIGHLIFE, P.85

L'Avenue
Corner of route de Targa and rue Capitaine Arrighi; tel : 0524-458 901; http://lavenue.blog.com; daily noon–2.30, 6pm–midnight; $$$
Popular meeting point, café and restaurant open for lunch and dinner.They offer a two-for-the-price-of-one early evening drink in the cool and brooding lounge-style restaurant with funky lighting. Menu highlights are the risotto with *gambas* and the super crusty pizzas.

Le Bis
6–7 rue Sakia el Hamra, Semlalia; tel: 0524-446 634; www.lebis-jardindesarts.com; Tue–Sat noon–2.30pm, Mon–Sat 8–11pm; $$$
Funky small restaurant with good French fusion food based on the best Moroccan produce. Alfresco garden dining for lunch and in the warmer evenings. Their mirror-walled toilets with piped birdsong are a local talking point, and they regularly display contemporary art collections for sale.

Le Chat qui rit
92 rue de Yougoslavie; tel: 0524-434 311; Tue–Sun 7.30–11pm; $$; map p.132 B3
Popular and reasonably priced Franco-Italian back-street restaurant, with a menu that boasts enough variety to satisfy most tastes. Recommended for a cheap, relaxed and unpretentious night out.

Oliveri
9 boulevard el Mansour el Dahabi; tel: 0524-448 913; daily 7am–10pm; $; map p.132 B4
A Marrakesh institution for the last 50 years, when the temperatures soar, the queues get longer. Simply the best ice cream, served in an old-fashioned ice cream parlour.

Villa Rosa
64 avenue Hassan II; tel: 0524-449 635; daily 7.30pm–midnight; $$$$; map p.132 B3
Trendy venue by the city's hippest restaurateur, Nourdine Fakir, with live

DJs, a Hôtel Costes vibe, Parisian decor with plenty of red velvet, a bamboo-lined alfresco terrace and a French menu. The bar area fills up quickly, particularly at weekends. Book ahead.
SEE ALSO NIGHTLIFE, P.86

HIVERNAGE

Alizia

Corner of rue Ahmed Chaouqi and avenue Echouhada; tel: 0524-438 360; daily noon–2.30pm, 7–11pm; $$–$$$; map p.133 D1

Old-fashioned Italian-Mediterranean restaurant popular with expats and local families. The food is traditional and reliable, with great pizzas, a large selection of well-prepared fish dishes, as well as a few Marrakchi specials like *tanjia*, slow-cooked lamb.

Crystal

Pacha Marrakesh, boulevard Mohammed VI; tel: 0524-388 480; www.pachamarrakesh.com; daily 7.30pm–midnight; $$$$

The highly acclaimed Crystal is one of the two places to eat at the very succesful Pacha club, serving refined Mediterranean cuisine in a stunning dining room. The menu, designed by the Michelin-starred Pourcell brothers from Montpellier, has a range of French and world food options; and the atmosphere is chic and chilled.
SEE ALSO NIGHTLIFE, P.87

During the holy month of Ramadan, most or at least many Moroccans don't eat or drink from sunrise to sunset. They break the day's fast with *iftour*, traditionally a few dates, some milk followed by a meal. Later in the night they have dinner, and another meal is had just before the sun comes up. Needless to say that nothing really works normal hours in Ramadan, as everyone is exhausted, particularly if it gets hot in the day, so many businesses and sights open late and close early afternoon. Many restaurants close for the month, others just open for *iftour*, but in Marrakesh many places remain open in the more touristy areas. Tourists are not expected to fast, but it is recommended to be discreet. *See also Food and Drink, p.61.*

Le Comptoir

Rue Echouhada; tel: 0524-437 702; www.comptoirdarna.com; daily 8pm–1am; $$$–$$$$; map p.133 D1

Probably Marrakesh's most famous nightspot, Le Comptoir is an exotic slice out of *The 1,001 Nights*, with traditional music every night, oriental dancers and then cool tunes until 1am, spun by the resident DJ. With both Moroccan and French options on the menu, the food is good but not extraordinary, but the ambience is guaranteed every night of the week.
SEE ALSO MUSIC, DANCE AND THEATRE, P.83; NIGHTLIFE, P.85

Price guide for a three-course meal for one, excluding alcoholic drinks:
$$$$ over 500Dh
$$$ 300–500Dh
$$ 150–300Dh
$ below 150Dh

OURIKA VALLEY

Au Sanglier qui Fume

Km61, 5 route Marrakech–Taroudant; tel: 0524-485 707; www.ausanglierquifume.com; daily noon–10.30pm; $$

This long-established old-fashioned auberge serves a blend of bistro French cuisine and traditional Moroccan food like tajines, couscous, fresh Berber bread and, above all, *tanourht*, lamb on a spit, alfresco in the garden or in the Moroccan dining room.

Bo&Zin

Km3.5 Douar Lahna, route de l'Ourika; tel: 0524-388 012; http://bo-zin.com; daily 8pm–1am or later; $$$

Despite its situation in a

Below: the idyllic garden retreat of Ourika Garden *(see p.106)*.

Above: the great view at Kasbah du Toubkal.

nondescript village on the Ourika road (on the edge of town), Bo&Zin is the height of Marrakesh chic. The restaurant for local movers and shakers, this haven of cool serves a range of specialities from Moroccan to Thai cuisine. Very popular outdoor dining and bar with fabulous bamboo and cactus garden in summer.
SEE ALSO NIGHTLIFE, P.84

Le Palmier Fou
Beldi Country Club; Km 6 route du barrage, Dar Jedida Tanchacht; tel: 0524-383 950; www.beldicountryclub.com; daily 11.20am–4pm, 8–11pm; $$–$$$
Beside Marrakesh's largest rose garden, the Beldi offers a day by the pool with a delicious light set-menu Mediterranean lunch on its airy terrace, or a romantic candlelit dinner.
SEE ALSO ACCOMMODATION, P.36

La Perle de l'Ourika
Setti Fatma; tel: 0661-567 239; daily noon–10.30pm; $–$$
Ammaria at this small hotel-restaurant prepares a couscous to write home about, worth the trip from Marrakesh, simple but just as it has to be. Book ahead.

Ourika Garden
Aghbalaou, on the road from Tnine to Setti Fatma; tel: 0524-484 441; www.ourika-garden.com; daily noon–3pm, 7–10pm; $$
This idyllic guesthouse with restaurant offers the perfect escape from Marrakesh. Set in an organic garden, the restaurant produces and cooks its own vegetables. Simple lunches and dinners. Book the day before.

TOUBKAL PARK

Kasbah du Toubkal
Imlil (60km/40 miles from Marrakesh); tel: 0524-485 611; www.kasbahdutoubkal.com; daily noon–3pm, 7–10pm; $–$$$$
Even if you are not staying at this eco-friendly kasbah, then at least come and have lunch at the lovely restaurant run by Berbers, which offers a good Moroccan set menu and spectacular views over the High Atlas.

Price guide for a three-course meal for one, excluding alcoholic drinks:
$$$$ over 500Dh
$$$ 300–500Dh
$$ 150–300Dh
$ below 150Dh

If you enjoy the cuisine then there are plenty of opportunities to learn how to cook it yourself. Many riads organise their own cookery mornings, where you can join the house chef going to the local market and learn how to cook tajines or couscous. More specific classes are available from **Souk Cuisine** (tel: 0673-804 955; www.soukcuisine.com), who organise culinary weeks in Marrakesh, **La Maison Arabe** (tel: 0524-387 010; www.lamaisonarabe.com) and in the Palmeraie the **Jnane Tamsna** (tel: 0524-329 423; www.jnanetamsna.com).

TIZI-N-TICHKA

Chez Bilal
Aït Benhaddou; tel: 0668-248 370; daily 8am–10pm; $
Simple café-restaurant serving a good set menu of salad, tajine and dessert, all with a view over the photogenic kasbah.
SEE ALSO KASBAHS AND PALACES, P.69

I Rocha
Douar Tisselday, Ighrem N'Oudal; tel: 0667-737 002; www.irocha.com; $–$$
Not really a restaurant, but you order a set menu lunch or dinner combining the best of French and Moroccan cuisine at this lovely guesthouse. Call ahead to make a reservation.
SEE ALSO ACCOMMODATION, P.37; SPORTS, P.119

La Pause
Douar Lmih Laroussième, Agafay; tel: 0661-306 494; htpp://lapause-marrakesh.com; daily, enquire for times when booking; $$
Have a Moroccan lunch or dinner alfresco or under a tent, to the gentle sounds of the wind and melan-

cholic Gnaoua music and the High Atlas peaks as a backdrop. Call ahead to make a reservation.
SEE ALSO ACCOMMODATION, P.37; SPORTS, P.118

ESSAOUIRA

A l'Araignée Gourmande

Oualidia; tel: 0523-366 447; daily 11.30am–10pm; $$–$$$

A large, airy restaurant with big windows that open on the Atlantic, and red-and-white gingham table cloths; this is the perfect place to sample a fabulous *plateau de fruits de mer* (seafood platter), for which Oualidia is famous, with a glass of white wine.

Chalet de la Plage

1 boulevard Mohammed V; tel: 0524-479 000; daily 11.30am–10pm; $$

With a grand terrace right on the sea, this is the place for a long lunch or slow dinner of no-nonsense fresh fish and seafood with some chilled white Moroccan wine.

Elizir

1 rue d'Agadir; tel: 0524-472 103; www.elizir.com; daily 7.30–11pm; $$–$$$

The delightful Abdellatif is passionate about food and 20th-century furniture, and he has united the two in this most charming restaurant where you will want to return every night. Set in a traditional Moroccan town house but furnished with 1960s–70s furniture, the food served is inventive and delicious Moroccan-Italian fusion such as tajine of dromedary or home made ravioli with fresh goat's cheese.

Ferdaous

27 rue Abdesslam Lebadi; tel: 0524-473 655; Tue–Sun noon–3pm, 7–10pm; $$

Authentic Moroccan eatery with old-fashioned decor but serving good inventive and fresh Moroccan dishes. Very friendly service, and away from the tourist traps.

Above: lunch at the Essaouira food stalls is not to be missed.

Fish Stalls

Port side of place Moulay Hassan; daily 11am–9pm; $

The freshest catch of fish and seafood can be chosen from the display (prices are up on the board) and grilled to perfection. The setting is perfect, with just a table per stall, and all fish is served with salad and bread. No alcohol served.

Below: dine under canopy at the atmospheric La Pause.

Riads

Until the early 1990s the medina was a pretty run-down place, and one wouldn't stroll too far off the main tourist drags. Riads, or courtyard houses, went for peanuts then; foreigners, drawn to the exotic city, started buying them up. First they restored them as homes, intrigued by working with the skilful artisans, but as many of the houses were large, they turned them into luxurious guesthouses. Today, while usually foreign-owned, the riad guesthouses are mostly run by Moroccan staff who welcome guests with the same hospitality as if it were their home. For further information about staying in riads, *see Accommodation, p.31*.

A GARDEN HOUSE

The word *riad* comes from the Arabic word for garden and means a traditional Moroccan house centred around an interior garden or courtyard filled with flowers and trees. The plan for these houses follows the plan of the Roman villa quite closely, in fact. There are few or no windows in the thick exterior mudbrick walls, all the rooms open up to a bright courtyard, and the walls are just pierced by a heavy entrance door. This inward focus suits the Muslim mentality perfectly, as family privacy is all important. Traditionally the riads were home to an extended family, and each family would have one or two rooms; cooking and other household chores were done in the communal space of the kitchen and the courtyard. The courtyard garden was a miniature version of paradise as described in the Quran. A water feature is usually de rigueur for a calming effect, as is birdsong, jasmine for perfume and orange trees for shade. Riads now have been redesigned and redecorated by some of the world's best-known interior designers and architects, but the basic structure and principles of the original riad remain the same.

> This small-scale tourism has many advantages: the medina has been saved from falling in disrepair, a lot of jobs have been created and there has been a revival of traditional crafts, and visitors have a closer relationship with the people and their surroundings. The disadvantage, however, is that prices for riads are now so high that Moroccans cannot afford them any more; they have moved into new apartment blocks and have a different lifestyle.

RIAD FEATURES

TADELAKHT

The traditional coating on the walls of palaces, hammams and riad bathrooms. The plaster is made of lime from the Marrakesh area, polished with stone and treated with a natural soap (often 'black' soap) to render the surface more water-resistant. It is also used to fashion any shape of bathtub or shower cubicle, allowing for some very fancy riad bathrooms.

ZELLIJ

The traditional Moroccan tile work that adorns rooms and courtyards. Terracotta tiles are cut and pieced together to make geometrical designs, as Islam forbids the representation of living things. *Zellij* making is a craft that is transmitted by *maâlems* (master craftsmen) from father to son.

Left: enjoying a dip at the Riad Farnatchi.

Many books have been devoted to the **'Marrakesh style'**: *Living in Morocco* by Barbara and René Stoeltie (2003) *Living in Morocco: Design from Casablanca to Marrakesh* by Lisl and Dennis Landt (2001) *Marrakesh: Fine Living in Riads and 'Maisons d'Hôtes'* by Pascal Defraire (2003) *Marrakesh: the Secret of the Courtyard Houses* by Quentin Wilbaux (2000) *Morocco: 5,000 Years of Culture* by Vincent Boele (2004)

OLD-STYLE RIADS

Dar Cherifa – Café Littéraire

8 derb Cherfa Lakbir, off rue Mouassine; tel: 0524-426 463; daily noon–pm; map p.138 C3

Beautifully restored 16th-century riad, with superb woodwork and a small pool in the courtyard.

SEE ALSO CAFÉS, P.43

Gallia

30 rue de la Recette; tel: 0524-445 913; www.ilove-marrakesh.com/hotelgallia; map p.139 C1

Old-fashioned riad with a well-kept garden courtyard with turtles for good luck.

SEE ALSO ACCOMMODATION, P.30

Hôtel du Trésor

77 derb Sidi Bouloukat, off rue Riad Zitoun el Kedim; tel: 0524-375 113; www.hotel-du-tresor.com; map p.139 C1

Cosy and intimate riad hotel with a tiny pool in the courtyard.

SEE ALSO ACCOMMODATION, P.30

Left: an example of *zellij*.

Maison Tiskiwin

8 rue de la Bahia; tel: 0524-389 192; daily 9am–12.30pm, 3–5.30pm; admission charge; map p.137 C3

Part home, part museum this is the wonderful riad restored by anthropologist Bert Flint.

SEE ALSO MUSEUMS AND GALLERIES, P.79

Villa de l'Ô

3 rue Mohamed ben Messouad, Essaouira; tel: 0524-476 375; www.villadelo.com

Spectacular 18th-century riad renovated as a hotel.

SEE ALSO ACCOMMODATION, P.37

CONTEMPORARY-DESIGN RIADS

Maison MKhotel

14 derb Sebaai, Ksour quarter; tel: 0524-376 173; www.maisonmk.com; map p.138 B3

One of the chicest riads, designed in a contemporary Moroccan style.

SEE ALSO ACCOMMODATION, P.33

Riad Akka

65 derb Lahbib Magni, off rue Riad Zitoun el Jedid; tel: 0524-375 767; www.riad-akka.com; map p.139 E1

Sleekly designed riad where the traditional Moroccan heritage blends in with strong colours and a contemporary style.

SEE ALSO ACCOMMODATION, P.32

Riad Dyor

1 derb Driba Jdida, Sidi ben Slimane; tel: 0524-375 980; www.ryaddyor.com; $$$$

Ibiza-based designer couple used a modern Moorish style for this relaxed boutique hotel.

SEE ALSO ACCOMMODATION, P.34

Riad Farnatchi

2 derb el Farnatchi; tel: 0524-384 910; www.riadfarnatchi.com; map p.134 C1

Jonathan Wix designed this fabulous hotel as a contemporary oriental fantasy with no expense spared.

SEE ALSO ACCOMMODATION, P.34

Shopping

If you have shopping in mind, the first place to head for after arriving in Marrakesh is the Ensemble Artisanal, to get an idea of what is available and at what price – general prices are fixed here. The next place is definitely the souks, traditionally arranged by trade. Within the souks are specialised shops, and in recent years trendy little boutiques have popped up everywhere, that are harder to just come across, although the city also has a sprinkling of chic boutiques in Guéliz and the out-of-town Industrial Zone, showcasing the best of modern Moroccan design. For further shops, *see also Literature, p.73*, *Pampering, p.91*, and *Souks, p.114*.

WHERE TO SHOP

The medina is the place to shop for traditional clothes, crafts and general souvenirs. Reflecting its more refined character, the Mouassine area has some individual boutiques selling more unusual items, such as clothes, gifts and tableware often based on traditional style but with a contemporary twist. East of the Jemaa el Fna, the rue Riad Zitoun el Jedid, also has some interesting shops, and if you are looking for typical Marrakchi lanterns head for the place des Ferblantiers. Some of the side streets off avenue Mohammed V in Guéliz are worth exploring, in particular rue de la Liberté, and near place du 16 Novembre, the Plaza Marrakesh, a new shopping precinct that is slowly filling with international fashion shops.

Traditionally it's the men who do most of the shopping, perhaps to shield the women from the cut and thrust of the marketplace, perhaps to control the purse strings, but there are plenty of women around. Vendors use many flattering words to attract the women in: *Entrez pour le plaisir des yeux...*(Come in just for the pleasure of your eyes), *'Venez la gazelle...'*(Come in oh gazelle...).

SIDI GHANEM INDUSTRIAL ZONE

If you are seriously interested in contemporary Moroccan design, or are looking to export larger furnishings for the house, pay a visit to the Sidi Ghanem Industrial Zone (www.pagespro-marrakesh.com), off route de Safi (northwest exit from the city).

Akkal

No. 322; tel: 0524-335 938; www.akkal.net; Mon–Sat 9am–1pm, 2.30–6pm

Stunning contemporary ceramic tableware, including some pretty funky teapots and tajines.

Amira

No. 277; tel: 0524-336 247; www.amirabougies.com; Mon–Sat 9am–1pm, 2.30–6pm

Candles are the thing for Marrakesh nights, and Amira candles are as hip and stylish as they come. Huge selection of candles in all shapes and colours.

Talamanzou

932 Résidence al Massar, route de Safi, on the right-hand side as you leave town; tel: 0524-335 335; www.talamanzou.com; Mon–Sat 9am–1pm, 2.30–6pm

Traditional Moroccan carpets with a contemporary twist.

ANTIQUES AND CARPETS

SEE ALSO SOUKS, P.114–15

Bab el Khemis Junk Market

Outside Bab el Khemis, Northern Medina; daily 7am–noon; map p.135 C3

Flea market that is good on some days, particularly on Thursdays, and less so otherwise, but also check out the shops nearby.

Left: a Marrakesh trader presides over his wares.

Chez Brahim
101 Rahba Kedima, Eastern Medina; tel: 0524-440 110; daily 9.30am–6.30pm; map p.139 D3
One of the best dealers in Moroccan textiles from all over the country.

Chez Les Nomades
32–34 Bradia Lakdima, Mouassine Quarter; tel: 0524-442 259/0661-344 162; www.chezlesnomades.com; Mon–Sat 9am–7pm; map p.139 C4
Excellent carpet shop with a huge selection of old and new carpets (from traditional kilims and knotted wool carpets to modern leather rugs), a great roof terrace, and an interesting clientele coming and going.

El Badii
54 boulevard Moulay Rachid, Guéliz; tel: 0524-431 693; daily 9am–7pm; map p.132 B3
Two floors of a museum-quality collection gathered by some of Marrakesh's top guides, Mr Aboufikr and his wife, including wonderful Berber jewellery, medieval manuscripts, Fès blue pottery, textiles and carpets.

Right: classic Moroccan furnishings at El Badii.

CRAFTS

Centre Artisanal
7 derb Baissi Kasbah, off the rue de Kasbah, Southern Medina; tel: 0524-381 853; daily 8.30am–8pm; map p.136 B2
This 'emporium' store sells nothing but traditional crafts, from jewellery and carpets to pottery and clothing, all at fixed prices. No haggling here.

Cherkaoui
120–122 rue Mouassine, Mouassine Quarter; tel: 0524-426 817; daily 9am–7.30pm; map p.138 C3
Cherkaoui has everything, apart from carpets, to create that Marrakesh feel in your house, with woodwork, pottery, leather and metalwork, produced by the shops own artisans.

Ensemble Artisanal
Avenue Mohammed V, Jemaa el Fna; tel: 0524-386 758; daily 8.30am–7pm; map p.138 A3
Government-run one-stop shopping centre with shops and workshops of the best artisans, all here by royal appointment. With some of the best crafts in Morocco on offer, from jewellery to embroidery and leatherwork, the prices are fixed, but higher than in the souks. This is one of the few places where one doesn't bargain.

Kasbah du Toubkal Shop
Kasbah du Toubkal, Imlil; daily 9am–noon, 4–7pm
Great store at the entrance of the kasbah selling the best of local crafts, including wonderful *babouches* (slippers) worn in the hotel, leatherwork and textiles.

Above: modern artisan metalwork at Yahya.

designs. Funky accessories too.

Saturday Market
Asni; Sat 6am–noon
Large market for all the surrounding villages with food, textiles, crafts and animals; come early to avoid tour buses.

FASHION

CONTEMPORARY FASHION

Akbar Delights
45 place Bab el Fteuh, Mouassine Quarter; tel: 0671-661 307; Tue–Sun 10am–1pm, 3–7.30pm; map p.138 C3
Super chic little boutique with very expensive but fine kaftans, shawls and accessories, embroidered in Kashmir.

Atika
34 rue de la Liberté, Guéliz; tel: 0524-431 693; Mon–Sat 8.30am–12.30pm, 3–7.30pm; map p.132 C4
Popular shoe store selling good-quality Western-style shoes at Moroccan prices.

If the souks and bargaining are too daunting, you can now go shopping with the city's hippest personal shopper, **Laetitia Trouillet**, a French fashion designer (see From Marrakech with Love, *opposite*; tel: 0661-477 228; www.lalla.fr) who knows the souks inside out. She arranges a car, haggles and navigates her clients through the souks, and saves you a fair bit of money if you plan to buy lots.

Kasbek
216 rue Riad Zitoun el Jedid, Southern Medina; tel: 0663-775 690/0669-952 030; www.kasbekaftans.com; Mon–Sat 10am–7pm; map p.139 D1
Two Aussie girls who make beautiful kaftans in vintage fabrics and sexy jersey gandura-style dresses.

Kifkif
8 rue des Ksour Bab Laksour, Mouassine Quarter; tel: 0661-082 041; daily 9.30am–7.30pm; map p.138 B3
Better-quality one-stop shop with a sense of humour, selling great T-shirts, jewellery, bags and homeware, all with a twist.

Kulchi
1 rue des Ksour Bab Laksour, Mouassine Quarter; daily 9am–1pm, 3.30–7pm; map p.138 B3
Great boho fashion by French designer perfect for the nights out in Marrakesh, using local and West African fabrics and designs. Funky accessories too.

TRADITIONAL CLOTHING

Au Fil d'Or
10 Souk Semmarine, Eastern Medina; tel: 0524-445 919; Sat–Thur 9am–1pm, 2.30–7.30pm, Fri 9am–1pm; map p.139 C3
The collection, hidden behind curtains, includes the finest handmade shirts, traditional and contemporary in beautiful cotton, woolen *djellabas* and kaftans, and *babouches* fit for a king.

Aya's
Derb Jedid Bab Mellah, off the place des Ferblantiers, Southern Medina; tel: 0524-383 428/0661-462 916; www.ayasmarrakesh.com; map p.137 C3
The wonderful Nawal creates wonderful kaftans, jackets and robes in the the finest fabrics, traditionally embroidered with silk. A good selection of accessories and girls' dresses.

Beldi
9–11 Soukiat Laksour Bab Fteuh, Mouassine Quarter; tel: 0524-441 076; daily 9.30am–1pm, 3.30–8pm; map p.138 C3
The two brothers offer a good selection of ready-to-wear kaftans, in silks and velvets, with an eye for Western tastes.

La Maison du Kaftan
65 rue Sidi el Yamami, Mouassine Quarter; tel: 0524-441 051; daily 9am–7.30pm; map p.138 C4
Huge collection of kaftans, and other traditional clothing for men, women and children, in all colours and styles.

Above: a souk trader buried in woven baskets.

JEWELLERY

Boutique Bel Hadj

First floor of the Foundouk Ourzazi, place de Bab Fteuh, Mouassine Quarter; tel: 0524-441 258; daily 9am–8pm; map p.138 C3

Mohammed has a huge collection of beads and semi-precious stones from all over Morocco and Africa. He is very knowledgeable and makes his own necklaces as well.

LEATHER

Moroccan leather has a good reputation and is widely available. The largest variety of the typical *babouches*, soft slippers with turned-down heels, is available in **Souk des Babouches** *(see p.114)*.

From Marrakesh with Love xxx

45, 1st floor Souk Chérifia, under the Terrasse des Epices, Mouassine Quarter; tel: 0661-477 228; www.lalla.com; daily 11am–7pm; map p.139 C4

Vintage-style handbags by Laetitia Trouillet *(see box, opposite)* hand-made in Morocco, and accessories like Moroccan belts and boho jewellery.

Place Vendôme

141 avenue Mohammed V, at the corner of rue de la Liberté, Guéliz; tel: 0524-435 263; Mon–Sat 9am–12.30pm, 3.30–7.30pm; map p.132 B4

A good selection of leather bags and the finest leather clothing.

Poupa Litza

Rue Mohammed el Qory, Essaouira; tel: 0524-783 565; daily 10am–7pm

Funky hand-made leather bags in a multitude of colours.

METALWARE

This is a speciality of Marrakesh. Items range from massive brass door-knockers and hinges to wrought-iron furniture and grilles, and from the curvy silver-coloured teapots (ideal souvenirs) to highly patterned copper or brass trays and vases. The **place des Ferblantiers** is the place to find the typical Marrakchi lanterns.

SEE ALSO SQUARES, P.120

Yahya

Shop 49–50, 61 rue de Yougoslavie, Guéliz; tel: 0524-422 776; www.yahyacreation.com; Mon–Sat 9.30am–noon, 4–7pm; map p.132 B4

One of the premier artisans making chiselled, sculpted and engraved copper, nickel, silver and wood objects, all reflecting a successful balance between tradition and modernity.

The **Ministerio del Gusto** (22 derb Azouz el Mouassine, near Villa Flore, off rue Sidi el Yamani; tel: 0524-426 455; Mon–Sat 9.30am–noon, 4–7pm; map p.138 B4) is a shop-cum-gallery like no other in Marrakesh, set up by the designer Fabrizio Bizzari and Alessandro Lippini, a former style editor for Italian *Vogue*. The shop, styled like a West African mud house, has a changing collection of outlandish furniture, contemporary art and vintage clothes and accessories.

Below: fun and stylish accessories at Kifkif.

Souks

Built on the crossroads of the caravan routes, Marrakesh has lived by trade from its earliest beginnings. Like other old Islamic cities, Marrakesh has an extensive network of souks, Arabic for 'markets', where goods are made and sold side by side. This chapter covers the Arab way of shopping in the different souks, while in *Shopping, p.110,* individual shops found in the souks and elsewhere in the city are listed, as is information on bargaining in the souks. *See also Walks, Drives and Views, p.126,* for a route through the main areas and arteries, perhaps for a first time approach.

MARRAKESH'S SOUKS

Stretching north of the Jemaa el Fna, the souks comprise an area of about 4 sq km (1½ sq miles), a vast labyrinth, partially roofed by makeshift mats or boards. This warren can sometimes disorientate first-time visitors, but getting lost in the souks, wandering off the main drags and admiring the architecture instead, soon becomes a pleasure.

SOUK SMARINE

There are several entrances to this souk, but the main approach is from the northern side of the Jemaa el Fna, which leads to the main drag, via the dried fruit souk, of the Souk Smarine. This broad and busy shopping street is now mainly taken over by some expensive antiques stores and cheap souvenir stalls, but a few shops still sell cater for locals making traditional circumcision outfits. **Au Fil d'Or** at no.10 *(see Shopping, p.112)* stands out for its fine-quality clothes.

The best times to shop are the morning, when trade is brisk and businesslike, and early evening when Marrakchis pour into the souks not just to buy but to browse and soak up the atmosphere: the gorgeous colours, the twinkling lights, the smell of mint and spices. It is no longer necessary to use a guide to the souks. The labyrinthine alleys may be confusing at first, but you are never more than a 10-minute walk from 'La Place' (Jemaa el Fna), and locals are always happy to point you in the right direction.

Just beyond the turn-off to the Rahba Kedima, the Souk Smarine divides to the right into the **Souk el Kebir** (the Large Souk), to the left to the **Souk des Babouches** (Souk of the Slippers). The Souk el Kebir has some wood workers who sell bowls and other wooden household implements, as well a traditional saddle maker. Further on is **Souk Cherratine**, with mostly leather shops, which leads to place Ben Youssef, with the Ben Youssef Medersa, and to the right, to Bab Debbagh and the pungent smelling **tanneries** nearby. There are several tanneries where leather is still tanned and dyed in a smelly mix of lime, pigeon droppings and now also toxic chemical dyes. The tanners work knee-deep in the vats.

An incredible range of slippers is on sale in the Souk des Babouches, in a rainbow of colours, but the utilitarian brown, red or yellow are the traditional colours for men.

RAHBA KEDIMA

One of the most attractive corners of the souk is the old corn market, the **Rahba Kedima**, the place des Epices, domain of the herbalists, but also filled with Berber women selling baskets, bags and hats (straw in summer and colourful rough woollen caps in winter). The spectacle can be watched from the terrace of the Café des

Left: the souks are a quintessential Marrakesh experience.

Bargaining is an intrinsic part of buying things in the souks, something visitors either embrace or loathe to such a degree that they avoid shopping altogether. There are no hard and fast rules to this mind-game, other than never start haggling for something you have no intention of buying (time-wasters are not tolerated kindly) and start your negotiations at well below the asking price (half to a third is often suggested). Some stores offer fixed prices, usually a bit higher than what you pay in the souks, including the **Ensemble Artisanal** on Avenue Mohammed V *(see Shopping, p.111)* and most shops in Guéliz.

Epices. Just north of the café are two entrance ways to the **Criée Berbère** (Berber Auction). Now the **Souk des Tapis** (Carpet Souk) is mostly taken over by carpet sellers, but until 1912 it was the location of a slave auction where sub-Saharan slaves were sold.
SEE ALSO CAFÉS, P.43; SQUARES, P.121

Bazar du Sud
117 Souk des Tapis; tel: 0524-443 004; daily 9am–7pm; map p.139 D3
One of the best carpet shops.

KISSARIA

Between the Souk el Kebir and the Souk des Babouches is the **Kissaria**, a covered market where originally the most expensive items were sold, but these days it's a place to look for less commercial souvenirs, cotton clothing, good kaftans and blankets.

Further along, the Souk des Babouches turns into the **Souk Kchachbia**. The noise of metal hammering will lead you into the dusty alley of the **Souk Haddadine,** the ironmongers' quarter where blacksmiths forge iron into lamp stands, furniture and window grilles used in the Marrakchi riads. Several alleys leading west of Souk Kchachbia lead to the picturesque **Souk Sebbaghine** or Dyers' Souk, where dyed wool and scarves are draped to dry across wires above the alleys. There are some junk shops here, and a few shops selling felt bags, carpets and elaborate silverware.

Below: lamps and *babouches* for sale *(left and centre)*; the colouful tanneries *(right)*.

Sports

The Marrakesh medina may get a bit claustrophobic after a few days, but no need to panic: it is very easy to get out of town. From the Jemaa el Fna café rooftops you can see the snow-capped Atlas Mountains, where it is possible to ski in winter, or hike for the rest of the year. The Ourika Valley offers wonderful landscapes with picturesque Berber villages clinging to the red rocks, and a patchwork of fields and orchards surrounding the Ourika River. Essaouira has a long sweep of a beach and is known as the 'Wind City of Africa', as it is a paradise for surfers and windsurfers.

BEACHES AND SWIMMING POOLS

Beldi Country Club

6km (4 miles) south of Marrakesh, route du Barrage, Cherifia; tel: 05240-383 950; www.beldicountryclub.com; admission charge; daily 10am–10pm

The Beldi gardens are open to visitors who pay a fixed fee for a day by the beautiful swimming pools in the garden with an excellent lunch.

SEE ALSO ACCOMMODATION, P.36; GARDENS, P.65

El Andalous

Avenue du Président Kennedy, Hivernage; tel: 0524-448 226; www.elandalous-marrakesh.com; map p.133 C1

This four-star hotel will let non-residents use the pool if you have lunch there.

It's easy and pleasant enough to get around Marrakesh by bicycle, particularly in the medina. For a bike ride near town head for the Menara gardens or the Palmeraie *(see Gardens, p.64)*.

Above: poolside glamour at Plage Rouge.

Essaouira Beach

Essaouira

Essaouira has a long, large beach along the Atlantic, which occasionally is good for swimming and sunbathing, but with so much wind it's often better for surfing *(see p.119)*.

Jnane Tamsna

Douar Abiad, Palmeraie; tel: 0524-329 423; www.jnanetamsna.com; daily 11am–7pm

Each villa in this wonderful garden has its own pool, with a few larger pools too, by which non-residents who buy lunch can spend the day.

SEE ALSO ACCOMMODATION, P.35

Lake Lalla Takerkoust

40km (25 miles) from Marrakesh

Large artificial lake with several public and private beaches, and a range of water sports facilities.

Nikki Beach

Circuit de la Palmeraie; tel: 0663-519 992; www.nikkibeach.com; late Mar–Sept daily noon–10pm

St Tropez and Miami have

Left: skiing, Berber-style, at Oukaïmeden *(see p.118)*.

Hôtel Toulousain
Rue Tarek ibn Ziad, Guéliz; tel: 0524-430 033; www.geocities.com/hotel_toulousain; map p.134 C4
Bike rental by the day.
SEE ALSO ACCOMMODATION, P.35

Maroc Nature Adventures
129 Résidence Elbakouri, rue Khalid ben el Oualid, Guéliz; tel: 0524-447 019; www.maroc-nature.com; www.vtt-maroc.com; map p.133 D3
Mountain-bike rental and trips in the countryside around Marrakesh.

one, and so does Marrakesh. This is a 'beach' to see and to be seen, attracting wealthy young Moroccans and the clubbing crowds. Make sure to bring your flashiest bikini.
SEE ALSO NIGHTLIFE, P.86

Plage Rouge
Km10 route de l'Ourika; tel: 0524-378 086; www.ilovemarrakesh.com/laplagerouge; daily noon–1am
A large beach of fine white sand, with sun beds and shaded areas, around a huge pool measuring 80m by 40m (260ft by 130ft). DJs take care of the music, there are several restaurants and bars, and you can dance the night away by the pool or in one of the elegant pavilions.
SEE ALSO NIGHTLIFE, P.86

The late King Hassan II was a passionate golfer, and, as a result, Morocco has some excellent courses should you fancy a game, including three in Marrakesh – each of them in a perfectly scenic location with the Atlas Mountains as a backdrop. The **Fédération Royale Marocaine de Golf** (tel: 0537-755 636; www.golfsmaroc.com) can provide information on tournaments.

CYCLING

Actions and Loisirs
1 avenue Yaqoub el Mansour, Guéliz; tel: 0524-430 931
Bicycles and motorbikes for rent by the day or half-day.

Cycleactive
Tel: 00 44 (0)1768-840 400 (UK); www.cycleactive.co.uk
UK-based company specialised in cycling holidays organises wonderful week-long mountain-bike trips in the Atlas Mountains.

Said Mountain Bike
Immeuble Akenouche, on the corner of avenue Moulay Rachid and rue de la Poste, Ouarzazate; tel: 0524-884 222/0661-434 217; www.saidmountainbike.com; Mon–Fri 9am–noon, 3–6pm, Sat 9am–noon
Said organises mountain bike tours in the desert in winter and in the mountains in summer.

GOLF

Amelkis Golf Course
Route de Ouarzazate; tel: 0524-404 414
Backed by the Atlas Mountains, Amelkis, the newest and perhaps the

Above: biking in the desert with Said Mountain Bike *(see p.117).*

most stunning of Marrakesh's golf courses, is an 18-hole course 7km (4 miles) south of the city.

Palmeraie Golf Club
Palmeraie; tel: 0524-301 010; www.pgpmarrakesh.com
The 18-hole masterpiece golf course designed by the internationally acclaimed master Robert Trent Jones in the Palmeraie. He has designed a spacious valley with thousands of palm trees and seven lakes.

Royal Golf Club Marrakesh
Route de Ouarzazate; tel: 0524-404 705
Just 5km (3 miles) south of the city at the foot of the Atlas Mountains, this 18-hole golf course was built in the 1920s by the pasha of Marrakesh. It has hosted famous statesmen such as Churchill and Eisenhower, and was a favourite of the late King Hassan II.

HORSE RIDING

Marrakesh's Palmeraie, Essaouira's beach, the Ourika Valley and the foothills of the Atlas Mountains all offer wonderful terrain for horse riding. There are also specialist tour companies offering one- and two-week riding holidays, and several hotels in the Atlas can arrange riding for their guests.

Atlas à Cheval
932 Résidence el Massar, Route de Safi; tel: 0524-368 610/0661-222 272; http://atlasacheval-marrakech.net
Situated among olive groves about 26km (16 miles) from Marrakesh, this company offers good half- and full-day treks into the surrounding hills.

Club Equestre de la Palmeraie Golf Palace
Circuit de la Palmeraie, tel: 0524-301 010; www.pgp.co.ma
Excellent, well-kept stables with good instructors.

Les Cavaliers de l'Atlas
Palmeraie; tel: 0672-845 579; www.lescavaliersdelatlas.com
The horses here are among the best in town, and a wide variety of excursions is available, from a one-hour class to full day trips, and longer overnight excursions.

Ranch de Diabat
Diabat, 6km (4 miles) north of Essaouira; tel: 0676-925 211; www.ranchdediabat.com

La Pause hotel near Marrakesh is the perfect place to get away from city traffic, and offers a range of outdoor activities, from cross golf, mountain biking and hiking to overnight trips on camel or horseback (Douar Lmih Laroussième, Agafay; tel: 0661-306 494; www.lapause-marrakesh.com) in its amazing surroundings. *See also Accommodation, p.37.*

Plenty of people go jogging in the Palmeraie, but more serious runners can join the annual **Marrakesh Marathon** (tel: 0524-446 822; www.marathon-marrakesh.com) and the **Marathon des Sables** (www.saharamarathon.co.uk) departing from Ouazarzate. *See also Festivals and Events, p.54.*

Provides a wide range of treks, including a half-day (five-hour) trek along the coast plus two, three- and six-day treks.

Ranch Equestre de la Palmeraie
6km (4 miles), Hotel Palmariva, route de Fès; tel: 0661-455 034/0660-405 034
This ranch in the Palmeraie offers trekking for 1½ hours or half a day at a reasonable cost.

SKIING

Morocco's only real ski resort is **Oukaïmeden**, 75km (45 miles) from Marrakesh, at a height of 2,650m (8,690ft). There is usually snow from January to March, and there is talk of Gulf Arab investors installing artificial snow-making machines, and turning this old-fashioned ski resort into a top resort that attracts the jet set. It has seven runs from nursery slope to black run, and the highest ski lift in Africa (3,243m/10,640ft). Information can be obtained from:

CAF (Club Alpin Français) Refuge
Oukaïmeden; tel: 0524-319 036; www.caf-maroc.com

TREKKING AND RUNNING

Marrakesh is the natural springboard for treks in

Right: a game of football on Essaouira beach *(see p.116)*.

the Atlas, and in particular the Toubkal National Park. If you have not come on a trekking holiday but would like to sample the Atlas terrain, it is easy enough to arrange something on the spot. The best time for hiking is late spring through to early autumn; in winter there is too much snow.

Bureau des Guides
Imlil; tel: 0524-485 626
Setti Fatma; tel: 0524-426 113

Dar Adrar
Imlil; tel: 0668-760 165/0670-726 809; www.guidedtrek.com
Mohammed Aztat, who owns this small guesthouse, is one of the best mountain guides around. He arranges treks, has a good team of guides, muleteers and cooks, as well as a small shop with equipment rental.
SEE ALSO ACCOMMODATION, P.36

Hotel Ali
Rue Moulay Ismail; tel: 0524-444 979
Used by many outdoor tour operators and a good place to find out about joining an organised hike (and mountain biking). Also **Hotel Foucauld** (Avenue el Mouahidine; tel: 0524-445 499).

I Rocha
Douar Tisselday, Ighrem N'Oudal; tel: 0667-737 002; www.irocha.com
From their hotel, geologist Ahmed and his partner Catherine organise interesting walks using the benefit of their excellent local knowledge.
SEE ALSO ACCOMMODATION, P.37

Kasbah du Toubkal
Imlil (60km/40 miles from Marrakesh); tel: 0524-485 611; www.kasbahdutoubkal.com
A popular destination for an easy mountain walk combined with lunch. A longer trek can be arranged, staying in the upmarket eco-lodge that also belongs to the Kasbah du Toubkal.
SEE ALSO ACCOMMODATION, P.36; RESTAURANTS, P.106

WATER SPORTS

Essaouira has been a popular destination for surfers for decades. The best conditions for surfing are at Moulay Bouzerktoun 20km (12 miles) to the north, and Sidi Kaouki 27km (17 miles) to the south.

Magic Fun Afrika
22 rue Ibn Azim, Essaouira; tel: 0524-473 856; www.magicfunafrika.com
A water sports centre offering lessons and equipment hire for kiteboarding, surfing, windsurfing and sea kayaking.

Ocean Vagabond Base Nautique
Essaouira beach; tel: 0524-783 934; www.oceanvagabond.com
A cool café on the beach to have lunch or hang out in and also a good place to find out about water sports in the area. They rent wind surfing and surfing equipment and body boards, and offer surfing, wind surfing and kiteboarding lessons.

Below: there are many riding opportunities near Marrakesh.

Squares

Squares are all-important in Morocco, as places to trade, to meet, to entertain and be entertained, and to come together as a community. The Mediterranean habit of the *paseo,* or late afternoon walk, is still popular, where everyone gets out of the house to a square, after the heat of the day and before the serious business of dinner. Berber villagers sometimes still have a weekly market in a 'square' in the middle of nowhere, then slowly a village grows around it, named after the day of the week the souk is held. No square is more quintessentially Morocco than the Jemaa el Fna, the mother of all squares.

JEMAA EL FNA

Medina; map 138–9 C2

The name Jemaa el Fna means the 'Assembly of the Dead', as it was once used for for public executions, but 'La Place', as locals refer to it, is very much alive nowadays, overwhelmingly so sometimes. Even Unesco has recognised its value as a unique showcase for popular and traditional culture, by making it the first World Heritage Site for Oral Heritage.

Have at least one meal in the Jemaa el Fna, sharing a bench and a laugh with locals around a food stall that grills fresh meat skewers or scoops up a pile of steaming couscous with vegetables. The after-show goes on for a while and eventually calms down around 11pm. Beware of pickpockets active in the evening crowds at night, and of scooters crossing totally oblivious through the pedestrian masses. Also beware of henna tattoos; now often chemical rather than natural henna, which can leave you with seriously itchy skin rashes.

Activity starts around 9am when orange juice vendors set up their stalls and start squeezing their tasty fresh juices, the sweetest around. They are soon followed by snake charmers, henna tattooists, photogenic water vendors festooned in pompons, love potion sellers and traditional apothecaries, etc. All are hoping to catch the camera lens of the tourists, on their way to the souks, who can take a pic in return for a few coins. In the late afternoon the place fills up with storytellers, reciting old Arab tales, Gnaoua musicians singing their trance songs and the acrobats building human pyramids. Tourists head for the café rooftops lining the square to watch a perfect sundown. Once the sun has set, the frenzy is turned up a few notches; with the locals joining in the crowds, transvestite belly dancers, more passionate storytellers, comic acts, all seemingly rising out of the swirling smoke and scents of the food stalls selling excellent street food, from kebabs and couscous to a soup of lamb trotters.

PLACE DES FERBLANTIERS

Southern medina; map 137 C3

The picturesque place des Ferblantiers (Tin Smiths' Square) was part of a souk in the Jewish Mellah. Originally a fondouk, it is now a small, intimate square – the best place to buy the typical Marrakchi metal lanterns. In recent years it has been cleaned up, and it is now a pleasant place for a mint tea or a good-value alfresco Moroccan lunch on one of the café terraces. On one side is the trendy **Kosybar**, while across the street is a small covered market with

Right: the sun sets over the place des Ferblantiers.

Left: the market in the Rahba Kedima.

mainly gold jewellery shops, and a few silver dealers.
SEE ALSO NIGHTLIFE, P.85; RESTAURANTS, P.100

PLACE MOULAY HASSAN

Essaouira

The main square in Essaouira, the large place Moulay Hassan between the port and the souks reflects the relaxed pace of the city. It's hard not to stop at the café terraces lining the square, which are always crowded with people meeting for breakfast, a drink, a cheap lunch or a game – locals all meet here. As locals stroll through the square, day-trippers arrive here looking lost, shoeshine boys operate their little racket and Gnaoua musicians swing their heads for a few coins.

RAHBA KEDIMA

Eastern medina; map 139 D3

The Rahba Kedima, also known as the place des Epices, is one of the most atmospheric squares in the medina. The old corn market is now the place to head for good luck amulets, magic potions and talismans made of crushed dried lizards, scorpions, hedgehogs and chameleons. You can watch Berber women haggle with locals and tourists over their hand-made wares from the rooftop of the **Café des Epices**, while listening to Bob Marley or Baaba Maal.
SEE ALSO CAFÉS, P.42

Transport

Marrakesh is easily reached from Europe by the major international airlines as well as some budget airlines. The city is well connected by train and bus with most major cities in Morocco. The centre is relatively small, although it has been spreading fast in recent years, and it is fairly easy to get around by foot or cycling. Public buses are far and few between, and not really used to travel in the city centre, where *petits taxis*, small taxis, are more practical and relatively good value. Due to tourists' overwhelming reliance on walking or taxis to get around, there are no transport suggestions given for any of the listings throughout this book.

GETTING TO MARRAKESH

BY AIR

Royal Air Maroc (RAM) operates daily flights to Marrakesh from London Gatwick, and from New York to Casablanca. British Airways operates daily flights to Marrakesh from Heathrow at competitive prices. Budget airlines lines Atlas Blue and Easy-Jet operate direct from London Gatwick, Ryanair from Luton and Thomson Fly from Manchester. There are no direct flights between Australia and Morocco.

Above: taxis, scooters and bicycles constantly zoom around Marrakesh's main streets.

Royal Air Maroc
In London: tel: 020-7307 5800; www.royalairmaroc.com
In Marrakesh: 197 avenue Mohammed V; tel: 0524-425 500. Reconfirm RAM flights 48 hours ahead

Atlas Blue
www.atlas-blue.com
British Airways
www.ba.com
EasyJet
www.easyjet.com
Ryanair
www.ryanair.com
Thomson Fly
www.thomsonfly.com

BY RAIL

Travel to Marrakesh by train via Paris (Eurostar to Gare du Nord and change to Gare d'Austerlitz) for Algeciras in Spain, where ferries leave for Tangier. Three daytime trains leave Tangier for Marrakesh (9–10 hours), and a sleeper leaves at 9.05pm and arrives at 8.30am (First-class compartments have four comfortable beds). Book ahead as there is just one sleeper carriage; check out schedules and fares on www.oncf.ma.

BY ROAD

From Tangier it is a 600km (370-mile) drive along a new toll motorway to Marrakesh.

Left: a standardly chaotic scene on Marrakesh's roads.

For information on where to hire bicycles or the Marrakchi's favourite – a moped – *see Sports, p.117.* The roads are in a pretty rough state, so only try this option if you're a confident rider – or just want to cruise in the calmer environs of a green space. Before hiring, be sure to check the brakes and gears are in a recently serviced state.

TO AND FROM THE AIRPORT

Marrakesh-Menara airport is situated 6km (4 miles) from the city centre. There are usually plenty of taxis outside the terminal. The fare into town should be no more than 100–130Dh, and if it is more be prepared to bargain. If it's your first time, arrange for a pick up when booking your riad, as some riads are hard to find in the medina. Bus (No.11) leaves for the Jemaa el Fna every 30 minutes.

TOURS

Diversity Excursions
Palmeraie; tel: 0524-329 423; www.diversity-excursions.co.uk
SEE ALSO ENVIRONMENT, P.47

Inside Morocco Travel
Riad Bledna, Palmeraie; tel: 0661-182 090; www.riadbledna.com
Eco-friendly tours.
SEE ALSO ENVIRONMENT, P.47

Marrakesh Tour
Departure outside tourist office on place Abdel Moumen ben Ali, Guéliz; tickets cost 130Dh (65Dh for children), valid for 24 hours; map p.132 B4
Hop-on-hop-off open-top tour bus service with two routes (tickets are valid for both): Marrakesh Monumental linking the main monuments, and Marrakesh Romantique, which takes in the Majorelle Garden and the Palmeraie.

Ribat Tours
6 rue des Vieux Marrakchis, Guéliz; tel: 0524-438 693; www.ribatours.com
Specialises in outdoor activities around Marrakesh.

Terres et Voyages
Immeuble D1, 8 avenue 11 Janvier, Bab Doukkala; tel: 0524-437 153; www.terresetvoyages.com; map p.134 A2
Reliable tour operator for treks, biking holidays and other outdoor pursuits.

GETTING AROUND

PETITS TAXIS

Petits taxis (small beige-and-black taxis) only take up to three passengers and can be hired on the street. Fares are very cheap, but to pay local prices you need to ensure that the meter is switched on from the start of your journey – not always easy. Most drivers will try to negotiate a set price for the journey; this will be at least double the meter price but will still be cheap by European standards.

GRANDS TAXIS

Grands taxis (large cream Mercedes) take up to six passengers. You can charter a *grand taxi* for the day or for a longer trip (easily arranged through your hotel, or more cheaply by

Below: bicycles are a popular way of getting around.

Above: *calèches* line up for business.

negotiating directly with drivers at the *grands taxis* stations). In Guéliz the main station is next door to the train station on avenue Hassan II.

CITY BUSES

There is a bus service, but buses get very crowded, and few tourists use them. (Tickets cost 3.5Dh and are sold on board.)

Route No. 1 runs from place de Foucauld to place Abdel Moumen ben Ali. Other useful routes include No. 2 and No. 10, which go to the bus station *(gare routière)*. No. 3 and No. 8 go to the train station.

CALECHES

Horse-drawn carriages congregate outside the larger hotels and at various points around the city, particularly on place de Foucauld. Official prices are posted inside the *calèche,* but be sure to check the price with the driver before boarding. There is usually a large congregation on the Jemaa el Fna, near the Koutoubia Mosque.

Inside the medina, the best mode of transport is really your own two legs. Narrow streets and a compact size make walking the ideal way to explore the Old City.

LONG-DISTANCE TRAVEL

Railway Station

Corner of avenue Hassan II and avenue Mohammed VI; tel: 0524-447 768/090-203 040; www.oncf.ma; map p.132 A3

There are good connections with the north: Tangier, Fès, Rabat and Casablanca, but no railway south.

Supratours

Avenue Hassan II, next door to the railway station; tel: 0524-435 525; map p.132 A3

Most reliable inter-city buses. The main bus station *(gare routière)* is just outside Bab Doukkala. This is the best form of public transport for travelling to Essaouira. Journeys are relatively quick, comfortable and cheap.

Right: taxis are the best way of getting around the city, especially outside of the Medina.

DRIVING

It is not worth hiring a car for getting around Marrakesh, as taxis are so cheap, but it is worth it if you want to get out of town, which is spectacular. It can work out cheaper than chartering a succession of *grands*

taxis, and will give you a lot more independence. However, if you only want to go to Essaouira you are probably better off getting the Supratours bus *(see opposite)*, which is cheap and efficient.

Speed limits are: 40kph (25mph) in urban areas, 100kph (60mph) on the open road and 120kph (74mph) on motorways (but look out for signs specifying other limits). Be careful to observe these limits: speed traps are common, especially on approaches to towns. You will receive a small on-the-spot fine for breaking the speed limit.

Car Hire

It is easier, and often cheaper, to book car hire in advance from home using one of the international companies. Otherwise, you can arrange something *in situ*; most companies have offices around place Abdel Moumen ben Ali on avenue Mohammed V in Guéliz. Do try haggling, especially for longer periods.

Avis
137 avenue Mohammed V, Guéliz; tel: 0524-432 525; www.avis.com; map p.132 B4

Europcar
63 boulevard Mohammed Zerktouni, Guéliz; tel: 0524-431 228; www.europcar.com; map p.132 B4

Hertz
154 avenue Mohammed V; tel: 0524-449 984; www.hertz.com; map p.132 B4

Roads

A toll motorway runs from Marrakesh to Tangier (600km/360 miles). This is cheap by European standards, but expensive for Moroccans (most of whom use the free A roads instead), so it is often fairly empty, other than around Casablanca and Rabat. Routes south and west are not dual carriageway and are much busier and slower.

If you are planning to drive through the Atlas you should expect twisting roads with steep drops below, especially on the narrow Tizi-n-Test. The Tizi-n-Tichka has a broader, better surface. Neither route requires four-wheel drive.

Above: shiny details on a *calèche*.

Parking

Your riad or hotel will be able to advise on parking. If they don't have their own car park, you will need to park in a public car park or on the street. Either way, a *gardien*, who wears an official badge, will keep an eye on your car for a small charge (3–4Dh is sufficient for an hour or two, but overnight parking usually costs 15–20Dh).

Walks, Drives and Views

The old medina of Marrakesh is relatively small, and easily discovered on foot. Don't worry about getting lost, the fun is finding treasures off the beaten track. Picturesque Essaouira is also best visited on foot, with its intimate medina surrounded by the thick sea walls. It would be a shame to miss out on the grand mountains that surround Marrakesh. Many tour companies organise trek or bike rides in the Atlas Mountains if you want something set up, but it's fairly easy to rent a car too. Within half an hour from Marrakesh you are out in wild, stunning scenery.

THE MARRAKESH MEDINA

Start: Place des Ferblantiers; map p.137 C3
End: Jemaa el Fna; map p.138 C2

The bustling medina can be daunting at first, so it is good to start with this walk, covering some obvious and some more hidden places, to realise that it's a small and very unthreatening place.

The **place des Ferblantiers** *(see Squares, p.120)* is a good starting point, easily reached by taxi from Guéliz or on foot from the Jemaa el Fna. After a coffee on a café terrace and a stroll through the **Mellah**, head for the rue Riad Zitoun el Jedid. Opposite the small car park, you will find to the right an archway that leads to **Dar Si Said** and **Maison Tiskiwin** *(see Museums and Galleries, p.79)*. Despite the many riad guesthouses, this feels like a very authentic part of town, with children playing in the street and little corner shops.

Return to the rue Riad Zitoun el Jedid and continue north past the wonderful posters of **Cinema Eden** *(see Films, p.57)* on the left, before arriving, via the rue des Banques, on the northern side of the **Jemaa el Fna** *(see Squares, p.120)*. Take a right and follow derb Debbachi, and then left on rue Biyadine leading to the **Rahba Kedima** *(see Squares, p.121)*. Stop for a mint tea at the **Café des Epices** *(see Cafés, p.42)* and then continue to the **Souk Smarine** *(see Souks, p.114)*. Take the left fork further, to the **Souk des Babouches,** and find to the left two entrances to the **Souk Sebbaghine** *(see Souks, p.115)*.

At the end of this Dyers' Souk turn left towards the **Mouassine Mosque** *(see Religion and Religious Sites, p.95)*, with its beautifully ornate

Essaouira was designed by the French architect Théodore Cornut. He was captured by Sultan Sidi Mohammed ben Abdallah in the 1760s. Cornut also designed the town of St-Malo in Brittany in France, and there are clear similarities between the two towns on the Atlantic. The sultan loved the blend of Moroccan and European styles, and it fitted perfectly with the cosmopolitan atmosphere in town where Europeans, Africans and Moors mixed together easily.

Left: the stunning drive over the Tizi-n-Tichka.

Left: in the Place des Ferblantiers.

fountain. Southwest along the rue Sidi el Yamani is some good shopping and a few unrestored **fondouks** *(see Architecture, p.38)*. Take a left on **rue Laksour** with some quirky boutiques and return to the rue Mouassine. Further south is the **Bab Fteuh**, boasting a large fondouk with jewellers' and artisans' workshops; from here, return to the Jemaa el Fna.

WALK IN ESSAOUIRA

Start: Skala du Port
End: Galerie Frédéric Damgaard

This pretty port town is just a three-hour drive west of Marrakesh. Its beaches attract a mix of windsurfers, artists and chilled-out travellers escaping the dust of the desert city. The port of Essaouira is always busy with the coming and going of the colourful fishing boats.

Climb up the tower of the **Skala du Port** *(see Monuments, p.76)* for good views over the port and the town. Walk across the **place Moulay Hassan** *(see Squares, p.121)*, and turn left on rue de la Skala between the towering town houses and the sea walls, to the **Skala de la Ville** *(see Monuments, p.77)* with cannons, lovers and views over the Atlantic.

Stroll through the shops and workshops underneath the Skala – be led by your nose as the **thuya** wood smells delicious. The rue Laalouj leads straight through the medina, but make a little detour for the **Musée Sidi Mohammed ben Abdallah** *(see Museums and Galleries, p.81)*.

Follow the main drag of the souk, avenue Sidi Mohammed ben Abdallah, northeast, and just before the **Mellah** take a right on rue Abdelaziz el Fechtali. At the end to the left is the entrance to the **market**, with vegetables, spices and, above all, masses of fish. Cross the main street into the **place du Marché de Grain**, now with some pleasant and tranquil café terraces. Across the rue Mohammed el Qory is a small gold **souk** that returns to the avenue de l'Istiklal. Follow this southwest towards the **kasbah** area, with to the right a small **clock tower** and,

Below: fishing boats tied up in Essaouira harbour.

The best places to get a good view of the medina are the café rooftops of the Jemaa el Fna, the **Kosybar** or the **Terrasse des Epices**. In the mountains the drive on the Tizi-n-Test road to Taroudant is one of the most scenic drives in the world, with varied mountain scenery, and so is the less dramatic Tizi-n-Tichka road. Climb to the top of **Aït Benhaddou** for the best view over this Kasbah of Hollywood fame and the magnificent surroundings. *See also Cafés, p.43; Kasbahs and Palaces, p.69; Nightlife, 85.*

further on, **Galerie Frédéric Damgaard** *(see Museums and Galleries, p.81)*.

WALK IN THE ATLAS MOUNTAINS

Start/end: Asni

Take a *grand taxi* or private car to **Asni** and continue along a road with great views to the higher up **Imlil**, a good start for treks. Follow your way through the village of Imlil, buying provisions and water for the day at the village grocery store. Go past the **Kasbah du Toubkal** hotel *(see Accommodation, p.36)* and follow the mule track on your left past apple and walnut orchards to the hilltop village of **Aremt**.

Once past Aremt head up the valley, and on the other side follow a mule path that clims up a huge rock that leads to the shrine of **Sidi Chamarouch** (2,310m/7,579ft). You will be joined along the way by local families who come to the shrine on a pilgrimage or to cure their mentally ill. Have a picnic by the little river near the shrine and return the same way. This makes for a nice day-trip from Marrakesh, or stay overnight at the wonderful Kasbah du Toubkal.

DRIVE IN THE OURIKA VALLEY

Many Marrakchis have a second home or farm in this valley, because the temperature in summer is often 10 to 15°C (18 to 27°F) cooler than in town. At weekends there is more traffic than other days as Marrakchis head out of town for lunch or a picnic along the riverbanks.

The Ourika Road (P2017) leads south of Marrakesh to the Ourika Valley, and the tourist office in **Tnine-l'Ourika** (34km/20 miles south of Marrakesh; tel: 0668-465 545) is a good first stop for information on trekking and the best vista points, and obtaining maps of the area.

Going through the village of Tnine, with a Monday morning souk, follow the signposts near the bridge to the **Jardins Bioaromatiques Nectarôme** and the **Jardin du Saffron** *(see Gardens,*

Below: there are many grand sights along the Tichka pass.

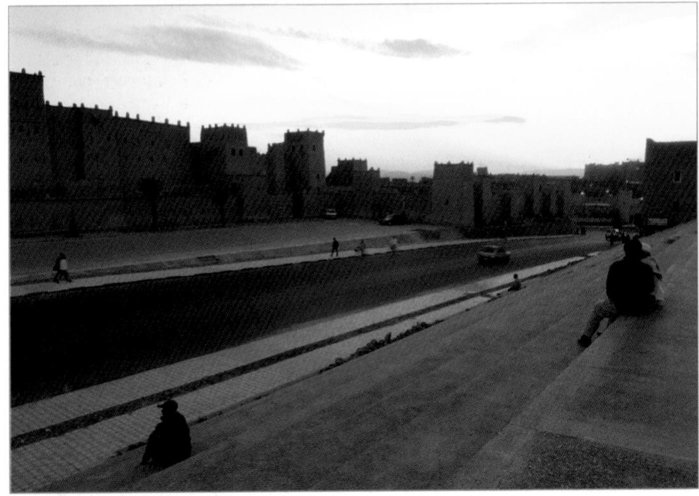

p.65). Return to the main road, and from here the Ourika River winds through lush orchards, gardens and fields, with great views of picturesque *douars*, tiny *pisé* villages. At the pretty village of **Aghbalou**, the road divides in two, with the left turn going to **Setti Fatma** and the right to the ski and trekking resort of **Oukaïmeden** *(see Sports, p.118)*. Setti Fatma is a pretty village with many trekking possibilities. The most popular option is the walk to the **Seven Falls**, about four hours away, for a swim and a picnic, but for longer treks contact the **Bureau des Guides** in the village (tel: 0668-562 340). Communal taxis leave Marrakesh every morning for Setti Fatma, and return in the afternoon to the *gare routière*.

DRIVE ON TIZI-N-TICHKA

If seeing the snow-capped mountains from Marrakesh rooftops is not satisfying enough, rent a car in Marrakesh and get closer. Head across the easier of the two mountain passes, the Tizi-n-Tichka, for a very different landscape from dramatic mountain scenery to the edge of the desert near Ouazarzate. This trip can also be done by communal taxi or bus, but leaving out visits off the road. It can be done in one day: travelling the length of the pass, it's a 200km (125-mile) trip from Marrakesh along the N9 highway.

The N9 out of Marrakesh leads to **Aït Ourir** (40km/25 miles) from Marrakesh), with a good Berber market on Tuesday or Saturday morning. For Telouet, turn left off the N9 (Km109) at the 'Ouarzazate 83km' sign, and drive for a further 25km (15 miles) to the **Glaoui Kasbah of Telouet** *(see Kasbahs and Palaces, p.69)*. Return to the main road and head further south to Ouazarzate, until the turn-off to the kasbah of **Aït Benhaddou** *(see Kasbahs and Palaces, p.69)*. The drive goes to the 'new' village on the west bank of the riverbed, where you have to walk across the river to the site. It is dry for most of the year, but in winter it is possible you will have to wade through some water. At the entrance to the town of Ouazarzate are the **Atlas Film Corporation Studios** *(see Tizi-n-Tichka, p.24)*.

Above: in the stunning Atlas Mountains.

As a rule, Moroccans drive quite chaotically but slowly. Dangerous overtaking on main roads is common, so be cautious. Your car hire company should provide you with the number of their breakdown company. Otherwise, flag down a fellow driver and ask for a lift to a repair garage in the nearest town to get assistance.

Atlas

The following streetplan of Marrakesh makes it easy to find the attractions listed in our A–Z section. A selective index to streets and sights will help you find other locations throughout the city.

Map Legend

	Notable building		Tourist information
	Park	★	Sight of interest
	Hotel		Statue / monument
	Souk/Market/Shopping		Mosque
	Urban area	✡	Synagogue
	Non urban area		Cathedral / church
	Transport hub		Library
	Cemetery		Bus station

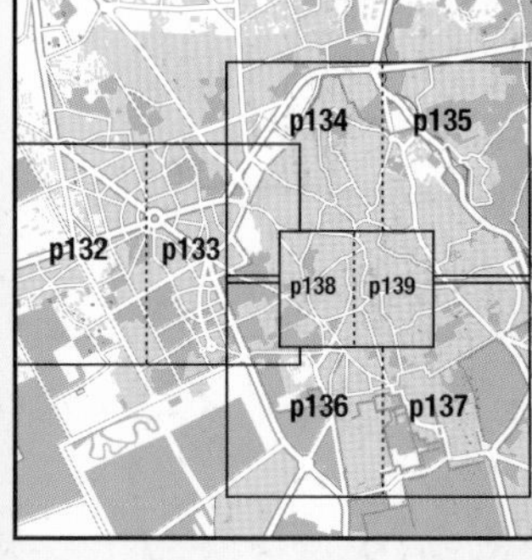

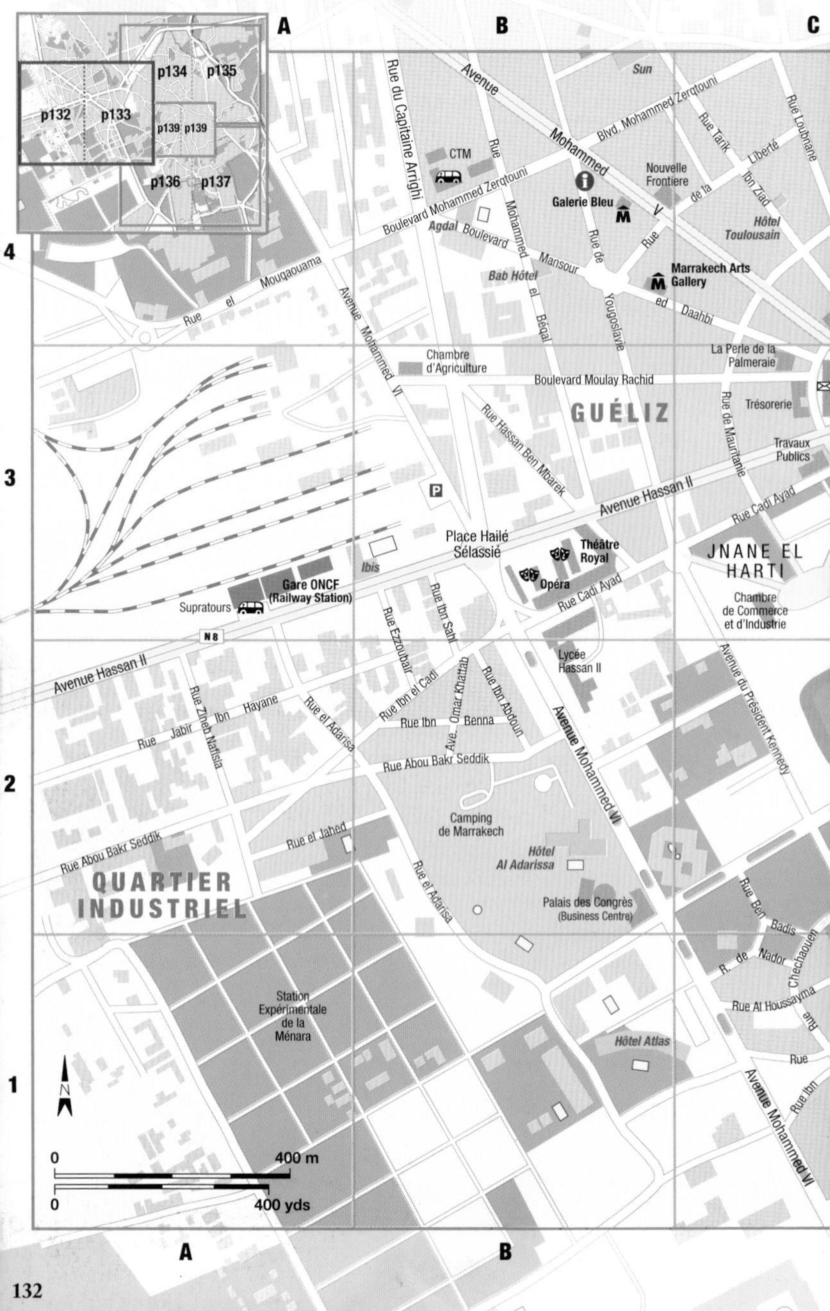
A
B
C
p134
p135
p132
p133
p139
p139
p136
p137
Avenue Mohammed V
Rue du Capitaine Arrighi
Sun
Blvd. Mohammed Zerqtouni
Rue Loubnane
Rue Tarik Ibn Ziad
CTM
Rue Mohammed el Béqal
Rue de la Liberté
Nouvelle Frontiere
Galerie Bleu
Boulevard Mohammed Zerqtouni
Agdal
Boulevard Mansour ed Daahbi
Rue de Yougoslavie
Hôtel Toulousain
Marrakech Arts Gallery
Bab Hôtel
Rue el Mouqaouama
Avenue Mohammed VI
Chambre d'Agriculture
La Perle de la Palmeraie
Boulevard Moulay Rachid
GUÉLIZ
Trésorerie
Rue Hassan Ben Mbarek
Rue de Mauritanie
Travaux Publics
Avenue Hassan II
Rue Cadi Ayad
Place Hailé Sélassié
Théâtre Royal
JNANE EL HARTI
Ibis
Opéra
Gare ONCF (Railway Station)
Supratours
Rue Ezzoubair
Rue Ibn Sahl
Chambre de Commerce et d'Industrie
N8
Lycée Hassan II
Avenue Hassan II
Rue Ibn el Cadi
Ave. Omar Khattab
Rue Ibn Abdoun
Rue Zineb Nafisia
Rue Jabir Ibn Hayane
Rue el Adarisa
Rue Ibn Benna
Avenue Mohammed VI
Avenue du Président Kennedy
Rue Abou Bakr Seddik
Camping de Marrakech
Rue el Jahed
Rue Abou Bakr Seddik
Hôtel Al Adarissa
QUARTIER INDUSTRIEL
Rue el Adarisa
Palais des Congrès (Business Centre)
Rue Ben Badis
R. de Nador
Chechaouen
Station Expérimentale de la Ménara
Rue Al Houssayma
Hôtel Atlas
Rue
Rue Ibn
Avenue Mohammed VI
N
0
400 m
0
400 yds
4
3
2
1

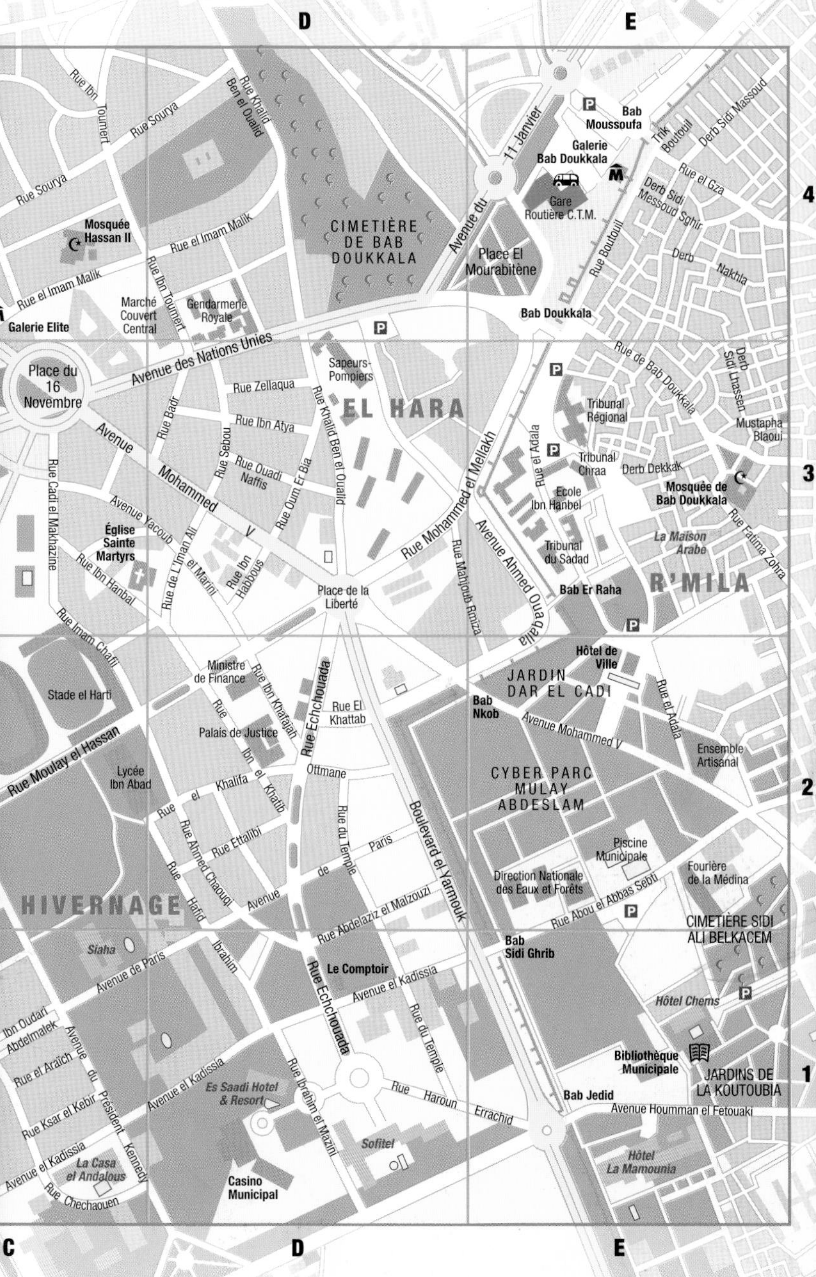
D
E
4
3
2
1
C
D
E
Rue Ibn Toumert
Rue Sourya
Rue Khalid Ben el Oualid
Mosquée Hassan II
Rue el Imam Malik
CIMETIÈRE DE BAB DOUKKALA
Avenue du 11 Janvier
Bab Moussoufa
Galerie Bab Doukkala
Gare Routière C.T.M.
Trik Boutouil
Derb Sidi Massoud
Rue el Gza
Derb Sidi Messoud Sghir
Derb Nakhla
Rue Boutouil
Place El Mourabitène
Bab Doukkala
Galerie Elite
Marché Couvert Central
Rue Ibn Toumert
Gendarmerie Royale
Avenue des Nations Unies
Place du 16 Novembre
Sapeurs-Pompiers
Rue Zellaqua
Rue Ibn Atya
Rue Badr
Rue Sebou
Rue Ouadi Naffis
Rue Oum Er Bia
Rue Khalid Ben el Oualid
EL HARA
Rue Mohammed el Mellakh
Rue de Bab Doukkala
Derb Sidi Lhassen
Tribunal Régional
Mustapha Blaoui
Rue el Adala
Tribunal Chraa
Derb Dekkak
Mosquée de Bab Doukkala
Ecole Ibn Hanbel
Avenue Mohammed V
Rue Cadi el Makhazine
Avenue Yacoub el Marini
Église Sainte Martyrs
Rue Ibn Hanbal
Rue de L'Iman Ali
Rue Ibn Habbous
Place de la Liberté
Rue Mahjoub Rmiza
Avenue Ahmed Ouagalla
Tribunal du Sadad
La Maison Arabe
Rue Fatima Zohra
Bab Er Raha
R'MILA
Rue Imam Chafii
Stade el Harti
Ministre de Finance
Rue Ibn Khafajah
Rue Echchouada
Rue El Khattab
Hôtel de Ville
JARDIN DAR EL CADI
Bab Nkob
Avenue Mohammed V
Rue el Adala
Ensemble Artisanal
Rue Moulay el Hassan
Palais de Justice
Rue Ibn el Khatib
Ottmane
Lycée Ibn Abad
Rue el Khalifa
CYBER PARC MULAY ABDESLAM
Rue du Temple
Boulevard el Yarmouk
Rue Ahmed Chaouqi
Rue Ettalibi
Avenue de Paris
Piscine Municipale
Direction Nationale des Eaux et Forêts
Fourière de la Médina
Rue Abou el Abbas Sebti
HIVERNAGE
Rue Hafid Ibrahim
Rue Abdelaziz el Malzouzi
CIMETIÈRE SIDI ALI BELKACEM
Siaha
Avenue de Paris
Le Comptoir
Bab Sidi Ghrib
Avenue el Kadissia
Hôtel Chems
Rue Echchouada
Rue du Temple
Ibn Oudari
Abdelmalek
Avenue du Président Kennedy
Rue el Araïch
Avenue el Kadissia
Es Saadi Hotel & Resort
Rue Ibrahim el Mazini
Bibliothèque Municipale
JARDINS DE LA KOUTOUBIA
Rue Haroun Errachid
Bab Jedid
Avenue Houmman el Fetouaki
Rue Ksar el Kebir
Sofitel
Avenue el Kadissia
La Casa el Andalous
Rue Chechaouen
Casino Municipal
Hôtel La Mamounia

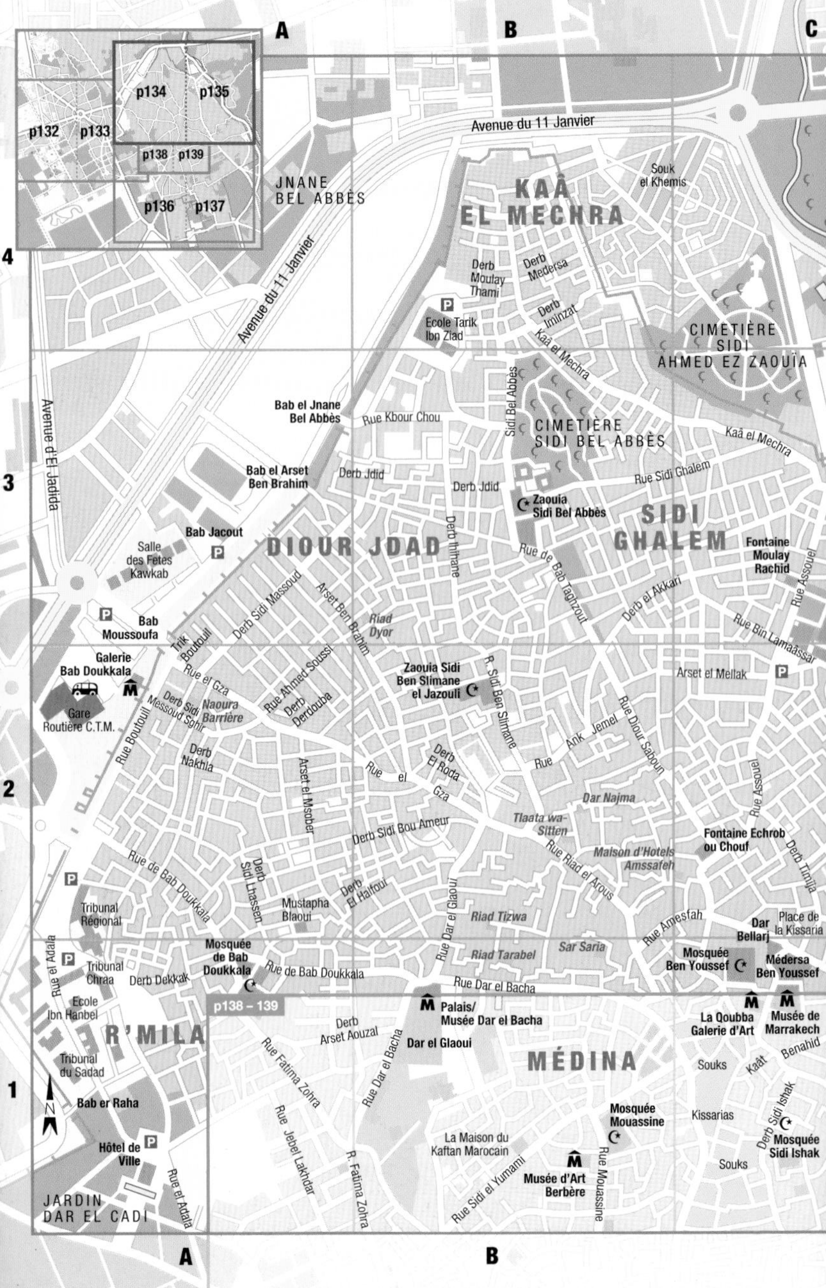
p132
p133
p134
p135
p138
p139
p136
p137
Avenue du 11 Janvier
JNANE BEL ABBÈS
KAÂ EL MECHRA
Souk el Khemis
Derb Moulay Thami
Derb Medersa
Ecole Tarik Ibn Ziad
Derb Iminzat
Kaâ el Mechra
CIMETIÈRE SIDI AHMED EZ ZAOUÏA
Avenue d'El Jadida
Bab el Jnane Bel Abbès
Rue Kbour Chou
CIMETIÈRE SIDI BEL ABBÈS
Sidi Bel Abbès
Bab el Arset Ben Brahim
Derb Jdid
Zaouia Sidi Bel Abbès
Rue Sidi Ghalem
SIDI GHALEM
Bab Jacout
Salle des Fetes Kawkab
DIOUR JDAD
Derb Ihihane
Rue de Bab Taghzout
Fontaine Moulay Rachid
Rue Assouel
Bab Moussoufa
Trik Boutouil
Derb Sidi Massoud
Arset Ben Brahim
Riad Dyor
Derb el Akkari
Rue Bin Lamaâssar
Galerie Bab Doukkala
Gare Routière C.T.M.
Rue el Gza
Derb Sidi Messoud Sghir
Naoura Barrière
Rue Ahmed Soussi
Derb Derdouba
Zaouia Sidi Ben Slimane el Jazouli
R. Sidi Ben Slimane
Arset el Mellak
Rue Boutouil
Derb Nakhla
Arset el Msober
Rue el Gza
Derb El Roda
Rue Ank Jemel
Rue Diour Saboun
Dar Najma
Tlaata wa-Sitten
Derb Sidi Bou Ameur
Rue Riad el Arous
Fontaine Echrob ou Chouf
Maison d'Hotels Amssafeh
Derb Timija
Rue de Bab Doukkala
Derb Sidi Lhassen
Mustapha Blaoui
Derb El Haifoui
Rue Dar el Glaoui
Riad Tizwa
Rue Amesfah
Place de la Kissaria
Dar Bellarj
Tribunal Régional
Rue el Adala
Tribunal Chraa
Derb Dekkak
Mosquée de Bab Doukkala
Riad Tarabel
Sar Saria
Mosquée Ben Youssef
Médersa Ben Youssef
Rue Dar el Bacha
p138 – 139
Ecole Ibn Hanbel
R'MILA
Derb Arset Aouzal
Palais/ Musée Dar el Bacha
Dar el Glaoui
La Qoubba Galerie d'Art
Musée de Marrakech
MÉDINA
Kaât Benahid
Souks
Tribunal du Sadad
Rue Fatima Zohra
Rue Dar el Bacha
Bab er Raha
Rue Jebel Lakhdar
Mosquée Mouassine
Kissarias
Derb Sidi Ishak
Mosquée Sidi Ishak
Hôtel de Ville
La Maison du Kaftan Marocain
Musée d'Art Berbère
Rue Mouassine
Souks
Rue el Adala
R. Fatima Zohra
Rue Sidi el Yumami
JARDIN DAR EL CADI
A
B
C
4
3
2
1
N

D
E
N8
Route de Fès
0
400 m
0
400 yds
CIMETIÈRE
DE TAGOURIANTE
DOUAR'AYN ITTI
4
Route des Remparts
Oued Issil
Collège
Ahmed Chaouki
Bab
el Khemis
Bab Kechich
3
Rue de Bab el Khemis
Collège
Abd el Moumen
Hôpital
Sheik Daoud
el Antaki
Bab
el Fakharine
DOUAR TABHIRT
CIMETIÈRE
SIDI ECH
CHEFFAJ
Place el
Antaki
Bine Laarassi
ASSOUEL
CIMETIÈRE
SIDI MAHTA
BEN SALAH
Toudgha Bab Debbagh
Tarik el Houri
EL
MOUKEF
Bab
Debbagh
2
Derb El
Baroud
Rue de Bab el Khemis
Rue el Fakhar
Tanneries
Tanneries
Route des Remparts
SIDI ALI
BENNAÇER
Rue de Bab Debbagh
Tarik Sidi Bouharba
Place du
Moukef
Derb Sebaat Ourijat
Derb Soussan
Derb
El Arsa
Bab
Lalla
Aouda
Mosquée
Eloussta
Ecole Moulay
Idriss I
Collège Lalla
Aouda daidia
ESSEBTIYNE
Derb el Kadi
Derb Ennajar
Oued Issil
1
Mosquée
Azebzed
Rue Essebtiyne
Ecole Moulay
Rachid
Soussane
Derb Kaid
Rasso
Hammam
el Grmai
Bab Aylen
Zaouia Sidi
Ben Salah
Zenket
Arset Sidi Youssef
Derb Ferran
Riad Caid
Rassai
Rue de Bab Aylen
Zaouia
Qadi Ayad
Derb
Boutouil
Mosquée
Cadi Ayad
Trik Boutouil
Place
Sidi Youb
Rue Fral Semar
C
D
E

p134
p135
p132
p133
p138
p139
p136
p137
A
B
C
4
3
2
1
R. Fatima Zohra
Bab Laksour
Zaouia Sidi Moulay el Ksour
Mosquée Quessabine
Place Bab Fteuh
Mosquée Kharbouch
Rue Jebel Lakhdar
Avenue Mohammed V
Trek el Koutoubia
R. des Banques
Rue Kennaria
Residence de la Place
Place Jemaa el Fna
Club Med La Medina
KENNARIA
CIMETIÈRE SIDI ALI BELKACEM
Bank Al Maghrib
Place Foucauld
Mosquée de la Koutoubia
Avenue el Mouahidine
Rue Ibn Khaldoun
Rue Tetouan
R. Moulay Ismail
R. Ben Marine
Rue de Bab Agnaou
Rue Riad Zitoun el Kedim
Hôtel Chems
Bibliothèque Municipale
JARDINS DE LA KOUTOUBIA
Avenue Houmman el Fetouakí
Bab Jedid
Hôpital Arset El Mokha
Sahara Pierre
R. Bani Marine
Place Youssef Ben Tachfine
Rue Lalla Rkia
Rue Ibn Rachid
Avenue Houmman el Fetouaki
Hôtel La Mamounia
Relais and Châteaux Villa des Orangers
JARDINS DE LA MAMOUNIA
Rue Sidi Mimoun
Rue Oqba Ben Nafaa
ARSET EL MAÄCH
JARDIN DE ROSIER
Régie Autonome de Distribution de L'Eau et d'Électricité
Marché Couvert
Rue Touareg
Avenue Bab Jedid
Pavilion Le Mamounia
Rue Essaadiyne
ARSET BEN DRISS
Rue Arset el Maâch
Green Pavilion
Hôpital Ibn Zohr
Bab Ech Charia
Mosquée de la Kasbah
Audience Pavilion
Palais El Badi
Zaouia Sidi es Souheili
Bab Agnaou
Pl. Yacoub el Mansur
Tombeaux Saadiens
Folklore Annuel
Bab er Rob
CIMETIÈRE SIDI ES SOHEILI
Rue de la Kasbah
La Sultana
Derb Harbil
Complexe d'Artisanal
Derb Abda
KASBAH
Riad Figaro
ARSET EL BAB ER ROB
Fourière Municipale
Derb Mnabha
Maison Mnabha
Rue Bab Méchouar
Bab Ksiba
Les Jardins de la Medina
Avenue Bab Jedid
Route d'Asni & Taroudant
Derb Chtouka
Rue de Bab Irhli
N
A
B

D
E
Rue Fral Semar
Derb Hammam
Rue Sidi Boulabada
Dabachi
Rue Bab Ahmad
ARSET EL HOUTA
ARSET EL MESFIOUI
Arset Moulay Bouazza
Derb el Makina
Rue el Cadi Ayad
Centre Cadi Ayad
Route des Remparts
Oued Issil
JNANE BOUSSEKRI
Riad Ifoulki
Derb Mqqadem
Derb Chemaa
Derb Chorfa
Derb Jdid
Rue Douar Graoua
Lycée Mohammed V
Derb Ferran
Rue el Cadi Ayad
Palais Moulay Idriss
Jnane Ben Chegra
Collège el Farabi
Derb Boujemaa
Poste de Police
FOOTBALL PITCHES
AGUEDAL BAB AHMAD
Lycée Hassan Ibn Tabit
Bab Ghemat
Dar Si Saïd Musée d'Art
p138 – 139
Préfecture Médina
Rue Riad Zitoun el Jedid
Maison Tiskiouine
Palais el Bahia
Jnane Ben Chegra
Rue Imam el Rhezoli
Zaouia Sidi Youssef Ben Ali
Trik Sidi Daoud
MELLAH
Marché de Lampe
CIMETIÈRE DE BAB GHEMAT
CIMETIÈRE JUIF DE MIÂARA
Place des Ferblantiers
Lazama Synagogue
Riad Assakina
Rue Belaïd
Avenue
BERRIMA
JNANE EL AFIA
Rue de Berrima
Mosquée Berrima
Palais Royal Dar el Makhzen
Bab Jnane el Afia
Bab el Harri
Rue Belaïd
Lycée
Rouis
Bab Er-Ryal
Ecole
Bab Hmar
Ecole
Méchouar extérieur
Rue de Bab Hmar
Bab La'Yal
Bab Er-Rih
Méchouar interieur
JARDINS DE L'AGUEDAL
Bab el Aghdar
Grand Méchouar
0
400 m
0
400 yds
C
D
E
1
2
3
4

p134
p135
p132
p133
p138
p139
p136
p137
A
B
C
4
3
2
1
Dar Moha
Palais/
Musée Dar el Bacha
Dar el Glaoui
R'MILA
MOUASSINE
Rue Dar el Bacha
Direction
des Affaires
Culturelles
Derb Abib Allah
Art Tuareg
Rue Mouassine
Derb Azouz
Bouganvillea
la Maison du
Kaftan Marocain
Mosquée
Mouassine
El Yed
Gallery
Rue Jebel Lakhdar
Derb Raouia
Rue Fatima Zohra
MÉDINA
Rue Sidi el Yamani
Dar Naima
Dar Attajmil
La Croix
d'Agadez
Derb
Tijani
Hammam
el Bacha
Al'anbar
Dar Bou
Ziane
Ksar
Essaoussan
Maison
MKhotel
Derb
Kadous
Derb Moulay
el Ghali
Rue el Ksour
Stylia
Kulchi
EL KSOUR
Ensemble
Artisanal
Dar Attajmil
Derb Fahal
Zefriti
Zaouia
Sidi Moulay
el Ksour
Mosquée
Quessabine
Haram Chikh
Place
Bab el Fteuh
Bab
Laksour
Riad el Fenn
Avenue Mohammed V
Rue Jebel Lakhdar
Riad Catalina
Le Tobsil
Les Jardins de
la Koutoubia
Trek el Koutoubia
Commissariat
Médina
Place
Jemaa el Fna
Hôtel
Islane
Fourière
de la Médina
Avenue Mohammed V
Club Med
La Medina
Poste Médina
Hôtel Ali
Koubba
de Zohra
Place
Foucauld
CIMETIÈRE SIDI
ALI BELKACEM
Dar el Hajar
Avenue el Mouahidine
Rue Moulay Ismail
Arsete
Albilk
Rue Bani Marine
Cinéma
Mabrouka
Mosquée
de la Koutoubia
Consulat
de France
Dar
Moulay Ali
Hôtel de
Foucauld
Hôtel
Chems
JARDINS DE
LA KOUTOUBIA
Rue Tetouan
Hôtel la
Gazelle
Bibliothèque
Municipale
Rue Ibn Khaldoun
Rue de Bab Agnaou
Rue de
0
200 m
0
200 yds
ARSET
EL BILK
Grand
Hôtel
Tazi

D
E
La Qoubba Galerie d'Art
Musée de Marrakech
Eloussta
Kaât Benahid
Derb Lakaâr
KAAT BENAHID
Souk Cherifa
Souk Kimakhine
Souk Haddadine
Artisanat Marocain
Souk Talaa
Souk Cherratine
Souk des Chaudronniers
Moulay el Arbi el Adlani
Souk Kchabbia
Souk Smata
Souk Serrajine
Derb El Aouli
Derb Sidi Ahmed
Tchai'kana
4
Souk Sebbaghine
Souk des Babouches
Kissaria
Souk el Kebir
Derb Sidi Ishak
Mosquée Azebzed
Derb Ferran
Fontaine Mouassine
Souk Attarine
La Brocante
Derb Amsegui
Souk des Teinturiers
Souk Tegmoutiene
Souk Milouda
Mosquée Sidi Ishak
Derb Herougui
AZBEZT
Place Ben Salah
Zaouia Sidi ben Salah
La Criée Berbère
L'Art de Goulimine
Derb Gnaiz
Souk Stailia
Bazar du Sud
Derb Nakhl
Derb Aznati
Derb Kadi
SOUKS
Place Rahba Kedima
Chez Brahim el Meskini
Riad Yima
Bordj Dar Lamane
BEN SALAH
Souk Nejjarine
Souk el Maazi
Art Quarzarzate
Rue Rahba el Biadyne
Riad Enija
Derb Faïd
Derb Chrifa
Derb Hidada
Traverse el Ksour
Belkhabir
Souk Btana
Derb el Toubib
Derb Mesioui
RAHBA KEDIMA
Taoulat Ben Saleh
3
Souk Laghzel
Derb Hajjaârbi
Hicham el Horre
Derb Moulay Abdelkader
Riad Magi
Derb Aarjane
Clothing crafts & textiles
Souk Smarine
Hôtel-Riad Rahha
Derb Zaouiat
Rue Sidi Boulabada
Abderrahim Bayzi
Souk Kchacha
Rue Dabachi
Palais Hadj Idder
Souk Qessabine
Kechla
Tanjia Stalls
Egg & Poultry Market
Souk el Henna
Mosquée Kharbouch
Grillade Chez Sbai
Hammam Mille et une Nuit
Trik Arset Loghzail
Les Terrasses de l'Alhambra
Chez Chegrouni
Derb Alaâdam
Rue Kennaria
Derb Sidi Ben Aissa
Derb Jamaâ
Derb Gachgach
Derb Hajra
Derb Djedid
Music Stalls
Juice & nuts
Rue des Banques
Riad Noga
Riad Laora
Derb Mqqadem
Derb Drouj
Food Stalls
Hôtel du Café de France
Mimosa
Riad Ifoulki
Derb Chemaa
Résidence de la Place
Derb Aâzzari
KENNARIA
Derb Jamaâ
Derb Jamae
2
Café du Grand Balcon
Covered Food Market
Derb Chorfa
Librairie Ghazali
Cinéma Eden
Derb el Arsa
Villa El Arsa
DOUAR GRAOUA
Derb Jdid
Rue Douar Graoua
Cecil
Café-Restaurant Toubkal
Bank Maghrib
Rue Riad Zitoun el Jedid
Tamouzigua Mustapha Mimani
Riad Al Moussika
Hôtel du Trésor
Médersa
Derb Kannaria
Chez Bahia
El Azhar
Palais Moulay Idriss
Central Palace
Zagora
Riad Maria
Derb Sidi Bouloukate
Jnane Mogadoray
Derb Djama
Riad Ella
Derb el Arsa
Sindi Sud
Derb Lakhdar
Casa Lalla
Rue Douar Graoua
Sahra
Sherazade
Riad Tamsna
Derb Zanka Daika
Dar Fakir
1
Chella
Riad Zinoun
Riad Akka
Rue de la Recette
Rue Riad Zitoun el Kedim
Gallia
Derb Sbatim
Dar Si Saïd Musée d'Art
Recette
Dar Mimoun
Rue Riad Zitoun el Jedid
Souria
Hôpital Arset El Mokha
Palais Gharnatta
Ksar el Hamra
Dar Mima
Derb Si Saïd
C
D
E

Atlas Index

PLACES OF INTEREST

STREETS

HOTELS

Index

V

W

Y

Z

Insight Smart Guide: Marrakesh
Compiled by: Sylvie Franquet
Edited by: Sarah Sweeney
Proofread and indexed by: Neil Titman

All Photography by: Clay Perry/APA, except: age fotostock /SuperStock 77B; akg-images 57; Nogues Alain/Corbis Sygma 67CR; Amenjena 104; Angsana Spa 91; blickwinkel/Alamy 44/45; Cafe Arabe 42/43; Café du Livre 42, 72/73; Carolyn Clarke/Alamy 54; Club Theatro 84/85, 87B; Nigel Cummings/fotoLibra 115L; Elizabeth Czitronyi/Alamy 22; Dar Fakir 30/31, 31; Dar Moha 100; Stéphane Frances/hemis.fr 81L; Patrick Esudero/hemis.fr 80; Mary Evans 67TL; Everett Collection/Rex Features 56/57; Face to Face/UPPA/ Photoshot 47; Le Fondouk 102(all); Kevin Foy/Rex Features 96; Getty Images 72; Ronald Grant Archive 56L; Hemis/Photoshot 15; Stephen Horsted/fotoLibra 122, 122/123; iStockphoto.com 9T, 11BR, 12, 38, 40/41, 46, 50B, 52T&B, 64L&R, 68, 115R; Jnane Mogaador 30; Kasbah du Toubkal 36T, 106; Kechmara 103; Alan Keohane 19T; Kif Kif 113BL&BR; Maxwell Knowles/fotoLibra 62/63; Kosybar 84; Lalla Mira 88; Alistair Laming/fotoLibra 39, 76; Rob Langhorst/fotoLibra 92/93; Greg Lubel/fotoLibra 110/111; Ludovic Maisant/hemis.fr 81R; Le Marrakchi 98; Giuseppe Masci/Alamy 78R; Anna Morris/fotoLibra 113T; Ourika Garden 105; La Pause 36B, 37B, 107B; Palais Rhoul 90L&R; Photolibary.com 78/79, 116/117; Photos 12/Alamy 56R; Pictures Colour Library 3BL, 17T, 19B, 23B, 38/39, 61, 62, 70L, 70/71, 92, 126/127; Andrea Pistolesi 112, 116; Riad Farnatchi 35BR, 108/109T; Riad Kniza 111; Riad Tarabel 33; Le Tanjia 98/99; Riad Tizwa 35BL; Silke Roetting/transit/Still Pictures 46/47; Es Saadi Hotel & Resort 37T, 88/89; Said Mountain Bike 118; Edwina Sassoon/fotoLibra 94B, 97; La Sultana 32T&B, 89; Eitan Simanor/Alamy 13B; Tchai'kana 35T; Treal-Ruiz/Gamma/ Eyedea/Camerapress 54/55; Patrick Tweddle/fotoLibra 93; Pierre Verdy/ AFP/Getty Images 55; Alan Ward/ fotoLibra 3BR, 40, 129, 130/131; Lee Winterbottom/fotoLibra 41; Phil Wood/APA 65, 66T, 67TR; World Pictures/Photoshot 44, 73; Worldwide Picture Library/Alamy 17B

Picture Manager: Steven Lawrence
Maps: James Macdonald
Series Editor: Jason Mitchell

First Edition 2009

Printed in Singapore by Insight Print Services (Pte) Ltd

Worldwide distribution enquiries:
Apa Publications GmbH & Co. Verlag KG (Singapore Branch) 38 Joo Koon Road, Singapore 628990;
tel: (65) 6865 1600;
e-mail: apasin@singnet.com.sg
Distributed in the UK and Ireland by:
GeoCenter International Ltd
Meridian House, Churchill Way West, Basingstoke, Hampshire RG21 6YR;
tel: (44 1256) 817 987;
e-mail: sales@geocenter.co.uk
Distributed in the United States by:
Langenscheidt Publishers, Inc.
36–36 33rd Street 4th Floor, Long Island City, New York 11106;
tel: (1 718) 784 0055;
e-mail: orders@langenscheidt.com

Contacting the Editors
We would appreciate it if readers would alert us to errors or outdated information by writing to:
Apa Publications, PO Box 7910, London SE1 1WE, UK; fax: (44 20) 7403 0290;
e-mail: insight@apaguide.co.uk

26
×12
240
72
1 2

Around Marrakech
0
50 km
0
50 miles
N
ATLANTIC
OCEAN
ESSAOUIRA
pages 26–27
Souk el Jemaa
Jemaa Sidi Brahim
Sidi Smail
Oualidia
Sebt Sais
Khemis des Zémamra
Beddouza
Cap Beddouza
Moul Bergui
Tnine Gharbia
Dar Caid Zerhouni
Had Harrara
Sebt Maarif
Lalla Fatna
Cap Safi
Jemaa Sahi
Arba Amrane
Safi
Bouguedra
Sidi Rosia
Youssoufia
Souira Kédima
Tnine Rhiate
Sebt des Gzoula
Nouasseur
Chemaia
Dar Caid Hadji
Khemis Nga
Dar Tahar ben Abbou
El Mehattat
Jemaa Laroum
Oulad Brahim
Talmest
Akermoud
Cap Hadid
Oum el Aioun
Sidi Chiker
Tensift
Had Mramer
Ounara
Sidi Mokhtar
Essaouira
Tleta Henchane
Chichaoua
Sebt Korimate
Cap Sim
El Khemis Meskala
Et Tnine
Zaouia Molay Lahsene
Rjal el Kheneg
Guemas
Dar Caid Zemzem
Zaouia Rahhal des Hassain
Bouabout
Had Smimou
Souk et Tnine Imi n Tlit
Imi n Tanoute
Bou Laouane
Amizmi
Dar Cheikh Taguent
Medersa Ichamrar
Irchalen
Tamanar
Adassil
Arba des Ida ou Trhouma
Khemis Igui Nilieud
Mzouzite
Tizza
Gouffre d'Agadir Imoucha
Touchka
Arhbalou
Sebt Talmakant
Tizi n Test 2092
Tamri
Jbel
Isk
Argana
Tassademt
Tasguinnt
Tamadant
Assafid
Barrage Abdelmoumen
Amesnaz
Taghazoute
Lgouz
Olad Berhil
Amcherk
Tamrhakht
Oulma
Ameskroud
Oued Issene
Taroudant
Sous
Agadir
Jbel
Arazane
Ben Sergaou
Inezgane
Ait Melloul
Oulad Teima
Tioute
Sebt Guerdane
Imariden
Sidi Toual
Ait Haida
Aguerka
Tifnite
Sidi Bibi
Biougra
Tidsi
Amagour
Souk Sebt de Tataoute
Souk el Had
Imi Mqourn
Et Tleta
Souk el Arba d'Assads
N 1
N 7
N 8
N 10
R 301
R 201
P 204
R 206
R 207
R 105
R 109